SIGNS
THAT MAKE YOU
WONDER

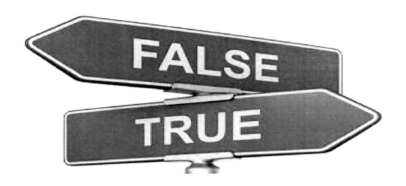

EXAMINING THE ROOTS, SHOOTS & FRUITS OF THE MODERN-DAY PROPHETIC MOVEMENT

by James P Smith

Printed by Kingsbridge Press Ltd, Cookstown, Northern Ireland.

What one generation tolerates,
the next generation will embrace (John Wesley).

SIGNS THAT MAKE YOU WONDER

Contents

FOREWORD

This book is deeply personal. It is born out of my personal experience of helplessly watching a close and much loved friend and brother in Christ slowly drown. When I say drown, I mean spiritually, not physically, but no less painful to watch. The content of this book is an expansion of the many conversations I had with my friend over many months in a vain attempt to stop him from wading deeper and deeper into dark and dangerous waters that eventually drowned him; dark and murky spiritual waters filled with the toxic doctrines and practices of dangerous apostate false teachers. What do I mean when I say apostate? The word itself is derived from the Greek word apostasia, meaning "defection", "withdrawal" or "falling away". The term is used in the New Testament to describe a defection, withdrawal or falling away from the key and true doctrines of the Christian faith in favour of deceiving spirits and doctrines of demons (e.g. 1 Timothy 4:1; 2 Thessalonians 2:3).

I tried to encourage my friend to be a good Berean and examine the Scriptures for himself to see if what I was saying was true (Acts 17:11), but he would not. I pleaded with him to prove me a liar, just as Job did with his friends (Job 24:25), but he would not, because he knew he could not. I tried to speak the truth in love to my friend and save him (and his family) from wading deeper into the toxic waters, but truth falls on deaf ears when they are being tickled so effectively by false teachers who tell the listener what they want to hear. And herein lies the root of the problem with my friend, because he was by no means an unwitting or helpless victim in his drowning. He wanted to have his ears tickled; he pursued teachers who would tickle his ears and tell him what he wanted to hear; he willingly waded into the dangerous waters to have his ears tickled more and more; his desire to wade deeper and deeper was so strong that it overwhelmed any honest pursuit of truth.

I tried desperately to hold out my hand to him, as anyone would do for a drowning man. Most drowning men would want to be saved and would gladly and gratefully firmly grab hold of any hand extended to them, but my friend did not, because the reality is that he was exactly where he wanted to be; he did not want to be saved from the dangerous waters he was wading deeper and deeper into. Instead of grabbing on to the hand I was holding out to him, he pushed it away and accused me of pointing the finger. Who knows, perhaps my increasing sense of desperation and frustration at being unable to save someone who did not want to be saved (and who despised my efforts to do so) did at times make the hand I was holding out resemble a pointing finger. But then again, perhaps my friend just used that as an excuse for pushing my hand away, because it was getting in the way of where he wanted to go.

The consequence of my very dear friend not wanting to be saved and having no genuine interest in pursuing truth is that I had to watch him drown; the word painful is not sufficient enough to describe the loss I felt. He is now in a position of pastoral leadership within one of the hugely successful organisations I refer to in my book, pastored by one of the men I mention throughout. It is an organisation I do not hesitate in describing as a pseudo-Christian cult masquerading as a mainstream evangelical ministry. My friend is now himself a dangerous apostate false teacher; he is exactly where he always wanted to be. We are now physically separated by the Atlantic Ocean, but that is nothing more than a puddle compared to the length and breadth of the spiritual waters that now separate us.

As I write this forward to my book I have the chorus of Carly Simon's famous song, "You're So Vain" running through my head, which goes:

> You're so vain,
> You probably think this song is about you;
> You're so vain,
> I'll bet you think this song is about you,
> Don't you?
> Don't you?

Why is this particular song running through my head? Because if my friend ever reads this book (which I pray he does) he is so vain that, in spite of the fact that I make no mention of his name anywhere in the book, he will immediately recognise it is about him. That being the case, it is only fair that I dedicate it to him in the desperate hope that it will wake him (and perhaps others) from his drowned state of wilful self-deception so we can once again share the faith which was once for all delivered to the saints.

I mourn the loss of my friend to the depths of the dark spiritual waters he drowned in; I mourn for what he has lost, even though he is (currently) too self-deceived to acknowledge it. This book is for you my friend.

He is your best friend who tells you the most truth (J. C. Ryle)

INTRODUCTION

It is almost impossible to name any part of the 21st century charismatic/evangelical church that has not been influenced by the teaching and so-called "signs and wonders" of the new "apostles" and "prophets" of the Prophetic Movement. The hearts and minds of millions of Christians around the world have been captured by larger-than-life personalities boldly claiming a special "anointing" giving them authority to "impart" the power of God on to whoever they wish, and making bold proclamations of private revelation directly from God; declarations of God raising up a special breed of "elite" Christian that will:

Move in the supernatural

Perform "signs and wonders"

Breakdown spiritual strongholds

Be the cause of a global End-Time revival

Take dominion over the earth and earthly governments

Usher in the kingdom of God and invite Jesus Christ to return to rule as king.

Sounds fantastic! Who would not want to be a part of that? But the question is: is it Biblical?

Is this movement that has captivated so much of the charismatic/evangelical church on the verge of ushering in a global End-Time revival or a widespread End-Time apostasy?

This, and other questions about this movement, demand an answer, but sadly Christians who do try to raise important questions are often silenced by being accused of quenching the work of the Holy Spirit, or even blaspheming the Holy Spirit[1]. No one wants to be accused, let alone be guilty, of doing that!

From a personal perspective, I feel I am well placed to both ask the necessary questions and propose some answers, because unlike most people who criticise the excesses of the charismatic/evangelical churches, I am **not** a cessationist[2] and

Christians who are cessationists should take no comfort or solace from the content of this book, because I believe cessationism to be no less of an unbiblical error than the spiritual excesses I address. I believe the gifts of the Spirit **are** for today, but - and this is a big but – only in a way that is based soundly on Scripture; as New Testament believers in Jesus Christ we should never go beyond what is written (1 Corinthians 4:6); this is our standard, not the experience itself. Our experience of the gifts of the Spirit should be in accordance with God's will and good pleasure, not ours.

I grew up in the House Churches of the *Charismatic Renewal Movement* of the 1970s and 1980s; I experienced first-hand its steady decline toward becoming inward looking and self-gratifying in the way the gifts of the Spirit were used in accordance with the will and good pleasure of the believer, not God, and how in the following decades it became increasingly infected by the teaching of so-called new "Prophets" and "Apostles"; teaching that steered the church away from objective doctrinal certainty toward a subjective experience based faith that fed its followers a diet of increasingly bizarre manifestations and "signs and wonders", and promises of the "imparting" of spiritual power that would usher in God's kingdom on earth.

The influence of men like John Wimber in the 1980s onward, with his Signs and Wonders movement, cannot be overstated. Then, in the 1990s we had the "Toronto Blessing" and the Pensacola Outpouring (also known as the Brownsville Revival), which in turn directly led to the Lakeland Revival with Todd Bentley in 2008. We have seen the emergence of hugely influential ministries such as the *International Coalition of Apostles, New Apostolic Reformation* (NAR), the *International House of Prayer* (IHOP), Bill Johnson's *Bethel Church* and *Jesus Culture*; all founded on the same fundamental doctrine and all committed to promoting ever-increasingly extreme manifestations as moves of the Holy Spirit.

Within the above paragraph I have made specific reference to a number of people by name, and I will continue to do so where appropriate throughout this book. Therefore, before I go any further I think it is important to address a number of objections commonly raised by some Christians who do not agree with judging other Christians and/or naming them personally and publicly.

JUDGE NOT

One of the most common Bible verses used by people who claim we should not be critical or judge other believers is Matthew 7:1, which says:

> *Judge not, that you be not judged.*

That is pretty clear isn't it, so I should cease and desist from going any further?

No, the Bible can be made to say pretty much anything someone wants it to say if it is taken out of context, so every Bible verse should be properly read in its context in order to correctly understand it and *"rightly divide the Word of truth"*(2 Timothy 2:15). Matthew 7:1 should therefore not be read or used in isolation to the surrounding verses which give it its context. Verses 2-5 clearly show that verse 1 is referring to **hypocritical** judgment. This is also true of Romans 2:3:

> *And do you think this, O man, you who judge those practicing such things, and doing the same, that you will escape the judgment of God?*

The lesson is clear: you cannot judge another for their sin if you are guilty of the same sin. If Matthew 7:1 means do not judge at all, it would render what Paul wrote in 2 Timothy 3:16 totally null and void, together with much of what Paul wrote in his epistles about correcting error that had arisen within the church. The fact is that Paul used Scripture in exactly the way he advised Timothy it should be used; Paul used Scripture for *"doctrine, reproof, correction, for instruction in righteousness"*. Notice Paul places **doctrine** first and that *"reproof, correction and instruction in righteousness"* can only come from right doctrine.

In 1 Corinthians 5:12-13 Paul makes clear that Christians **are** to judge each other; it is people outside the Body of Christ we are to leave in the hands of God to judge.

GO TO THEM PRIVATELY

Whilst it is clear from Scripture that believers in Christ are to judge each other, is it right to do so publicly, or should it be done in private? Many Christians do not think it is Biblical to judge publicly and use Matthew 18:15-17 as a proof text for that view:

> *15 "Moreover if your brother sins against you, go and tell him his fault between you and him alone. If he hears you, you have gained your brother. 16 But if he will not hear, take with you one or two more, that 'by the mouth of two or three witnesses every word may be established.' 17 And if he refuses to hear them, tell it to the church. But if he refuses even to hear the church, let him be to you like a heathen and a tax collector.*

The argument using the above passage in Matthew 18 is that we should go privately to the person teaching false doctrine, rather than expose them publicly. However, this passage has **nothing** to do with how we should deal with people publicly teaching false doctrine. The above passage in Matthew is instructing us how to do deal with private sin committed by one brother or sister in the Body against another.

False doctrine is **never** a private matter in Scripture and is always to be dealt with publicly for the protection and edification of the wider Body of Christ; just consider the open letters of correction and rebuke Paul (and Jesus through revelation given to the apostle John) wrote to New Testament churches. Furthermore, false teachers (like the people I will name throughout this book) peddle their false doctrine **publicly** via (best-selling) books, video, television, the internet and radio programmes, and what has been written in books and said on video, television, the internet and radio programmes is very deliberately in the **public** domain (often making the false teacher very wealthy). Because of this, it is very much subject to **public** review, analysis, critique and judgment. Anyone making **public** declarations intended to influence large audiences should know that he or she is responsible for what they say and should be held accountable (and that includes the author of **this** book!).

There is a clear and consistent **Biblical** precedent for exposing error publicly, and here are just some examples:

Paul named Peter publicly. Peter was guilty of unscriptural practice:

> *Now when Peter had come to Antioch, I withstood him to his face, because he was to be blamed; for before certain men came from James, he would eat with the Gentiles; but when they came, he withdrew and separated himself, fearing those who were of the circumcision. And the rest of the Jews also played the hypocrite with him, so that even Barnabas was carried away with their hypocrisy. But when I saw that they were not straightforward about the truth of the gospel, I said to Peter before them all, "If you, being a Jew, live in the manner of Gentiles and not as the Jews, why do you compel Gentiles to live as Jews? (Galatians 2:11-14).*

The issue Paul addresses in his letter to the church at Galatia revolved around salvation by the law or by grace. When the integrity and purity of the Gospel is at stake, we have no choice but to follow Paul's example and expose error and name those preaching the error, no matter who it may concern.

Paul named Hymenaeus and Alexander. Paul told Timothy to:

> *This charge I commit to you, son Timothy, according to the prophecies previously made concerning you, that by them you may wage the good warfare, having faith and a good conscience, which some having rejected, concerning the faith have suffered shipwreck, of whom are Hymenaeus and Alexander, whom I delivered to Satan that they may learn not to blaspheme. (1 Timothy 1:18-20).*

God's true servants should *"wage the good warfare"*, and name those who have departed from the faith that was once delivered to the Saints (Jude 3). Paul is not discussing here the faith of salvation but the faith as a system of **doctrine**. These men had made a *"shipwreck"* of it and Paul was calling them out by name; we are obligated to follow Paul's example.

Paul named Hymenaeus and Philetus. He told Timothy to:

> Be diligent to present yourself approved to God, a worker who does not need to be ashamed, rightly dividing the word of truth. But shun profane and idle babblings, for they will increase to more ungodliness. And their message will spread like cancer. Hymenaeus and Philetus are of this sort, who have strayed concerning the truth, saying that the resurrection is already past; and they overthrow the faith of some (2 Timothy 2:15-18).

False doctrine must be exposed and those teaching it must be exposed by name, otherwise "*their message will spread like cancer*".

Pauls named Alexander the Coppersmith:

> Alexander the coppersmith did me much harm. May the Lord repay him according to his works. You also must beware of him, for he has greatly resisted our words (2 Timothy 4:14-15).

It is clear that this is not a personality problem between Paul and Alexander, but a **doctrinal** problem. Alexander had withstood the words and doctrine of Paul. He was an enemy of the truth.

Paul is not the only one who called people out by name. John named Diotrephes:

> I wrote to the church, but Diotrephes, who loves to have the preeminence among them, does not receive us (3 John 1:9).

John relates how this man prated [talked foolishly] against him "*with malicious words*" (verse 10). He further said:

> Beloved, do not imitate what is evil, but what is good. He who does good is of God, but he who does evil has not seen God (3 John 1:11).

There are many more examples, both in the Old and New Testament, but the ones I have mentioned are sufficient for making my point. It is **not** wrong to name and criticise those whose doctrine and practice is contrary to the Word of God. In fact, the whole Bible abounds with examples of false prophets, false teachers and people practising false things being exposed and named. Faithful messengers will warn the sheep of false teachers and identify them by name; it is not enough to broadly hint at their identity. Peter describes well the kind of people I will openly name and quote in the pages of this book:

> But there were also false prophets among the people, even as there will be false teachers among you, who will secretly bring in destructive heresies, even denying the Lord who bought them, and bring on themselves swift destruction (2 Peter 2:1).

JUST LEAVE THEM ALONE

This argument is often called the "Gamaliel approach" due to it being based on the words of Gamaliel, a first-century Jewish rabbi and leader in the Sanhedrin. He was a Pharisee and a grandson of the famous Rabbi Hillel and is mentioned in the New Testament a number of times. For example, Acts 22:3 tells us that Saul of Tarsus (who later became the apostle Paul) trained to be a Pharisee under Gamaliel. However, it is what Gamaliel said in Acts chapter 5 that is appealed to by people who claim false teachers should be left alone.

Acts chapter 5 describes a meeting of the Sanhedrin where John and Peter are standing trial for preaching the Gospel of Jesus Christ and their refusal to stop doing so enrages the Jewish council to the point where they begin to call for the apostles to be put to death. This is where Gamaliel steps in. After first ordering the apostles to be removed from the room, Gamaliel advises the council to:

> *Keep away from these men and let them alone; for if this plan or this work is of men, it will come to nothing, but if it is of God, you cannot overthrow it – lest you even be found to fight against God* (Acts 5:38-39).

Based on the advice given by an unbelieving Pharisee on how to deal with true teachers, the argument is constructed by apologists for false teachers that they should just be left alone, because if their ministry is not from God, it will come to nothing.

Is that true?

Does false teaching come to nothing if left alone?

Of course not.

What about Islam for example, a most diabolical anti-Christ religion. Has it come to nothing over the last 1,000 years?

What about Hinduism, Buddhism, Taoism, Roman Catholicism, Mormonism or the Jehovah's Witnesses cult?

Have they all come to nothing?

The words of Gamaliel cannot be used as Biblical justification for telling discerning Christians to leave false teachers alone. Proponents of the "Gamaliel approach" confuse the Pharisaical response to true teachers with the apostolic response to false teachers; instead of following the instruction of Gamaliel, a Pharisee who never believed the Truth, we should follow the instruction of Paul, the most famous Pharisee to convert to the Truth, who never tells us to leave false teachers alone.

BUT THEY ARE SO SINCERE

Let me be clear, I have no interest in, or mandate for, questioning the sincerity of any of the people I name in this book. I know Christians who have met a number of the people I name and testify to them being most personable, humble and sincere. I do not judge anyone on the basis of their sincerity; only God can do that (1 Samuel 16:7; Jeremiah 17:10; Proverbs 16:2). I judge these people as the Bible mandates me to judge them: on their doctrine and the corrupt spiritual practices that result from their corrupt doctrine, which makes shipwreck of the true faith. Much of Paul's epistles were written to correct error in doctrine and practices that had already infiltrated the Body of Christ. The seven letters from Jesus to the seven churches in Revelation chapters 2 and 3 were predominantly admonishing false doctrine within the churches.

Sincerity is a most unreliable, unbiblical and naive litmus test for determining TRUTH; sincerity is no defence against being deceived. For example, I have met Mormons, JWs, Hindus and Muslims who all outwardly appear sincere and have no intention of taking advantage of their flock for evil gain. But they are all sincerely wrong!

Exposing error and *"contending earnestly for the faith"* (Jude 3) **is** a Biblical mandate. Paul instructs us to:

> *Note those that cause divisions and offences, contrary to the doctrine which you learned, and avoid them* (Romans 16:17).

Paul says to *"note"* (i.e. point out) and *"avoid"* those that teach contrary to the doctrine you have learned; he doesn't say to give some slack to those false teachers who at least appear sincere in their false beliefs.

The sad reality is that false teachers like the people I name in this book would not exist if they did not have a willing audience of Christians eager to have their ears tickled with false teaching. But Paul warned us it would be this way:

> *For the time will come when they will not endure sound doctrine, but according to their own desires, because they have itching ears, they will heap up for themselves teachers; and they will turn their ears away from the truth…* (2 Timothy 4:3-4).

Jesus also warned us it would be this way. We therefore have a definite Biblical mandate to expose false teachers and protect the flock from *"ravenous wolves"* (Matthew 7:15).

BUT THEY LOVE JESUS!

This argument is an extension of the one above, with the implication being that we should overlook someone's error or disobedience to God's Word because they profess to love Jesus; their profession of love for Jesus somehow trumps their need to be obedient to God's Word. In response, let us look carefully at what Jesus said on this very issue. Jesus said:

> *If you love Me, keep My commandments"* (John 14:15).

> *If anyone loves Me, he will keep My Word"* (John 14:23).

John declared, *"This is love, that we walk according to His commandments"* (2 John 1:6). Those who love and follow Jesus demonstrate they love and follow Him by keeping His commandments, and conversely, *"He who says, 'I know Him' and does not keep His commandments, is a liar, and the truth is not in Him"* (1 John 2:4). No matter how much someone professes a love for Jesus, their profession is to be judged in light of how obedient they are to Jesus. That is how Jesus Himself judges someone's profession of love for Him.

THE DOWN GRADE

To understand where the charismatic/evangelical church is today, we must go back further than the 1970s. There is a doctrine and theology deep at the root of today's experience based version of Christianity with its self-appointed "apostles" and "prophets" that goes back much further than the decade made famous for bad music (did anyone ever really think glam rock was good?!?), even worse fashion (tie-dye shirts, folk-embroidered Hungarian blouses, bell-bottom trousers – need I go on?), and introducing the world to the film franchise that began "A long time ago in a galaxy far, far away…"[3]. The fruit of the shoot is directly traceable to the root, so we must go back and examine the root to understand from where the shoots sprouted in order to establish the quality of the fruit produced. Let us start by going back to the state of the church near the end of the 19th century and then journey forward from there.

In March 1887 Charles H. Spurgeon (19/6/1834-31/1/1892) published in his monthly magazine, *The Sword and the Trowel*, an article titled *"The Down Grade"*[4] that exposed the way in which much of the church at that time was on a slippery slope, or "down grade" away from essential Christian evangelical doctrines and were denying the inspiration of Holy Scripture. In the following months editions of *The Sword and the Trowel*, Spurgeon wrote:

> Biblical truth is like the pinnacle of a steep, slippery mountain. One step away, and you find yourself on the down grade. Once a church or individual Christian gets on the down grade, momentum takes over and the down slide gets worse.

He warned that once a church or individual Christian starts compromising and allows unbiblical views and philosophies in, "recovery is unusual", and recovery only occurs when the church or individual Christian gets on to what he described as the "up-line" or "getting back in the right direction through [genuine] spiritual revival".

The first step toward addressing a problem is recognising there is one!

Both the original article and Spurgeon's subsequent comments caused much controversy and trouble for him, eventually resulting in him receiving an official censure [a formal expression of severe disapproval] from the Baptist Union and being forced to resign. Such articles today would barely cause even a ripple. The controversy took its toll on Spurgeon's health; so much so that, after his death, his wife wrote:

> His fight for the faith… cost him his life.

Such was the poor spiritual state of the Baptist Union that after Spurgeon's death, his wife wrote:

> So far as the Baptist Union was concerned, little was accomplished by Mr Spurgeon's witness-bearing and withdrawal.

It was not as if Spurgeon was against revival in the church; far from it, but he recognised the growing dangers of chasing after signs and wonders:

> I am glad of any signs of life, even if they should be feverish and transient, and I am slow to judge any well intended movement, but I am very fearful that many so called revivals in the long run wrought more harm than good. A species of religious gambling has fascinated many men, and given them a distaste for the sober business of true godliness. But if I would nail down counterfeits upon the counter, I do not therefore undervalue true gold. Far from it. It is to be desired beyond measure that the Lord would send a real and lasting revival of spiritual life.

The "down grade" from the certainty of Scripture observed by Spurgeon was directly responsible for the growing decline in the way in which professing Christians were able to recognise false revivals and false doctrine, and on this travesty Bishop of Liverpool, J. C. Ryle (10/5/1816-10/6/1900), lamented:

> We cannot withhold our conviction that the professing church is as much by laxity and indistinctiveness about matters of doctrine within as it is by sceptics and unbelievers without. Myriads of professing Christians nowadays seem utterly unable to distinguish… what is true and what is false… If a preacher… is only clever and eloquent and earnest… he is all right, however strange… his sermons… They… cannot detect error.

There can be no better examples of the kind of clever and eloquent false teachers who were enchanting Christians during the late 1800s and into the turn of the century than two forerunners to the Pentecostal Movement, John Alexander Dowie (1847-1907) and Maria Woodworth-Etter (1844-1924).

JOHN ALEXANDER DOWIE

Regarded as the "father of healing evangelism", John Alexander Dowie's latter days healing theology paved the way for Pentecostalism, which in turn was to spawn the Charismatic Movement that dominates so much of evangelical Christianity today; many subsequent Pentecostal teachers were to come out of Dowie's movement. Dowie's magazine, *Leaves of Healing*, had a worldwide distribution which made him one of the most influential Christians of his day around the world.

The basis of Dowie's healing theology was that physical healing is **promised** in the atonement, sickness is always from the Devil and never within the will of God. This theology continues to be the foundation on which most of today's charismatic/ evangelical teacher's healing ministries are built [see Appendix 1]. It is worthy of note that Smith Wigglesworth (1859-1947) shared Dowie's theology on healing in the atonement and was central to his ministry.

Dowie believed that divine healing was only available to Christians so he refused to pray for the healing of anyone he did not believe was born again. Did Jesus or His disciples restrict healing to only those who were already born again? Of course not. Dowie's approach was completely unbiblical. He would question those who came for prayer and turn away those he did not believe were born again. He also insisted that those who sought faith healing should give up medical care, and flatly refused to pray for anyone who would not promise to give up their medical care afterwards; he viewed doctors as instruments of the Devil. When his own daughter suffered severe burns from knocking over an alcohol lamp, he stopped one of his followers from trying to alleviate the poor girl's pain by administering Vaseline, and refused to allow her any medical treatment. His daughter died from her injuries.

Dowie opened up over a dozen "faith cure homes" where he would admit sick people as in-patients, providing they agreed to reject any further secular medical treatment. Many of his patients died of their illnesses and in 1895 he was charged and convicted for manslaughter and neglect by the city of Chicago, but the courts ruled the conviction was unconstitutional.

He spent much of his ministry time in Chicago and claimed God had given him special apostolic governance over the city; he believed God had made him spiritual Mayor over the city, with all residents his spiritual responsibility. American evangelist D. L. Moody (5/2/1837-22/12/1899), who also spent much of his ministry time in Chicago, took a strong stand against Dowie. In response, Dowie declared that Moody would die under God's judgment, and when Moody did die in 1899 Dowie claimed it was at the hand of God.

Dowie's following grew to several hundred thousand and effectively took over a large section of the city. He took to purchasing land approximately 40 miles outside of Chicago and started to call it Zion, which he said would be a moral utopia where Christians could come and live and create heaven on earth with the Devil banished. This was never going to succeed for two keys reasons:

1. Jesus commanded His followers to *"Go into all the world and preach the gospel"* (Mark 16:15), not shut themselves away in a closed community. This venture was therefore at its core disobedient to a fundamental command given by Jesus.

2. A moral utopia on earth with the Devil banished will never be achieved until Jesus returns to earth as king to instigate His Millennial Kingdom. Dowie put the "cart before the horse" by believing this could be achieved without Christ first returning to rule.

Whilst the duration of Christ's reign on earth was not revealed until the last book of the New Testament (Revelation 20:1-7), the Old Testament is full of descriptions of what conditions will characterise Christ's 1000 year reign on earth. For example:

Psalm 15:1-5 describes the righteousness that will characterise a citizen of the Millennial Kingdom.

Psalm 24:1-6 describes the establishment of the Kingdom and the righteousness that will characterise the person in right relationship with God during the Millennial Kingdom.

Isaiah 2:2-4 describes a universal peace between nations that will characterise the Millennial Kingdom.

Micah 4:1-5 describes a similar scene to Isaiah 2:2-4, but then also adds that the Millennial Kingdom will also be a time of personal peace and prosperity.

Isaiah 11:6-9 describes how this universal peace will even extend to the animal kingdom, with all animals returning to being vegetarian, as they were originally in the Garden of Eden.

Dowie had a "kingdom now" theology in which he thought he could create on earth now the utopian conditions of the Millennial Kingdom that will only be possible when Jesus returns to rule and binds the Devil. In spite of Dowie's plan for Zion being completely unbiblical, over 20,000 professing Christians settled there. Dowie was the owner of all the property in Zion, with tenants leasing the land from him they built their houses on. Their savings were deposited in Zion bank and Dowie used this money to fund his tours overseas. He ruled Zion with a rod of iron and told his followers to expect a full restoration of apostolic Christianity and claimed he had been commissioned as the first apostle of a renewed End-Times church. He claimed he was visited by an angel who told him he would be the forerunner of the Second Coming of Christ, just as John the Baptist was the forerunner of Christ's First Coming. He claimed he was Elijah and walked around Zion in an Old Testament-like priests outfit (as shown below).

In a 1903 publication of his magazine, Dowie arrogantly wrote, "If I am not a messenger of God on this earth, then no one is". Dowie's life ended in shame and ignominy after it was found that he had misappropriated over half a million dollars, including (an investigation found) giving presents worth more than $300,000.00 to young girls in the town. Zion ended in financial ruin and his marriage in tatters with his wife claiming he was promoting polygamy. In spite of this, and his obvious false teaching, he is still revered today by the charismatic/evangelical world.

MARIA WOODWORTH-ETTER

Faith healer evangelist Maria Woodworth Etter (commonly referred to as "Mother Etter" in Pentecostal circles) had a vast influence on the development of the Pentecostal Movement. The *Dictionary of the Pentecostal and Charismatic Movements* describes Etter as "a monumental figure in terms of spreading the Pentecostal message" and notes that "most early Pentecostals looked at Woodworth-Etter as a godsend to the movement and accepted her uncritically".

Mother Etter was famous for holding meetings where there would be supernatural manifestations reminiscent of what has been seen time and time again at modern-day "revival" meetings. However, in spite of Etter sharing Dowie's doctrine on good health being guaranteed to the believer in the atonement, even Dowie took a stand against her ministry, calling her methods "trance evangelism" and was reported to have said her meetings were "something of the Devil" and was the "worst deception" he had seen in his life. In her meetings, people would go in to trances, standing perfectly still like statues for lengths of time; this was considered evidence of being "slain in the Spirit". Her powers, which were without doubt potent and real, bore more resemblance to those displayed by the Shamans and Magicians of primitive cultures rather than anything that could be justified as being Biblical.

She authored numerous books, one of which was titled, *A Diary of Signs and Wonders* (1916). She eventually established something like a "temple" in Indiana, took it upon herself to establish her own church and ordain her own ministers (something which is clearly contrary to the teaching of the New Testament).

Those within modern-day charismatic/evangelical circles who a) accept the false teaching that some Christians have a special "anointing" and b) believe it can be "imparted" to others, claim Mother Etter's "anointing" was "imparted" first to Aimee Semple McPherson, then to Kathryn Kuhlman and then to Benny Hinn. Those names alone should ring alarm bells with every Bible-believing Christian.

AIMEE SEMPLE MCPHERSON

A firm believer that good health is guaranteed to the believer in the atonement, Aimee Semple McPherson (1890-1944) was another very influential figure in the development of the Pentecostal Movement, with the *Dictionary of Pentecostal and Charismatic Movements* describing her as "the most prominent woman leader Pentecostalism has produced to date". Her meetings were famous for people being "slain in the spirit" and being "drunk in the spirit".

She was married three times and divorced twice and controversy followed her wherever she went. For example, in the May of 1926 she went missing from a beach in California and after a massive search was presumed drowned.

However, a month later she turned up in Mexico, claiming to have been abducted, but evidence strongly indicating she had in fact eloped with her lover, Kenneth Ormiston, whom was married at the time; the pair had been seen together earlier in the year during McPherson's trip to Europe and had been seen checking in together at hotels in California at various times. In addition, a grocery receipt signed by McPherson was found in a cottage in Carmel, California, where it appears she had met up with Ormiston at the time she claimed she had been abducted and taken to Mexico. Several eye-witnesses testified to seeing them together during that period.

McPherson's third husband, David Hutton, left his wife and children to marry her. Hutton then divorced McPherson in 1934.

McPherson started her own denomination, Foursquare, and built her own church, Angelus temple, which was owned on a 50/50 basis with her mother.

In spite of her positive confession, health and wealth gospel, McPherson died of an overdose of prescription drugs in 1944.

KATHRYN KUHLMAN

Just like Mother Etter and Aimee Semple McPherson before her, Kathryn Kuhlman (1907-1976) was famous for holding meetings in which people would be "slain in the Spirit" and fall down when she prayed for them. She was embraced by the Pentecostal Movement and then by the budding shoots of the Charismatic Renewal Movement in the 1960s. She committed adultery with a married man, who left his wife and children to marry Kuhlman. A few years later Kuhlman divorced him. She died of heart disease in 1976.

Even ignoring the false doctrine taught by Mother Etter, Aimee Semple McPherson and Kathryn Kuhlman, and the unbiblical supernatural experiences manifested at their meetings, all three women were divorcees (several times over for McPherson), which the Bible makes clear God hates, and they were all church leaders, which completely contradicts New Testament teaching [see Appendix 2].

BENNY HINN

Benny Hinn was born and raised in Israel, which leads many to believe he is an authority in Biblical Hebrew; he is not. He claimed his father was Mayor of Jaffa; he was not. He is ordained by the *International Convention of Faith Churches and Ministers,* the chief proponents of which are Word of Faith heretics Kenneth Hagin and Kenneth Copeland. He is also fully endorsed by Oral Roberts. Benny Hinn was a key proponent of the so-called "Toronto Blessing", with particular influence on John Arnott, pastor of the Toronto Airport Vineyard Fellowship. Hinn claims to have received his "anointing" from the grave of Kathryn Kuhlman, and regularly visits her grave for further "anointing". This is nothing less than the sin of necromancy (Leviticus 19:26; Deuteronomy 18:10-11; Galatians 5:19-20). It is an abomination to God.

What does Benny say himself? The following is a mere taster:

On the Trinity - "Each one of them is a triune being by Himself... there's nine of them" (Trinity Broadcast Network (TBN) 3/10/1990). "...Do you know that the Holy Spirit has a soul and a body separate from that of Jesus and the Father?" (Orlando Christian Centre, 13/10/1990).

On Adam - "Adam was a super-being when God created him. ...The Scriptures declare clearly that he had dominion over the fowls of the air. ...Adam not only flew, he flew to space. He was – with one thought he would be on the moon" (TBN, 26/12/1991).

On health - "There will be no sickness for the saint of God" (Rise and Be Healed! 1991, p14).

On wealth - "The Lord giveth and never taketh away. And just because he [Job] said, 'Blessed be the name of the Lord,' don't mean that he's right, he was just being religious" (TBN November, 1990).

On poverty – "Poverty is a demon. God had to show me in a vision of a demon literally to prove this to me (TBN, 1990).

On treatment of enemies – "The Holy Ghost is upon me... the day is coming when those that attack us will drop down dead... don't touch God's servants: it's deadly... Woe to you that touches God's servants. You're going to pay. (Miracle Invasion Rally 22/11/1991). "Now I'm pointing my finger with the mighty power of God on me... you hear this: there are men and women in California attacking me. I will tell you all under the anointing now, you'll reap it in your children unless you stop... and your children will suffer. You're attacking me on the radio every night – you'll pay and you're children will. Hear this from the lips of God's servant. You are in danger. Repent! Or God Almighty will move His hand. Touch not my anointed..." (World Charismatic Conference 7/8/1992)

On the sinful nature of man – "When you say, 'I am a Christian,' you are saying, 'I am Mashiach,' in the Hebrew. I am a little messiah walking on earth, in other words. That is a shocking revelation. ...May I say it like this? You are a little god on earth running around" (Praise-a-Thon, TBN, 6/11/1990).

On discernment – "So don't question this teaching. Only the immature question it" (Our Position in Christ).

On prophecy – "The spirit tells me, Fidel Castro will die – in the 90's. Oooh my! Some will try to kill him and they will not succeed. But there will come a change in his physical health, and he will not stay in power, and Cuba will be visited by God" (Orlando Christian Centre 31/12/1989). In spite of Hinn's prophecy, Castro managed to hang on to life until November 2016.

On the same night as the Castro (false) prophecy, Benny Hinn also gave this prophecy:

> The Lord also tells me to tell you in the mid 90's, about 94-95, no later than that, God will destroy the homosexual community of America. But He will not destroy it with what many minds have thought Him to be, He will destroy it with fire. And many will turn and be saved, and many will rebel and be destroyed.

Since then we have of course seen the legalisation of same-sex marriage in all 50

States of America; not exactly the destruction of homosexuality prophesied.

Benny Hinn remains a very successful and prominent figurehead within the Pentecostal Church.

The level of fame and adoration enjoyed by John Alexander Dowie and Maria Woodworth Etter, and the huge influence they had on the church is a clear indication of the general poor spiritual state of the church as it approached the turn of the century; this is the general spiritual state of the church when it embraced an event widely heralded as the beginning of modern-day Pentecostalism; an event in church history that millions of Christians around the world today regard as a hugely significant and genuine move of God, and has been used as the model and "blueprint" for every Charismatic revival since. That event was the *Azusa Street Revival.*

AZUSA STREET

Azusa Street   Rev. William Seymour

The *Azusa Street Revival* (also known as the Latter Rain Outpouring) in Los Angeles, was founded by a man called William Seymour (1870-1922) in the spring of 1906. In establishing whether or not the events at the *Azusa Street Revival* meetings were a genuine move of the Holy Spirit, it is important to examine not only what happened at the revival meetings themselves, but also William Seymour's own doctrine, because one's actions are determined by one's doctrine, and God does not honour false doctrine.

William Joseph Seymour was born on 2nd May 1870 in the town of Centerville, Louisiana to former slaves Simon and Phillis Seymour. The region was noted for its sugar plantations, the dominance of Roman Catholicism and its syncretism with voodoo, a heavily Cajun culture, and the presence of white supremacist groups. At the time of young William Seymour growing up, Louisiana had one of the highest rates of lynching in the nation.

Seymour was baptised as a child in a Roman Catholic Church in Franklin, but as a young boy attended a Baptist church in Centerville with his family. However, it was not until after 1895 that he became born-again through attending a Methodist church in Indianapolis. Soon after his conversion he joined the Church of God Reformation movement in Anderson, Indiana. At the time, the group was called *The Evening Light Saints*.

Four years before the *Azusa Street Revival* began, Seymour attended a Bible School in Cincinnati. It was during his time at this Bible School that he embraced the false doctrine of "entire sanctification", in which it is taught that two "works of grace" are required to save and cleanse a believer; the believer has to be first born again through faith in Jesus Christ, but then subsequently has to be sanctified and made perfect through baptism in the Holy Spirit. Being sanctified is a Biblical doctrine, but **not** in the way Seymour believed. The Bible teaches that sanctification is progressive throughout the life of the believer, whereas Seymour believed and taught it was fully achieved and completed in the believer through being baptised in the Holy Spirit. Smith Wigglesworth (1859-1947) would teach something similar when he came on the Pentecostal scene a short time later. He taught a form of sinless perfection. He stated:

> I am realising very truly these days that there is a sanctification of the Spirit where the thoughts are holy, where the life is beautiful, with no blemish (*Count It All Joy*, August 1925, reprinted in *The Anointing of His Spirit*, page 226).

The Greek word translated "sanctification" (*hagiasmos*) means "holiness". To sanctify therefore simply means "to make holy" or "to set apart". In Christianity, sanctification means to be set apart for God; Jesus said a lot about being sanctified in John 17. Biblical sanctification is a progressive work as a result of the believer being obedient to God's Word throughout their lifetime; it is precisely what Peter is referring to in 2 Peter 3:18:

> *…but grow in the grace and knowledge of our Lord and Saviour Jesus Christ.*

Sanctification is a word that describes the Christian growing in their spiritual maturity; God began the work of making us "holy" ("set apart") and being Christ-like at the point of salvation, but He continues to progressively sanctify the believer:

> *…He who has begun a good work in you will complete it until the day of Jesus Christ* (Philippians 1:6).

Sanctification is to be pursued by the believer earnestly (1 Peter 1:15; Hebrews 12:14) and is effected by the application of the Word of God (John 17:17). Sanctification of the believer will only be complete when their life on earth is finished and their salvation is complete and they are finally glorified. This is evidenced by the words of Paul in Romans 7:18, 24:

> *For I know that in me (that is, in my flesh) nothing good dwells; for to will is present with me, but how to perform what is good I do not find… Oh wretched man that I am! Who will deliver me from this body of death.*

Seymour (and those who followed him like Wigglesworth) failed to distinguish properly between what we can expect God to fulfil in this present life and what He will fulfil in the resurrection life which is to come. He did this both in respect of his theology on sanctification and healing.

Seymour was motivated by a belief that the true church was being restored in an End-Times miracle revival, and he was on the hunt for the beginning of this revival.

This is the same belief that has driven millions of Christians over the last few decades to travel all over the world at the mere suggestion that the next great revival has begun (such as the previously mentioned "Toronto Blessing", Pensacola Outpouring and Lakeland Revival)

In 1903 (three years before the *Azusa Street Revival* began), Seymour attended in Texas, Houston, the Bible school of his mentor, Charles Fox Parham (4/6/1873-29/1/1929), and it was here that he became committed to another false doctrine: the belief that speaking in tongues is the evidence of being baptised in the Holy Spirit and if someone did not speak in tongues then they had not received the Holy Spirit[5].

Charles Parham was the founder of the Apostolic Faith Movement, and at his Bible school in Topeka, Kansas, his followers had reportedly experienced a "Holy Spirit revival" where they had manifested receiving the Holy Spirit by speaking in tongues; within Pentecostal circles this is known as the Topeka Outpouring of 1901, and events at Azusa Street just five years later are regarded by many as a continuation of the Topeka Outpouring. It began on 1st January 1901 when a student called Agnes Ozman spoke in tongues after Parham had laid hands on her. Parham claimed Ozman spoke in Chinese for three days, unable to speak English, and then spoke in Bohemian  (a language that became extinct after World War II). Soon many other students were reportedly speaking in tongues, with Parham claiming language professors were confirming the tongues spoken as genuine and recognised languages. However, this was never confirmed by anyone outside the school. The students also began to write down what they claimed to be the product of the gift of tongues; they claimed they were recognised languages, but when examined were found to be indecipherable nonsense.

Fascinatingly, on the very same day that Agnes Ozman spoke in tongues, thus starting the Topeka Revival, Pope Leo XIII "invoked" the Holy Spirit, having claimed to have received instruction from Mary to do so. In her 1992 book, *As by a New Pentecost*, Patti Gallagher Mansfield records this "invoking" by Pope Leo XIII as the birthing of what would eventually become known in the 1960s onwards as the *Catholic Charismatic Renewal Movement*, a movement that has been hugely influential in bringing Catholics and Protestants together through the shared experience of supposedly being baptised in the Holy Spirit.

Because of the strict segregation laws in place at the time, Seymour was not allowed to sit in the classroom where Parham taught, so he instead sat and listened from the hall. However, he did not do this for any more than a few weeks before deciding he had learned enough to teach himself from then on.

Seymour and Parham held joint meetings in Houston, with Seymour preaching to black audiences and Parham speaking to the white groups; Parham was keen to use his younger protégé to spread his Apostolic Faith message to the African-Americans in Texas.

Whilst Charles Parham is regarded as one of the two main figures in the development of Pentecostalism (with Seymour being the other), he was by no means "orthodox" in his Christian doctrine; a fact he readily acknowledged himself. For example:

He believed in the annihilation of the unsaved and denied the doctrine of eternal torment; annihilationism is the belief that unbelievers will not experience an eternity of suffering in hell[6], but will instead be "extinguished" after death. Parham stated:

> Orthodoxy would cast this entire company into an eternal burning hell; but our God is a God of love and justice, and the flames will reach those only who are utterly reprobate.

He was a supporter of the false doctrine of British-Israelism (also known as Anglo-Israelism), which teaches that the "lost ten tribes" of Israel migrated to Europe and then to England and became the primary ancestors of the British people and, thereby, the United States of America. This doctrine was also supported by Dowie.

Parham taught there were two separate creations, and that Adam and Eve were of a different race to the people he claimed lived simultaneously outside the Garden of Eden. He claimed the first race of people did not have souls and were destroyed by God in the Flood.

He taught that those who received the latter days spirit baptism and spoke in tongues would make up the Bride of Christ and would have a special place of authority at Christ's return.

He believed in a partial Rapture composed of those believers who spoke in tongues.

Parham was a keen follower of the teachings of John Alexander Dowie and believed that health is a guaranteed part of the apostolic Christian life through healing in the atonement. However, in spite of his firm belief that it is always God's will to heal and medicine and doctors must be shunned, one of Parham's sons died at the age of 16 from a sickness that God did not heal him from. His other son died at the age of 37. There is also the well-documented case of Nettie Smith, the nine year daughter of one of Parham's followers, who died after her father denied her medical treatment in the belief God would heal her if he did not seek medical treatment for her. The young girl's death was completely avoidable because her illness was easily treatable. Parham himself suffered with various illnesses throughout his life and was at times so sick it prevented him from teaching and preaching. Parham was the first Pentecostal preacher to pray over handkerchiefs and post them to those who desired manifestations. He also spent time at Dowie's city of Zion.

In 1907 Charles Parham was arrested for the crime of sodomy.

In early 1906 William Seymour was invited to pastor a small holiness group in Los Angeles led by a female pastor called Julia Hutchinson, a fellowship that had been formed from a group of people who had been disciplined and thrown out of the Second Baptist Church for professing a belief in the same false doctrine of "entire sanctification" that Seymour believed in. On his way to Los Angeles, Seymour visited Alma White's *Pillar* of Fire movement in Denver, Colorado, who also taught the false doctrine of "entire sanctification". However, Alma White was not impressed with Seymour and later said of him:

> I had met all kinds of religious fakers and tramps, but I felt he excelled them all.

White records that Seymour introduced himself as a "man of God", and she asked him to lead a prayer at the close of a meal:

> He responded with a good deal of fervour, but before he had finished I felt that serpents and other slimy creatures were creeping all around me. After he had left the room, a number of the students said they felt he was devil possessed (*Devil and Tongues*, page 67).

Upon arrival in Los Angeles, Seymour managed to give only one sermon at Julia Hutchinson's group before being thrown out for preaching that tongues was the evidence of receiving the Holy Spirit. Much of their distrust of him was because he admitted he had never spoken in tongues himself!

He was locked out of the building, which posed quite a problem for him, because it was also the mission where he was supposed to be living. He was offered accommodation at the home of Edward Lee, a janitor at a local bank, and started meetings at the home of Richard and Ruth Asbery, at 214 North Bonnie Brae; Richard Asbery was also a janitor. After many weeks of meetings of fasting, praying and emotionally charged worship, Edward Lee was the first to speak in tongues, and from that point on numerous strange manifestations began that were attributed to the work of the Holy Spirit without any critical testing.

As a result of the supernatural manifestations attracting more and more people, they moved the meetings to an abandoned building at 312 Azusa Street. It was here that the strange phenomena increased as the numbers attending increased which, according to first-hand accounts included wild dancing, jumping up and down, imitation of various animals, trances, being "slain in the Spirit" (as it came to be known in Pentecostal circles) and falling down, jerking, hysteria, "tongues", strange noises and "holy laughter".

Alma White was personally and deeply affected by events at 312 Azusa Street, because whilst she made a strong stand against it, her husband deserted the *Pillar of Fire* movement to fully embrace it. Such was the division this caused in their marriage that it resulted in them separating. Her husband moved to England in 1922 and served as a pastor and teacher until 1939. Alma White could not be accused of taking a stand against events at Azusa Street because of any pre-disposed opposition to expressions of emotion during meetings, because her *Pillar of Fire* group was often derogatively referred to as the "Holy Jumpers" due to their habit of "working themselves up to a state of religious frenzy which calls for groans and dancing and laughing and shouts to give adequate vent" (*New York Times*). White catalogued in a book titled *Demons and Tongues*, the personal testimonies of people who had witnessed first-hand events at Azusa Street, and here are just a few examples:

> …a woman…stood shaking from head to foot…a man in front of her slid down out of his chair and became unconscious…the man…was…under high nerve pressure.. He arose, staggered to them and began to shake his hand in front of their faces and wave his arms over their heads and moan… Then he put his hands on the heads of the women and began to shake their hair. Some of them lost control of themselves and went under a hypnotic spell. He rubbed a man's jaw until the victim tumbled over on the floor and lay for half an hour, then suddenly began to jabber. Those who had received their 'Pentecost' cried out, 'He has the baptism, he has the baptism!'

> A young coloured woman, doing her best to get the gibberish, went through all kinds of contortions in her effort to get her tongue to work.

> …a coloured woman had her arms around a white man's neck, praying for him. A man of mature years leaped up out of his chair and began to stutter. He did not utter a distinct syllable… 'tut-tut-tut-tut-tut-tut-tut-tut'. This was evidence he had the 'baptism'.

> When the alter call was made, a woman walked up to the front and kissed a man… Kissing between sexes is a common occurrence in the tongue meetings.

> One of the three men…leading the meeting…kneeling upon an open Bible… He was almost beside himself with excitement. His arms waved and his body swayed. I thought…that he might be heard two blocks away. In this meeting there was barking like dogs, hooting like owls, and the like… After

adjourning, one of the leaders remarked in my hearing 'God had a wonderful hold on this meeting for a little while, didn't He?'

I found men and women lying on the floor in all shapes… jabbering all at once in what they called unknown tongues. While I was praying, one of the workers took hold of me and said, 'Holy Ghost, we command thee to go into this soul'. The workers were jabbering and shaking their hands at me, and a demonic power (as I now know) took possession of me, and I fell among people on the floor and knew nothing for ten hours. When I came to my senses I was weak and my jaws were so tired they ached. I believed then that this was of God. They said I was wonderfully blessed, and the leader sent me from one place to another so that I could jabber in tongues.

It would be impossible to publish the things that have occurred there. The familiarity between sexes in the public meetings has been shocking, to say the least. Hell has reaped an awful harvest and in-fidelity has become more strongly rooted…than ever before.

Ask yourself how **any** of these first-hand accounts of events at Azusa Street compare to the Pentecost described in the New Testament, yet Azusa Street is regarded by millions of professing Christians as the "Second Pentecost".

Apologists for Seymour and events at Azusa Street have tried to discredit Alma White's criticism by accusing her of being motivated by racism and pointing to her well-documented sympathies toward white supremacist groups of the time. Whilst it would be wrong to ignore or condone these well-documented connections, they should to be seen in their proper context, which was a period in American history framed by statutes enacted by Southern states (beginning in the 1880s) that legalised segregation between blacks and whites; these statutes were called the Jim Crow laws, named after a character in a popular minstrel song. The effect of these segregation laws is evident by the fact that as much as Charles Parham very clearly supported Seymour's studies at his Bible school, he could not allow Seymour to sit in his class with the white students, thus forcing Seymour to listen from the hall. Does that in any way suggest Parham was a racist? Of course not. He was merely abiding by the (abhorrent) Jim Crow laws. If Alma White's opposition to Seymour was rooted in racial prejudice, why did she have him speak at her *Pillar of Fire* fellowship in the first place? The fact is that White's sympathies toward white supremacist groups were by no means unusual in the context of where and when she lived, and in no way undermines the validity of the independent testimonies she compiled in her book of what occurred at Azusa Street; what happened at Azusa Street does **not** stand up to Biblical scrutiny and she was right to stand against it.

There was little or no order to the Azusa Street meetings and rarely any preaching from Seymour, who instead encouraged people to cry out to God and demand sanctification, the baptism of the Spirit and the divine healing that he believed was every Christian's right to claim. However, even Seymour quickly realised the meetings were getting out of hand and in fact had been filled up with spiritualist mediums, hypnotists and occultists, who had been attracted by the bizarre manifestations. A "*different spirit*" (2 Corinthians 11:4) had infiltrated the so-called move of God; so much so that Seymour wrote frantically to his mentor Charles Parham, begging him to visit to sort things out. When Parham did visit in October 1906, even he was shocked by the confusion he witnessed in the meetings. He was dismayed by the "awful fits and spasms" of the "holy rollers and hypnotists". In *The Life of Charles F. Parham*, his wife Sarah testifies that he saw "hypnotic influences, familiar spirits influences, spiritualistic influences, mesmeric influences and all kinds of spells and spasms, falling in trances etc".

As a man who preached that speaking in tongues was evidence of receiving the Holy Spirit, even Parham described the tongues manifested in the meetings as "chattering, jabbering and sputtering, speaking no language at all". Parham tried to counter the evil he identified at Azusa Street by holding alternative meetings elsewhere to deliver people from the influence of the spirits manifesting at Azusa Street. He said:

> Between two and three hundred who had been possessed of awful fits and spasms and controls in the Azusa Street work were delivered, and received the real Pentecost teaching and many spake with other tongues.

The manifestations Parham documented independently corroborate the accounts compiled in Alma White's book. Parham declared that "God is sick to His stomach" because of the "animalism" going on in the meetings, i.e. people imitating the behaviour and characteristics of animals. In his writings about what he had witnessed at the *Azusa Street Revival* meetings he described men and women falling on each other in a morally compromising manner. Parham never changed his mind about what he witnessed at Azusa Street, denouncing it as a case of "spiritual power prostituted", and in *The Life of Charles F. Parham*, his wife Sarah quotes her husband as saying that two-thirds of the people professing Pentecostalism in his day "are either hypnotised or spook driven" (page 164).

American Pentecostal writer Frank Bartleman made events at Azusa Street famous around the world through his journals about it and in 1925 published a book titled, *How Pentecost Came to Los Angeles* (reprinted in 1955 and 1980). He was an enthusiastic supporter of Azusa Street and experienced being "slain in the spirit", but still admitted people at the meetings were petrified by the occultists who had infiltrated the meetings:

> …spiritualists, hypnotists… all the religious soreheads and crooks and cranks

came… We had the most to fear from these… This condition cast a fear over many which was hard to overcome. It hindered the spirit too much. Many were afraid to seek God for fear the devil might get them.

Other scholarly preachers of the day spoke out against what was going on at Azusa Street. Harry A. Ironside (1876-1941) for example, described it as, "disgusting… delusions and insanities", and R. A. Torrey (1856-1928), the man whom D. L. Moody asked to head the *Bible Institute* in Chicago (now called *Moody Bible Institute*), said that it was, "emphatically not of God, and [referring to Charles Parham] founded by a Sodomite".

Jesus warned that we would know whether or not a teacher, ministry or movement is from God by the fruit produced (Matthew 7:15-20), and the fruit of the Azusa Street Revival has shown itself to be utterly rotten and founded on false doctrine. The Azusa Street Revival was the seedbed from which sprouted several decades later the *Latter Rain* and *Manifest Sons of God* [7] movements, which have in turn spawned every false charismatic revival since. In spite of the manifestations taking place at Azusa Street being recognised by both Seymour and Parham as being absolutely **not** of God, they have been used by subsequent so-called revivals and charismatic ministries as the very thing to aspire to! The "Toronto Blessing", Pensacola, John Wimber's Signs and Wonders movement and Lakeland with Todd Bentley, **all** attributing to the work of the Holy Spirit the kind of ecstatic, out of control manifestations that Seymour and Parham tried to stop. In spite of the accounts of what occurred during the revival meetings at Azusa Street having absolutely no Biblical justification, they are identical to what has been manifested at every false revival since, including the "animalism" documented by Charles Parham and the complete lack of self-control. How can I say the manifestations have no Biblical justification? Because Paul tells us in Galatians 5:23 that the fruit of the Spirit is **self-control** - *egkrateia* in Greek, which is defined in Strong's Concordance as:

Self-mastery, self-restraint, self-control (1466).

The Word of God could not be any clearer.

Doctrinal disagreements eventually caused a split between Parham and Seymour in 1913, which resulted in several independent Pentecostal organisations being formed out of the *Azusa Street Revival*, including the Assemblies of God in 1914 and the Pentecostal Church of God in 1919, which was formed at the *Sharon Bible School* in Canada. In spite of most Pentecostals and Charismatics having never heard of the *Sharon Bible School*, what happened there is just as instrumental as Azusa Street in the development of key heresies that continue to influence much of the charismatic/ evangelical church today.

SHARON BIBLE SCHOOL

In 1947, two men called George Hawtin and Percy Hunt launched an independent Bible School called the *Sharon Bible School* in North Battlefield, Canada. Both were part of the faculty at another Bible school called the *Bethel Bible Institute*, but due to doctrinal disagreements, fell out with the board there, so left and formed their own Bible school so they could freely teach what they wanted to. Most of the students returning after the summer break followed these two influential men to their new Bible school.

The foundation to what was taught at this new Bible school was a coming *Latter Rain*; an outpouring of the Holy Spirit that would change Christianity forever. After a time of corporate prayer and fasting at the school (under the guidance of Hawtin and Hunt, lessons had taken a back seat to more "spiritual" pursuits) a prophecy came forth in one of the classes proclaiming a "new thing" in which God would restore to the church the ministries of the apostle and the prophet, and gifts of the Spirit would be "imparted" by the laying on of hands by certain people chosen by God. Classes at the school were cancelled in order to allow their "revival" meetings to be extended.

Perhaps the first expression of this was reported in the April 1949 issue of the *Sharon Star*, the official publication of the *Latter Rain*. The publication quotes George Hawtin recount the following:

> Suddenly without warning a mighty wind swept through the building, Brother Crane was standing teaching the class when he was almost swept off his feet… This great demonstration was accompanied by a vision of the Manifest Sons of God in the last days of this dispensation. This mighty army was seen conquering all before it. Sickness and disease were vanishing and all evil spirits were scattered before the triumphant power of God's people.

Notice the vision was of sickness, disease and all evil spirits being dispensed with before the "triumphant power of God's people", not God Himself.

News of these "revival" meetings soon spread beyond the gates of the school and began to attract people from far and wide, until eventually thousands were descending on the school from all over the world seeking the "anointing" that was being preached and manifested and the promise of power for God's people. This was the birth of what later became known as the *Latter Rain Revival*. Just like the *Azusa Street Revival* four decades earlier, what happened at the *Sharon Bible School* "revival", and the false doctrine that came out of it, has provided the blueprint for **every** false revival that has followed down the years.

As it was a Bible school you would perhaps be forgiven for thinking that the influence for what went on at the *Sharon Bible School* was the Bible. Tragically, you would be **very** wrong, because George Hawtin and Percy Hunt were directly influenced not by the Bible, but by two men in particular:

Franklin Hall and William Branham.

FRANKLIN HALL

In 1946, convinced the world was on the verge of experiencing a spiritual revival, Franklin Hall authored and published a book titled, *Atomic Power with God through Fasting and Prayer*. Hall was convinced that as a result of the coming world revival the church would emerge victorious and perfected and would produce a new breed of believer called "overcomers" who would not only be immortal, but would also be free from the imprisonment of all gravitational forces (i.e. they would be able to fly!) and be impervious to all sickness and harmful accidents. All this, he believed, would be in fulfilment of the Joel's Army prophecy of Joel 2:3-11, with these "super Christians" being the "Manifest Sons of God". He promoted the doctrine of "body-felt salvation", declaring that it was 700% greater than ordinary healing power. According to Hall, it took around 30 days for the "body-felt salvation" to get established in a person's body in order for them to live completely above both all sickness and tiredness. He claimed a glory cloud hovered over his meetings and when the congregation raised their left hands and said, "Hello Jesus", they would smell the fragrance of Jesus. He further claimed that those who had basked in the fragrance of Jesus would not be recognised by their pets because they would smell differently, and that their homes would be free from insects because the fragrance of Jesus was a "Holy Ghost exterminator". In 1960 Hall published his *Formula for Raising the Dead and the Baptism of Fire*.

The basic premise of Hall's book was that God always responds to prayer when it is accompanied by fasting, and that without fasting, prayer is ineffectual. However, he went even further by claiming that **all** prayer was effectual when accompanied by fasting, irrespective of to whom the prayer was made. Hall would quote the Native American Indian tribes as examples of how their prayers to the Great Spirit were always answered when accompanied by fasting.

In a similarity with the Native American Indian tribes who claimed the Great Spirit manifested itself in fire and smoke, Hall claimed the Holy Spirit manifested itself in the same way.

Hall taught that the restoration of the church would be preceded by psycho-spiritual encounters with UFOs and UHO's (Unidentified Heavenly Objects), and he assigned spiritual significance to the signs of the Zodiac.

The founders of the *Sharon Bible School* put into practice what Franklin Hall taught in his book and all kinds of supernatural manifestations started happening that they attributed to the Holy Spirit.

WILLIAM BRANHAM

Even though he has been dead for over half a century, William Marion Branham (6/4/1909-24/12/1965) continues to cast a long and dark shadow over much of Pentecostal and Charismatic Christianity, with many churches in Canada, South Africa and Europe (including Britain) claiming him as their spiritual leader. Branham's broad and powerful influence is summarised well by the *Dictionary of Pentecostal and Charismatic Movements* as follows:

> The persona universally acknowledged as the revival's 'father' and 'pacesetter' was William Branham. The sudden appearance of his miraculous healing campaigns in 1946 set off a spiritual explosion in the Pentecostal movement which was to move to Main Street, U.S.A., by the 1950s and give birth to a broader charismatic movement in the 1960s, which currently affects almost every denomination in the country. ... Branham filled the largest stadiums and meeting halls in the world. ... As the pacesetter for the healing revival, Branham was the primary source of inspiration in the development of other healing ministries. He inspired hundreds of ministers to enter the healing ministry and a multitude of evangelists paid tribute to him for the impact he had upon their work. As early as 1950, over 1,000 healing evangelists gathered at a *Voice of Healing* [the name of Branham's magazine] convention to acknowledge the profound influence of Branham on the healing movement (page 372).

Branham's influence is further confirmed by modern-day "prophet" Bob Jones:

> There was a man by the name of Jack Moore in Shreveport, Louisiana in 1946. This angel spoke to him and told him to begin to bring people together and so he brought Gordon Lindsay, A. A. Allen, William Branham, Oral Roberts, and Jack Coe...all together and they started the 'Voice of Healing'.

Five years later when the power hit (William Branham was commissioned in May 1946 but the corporate anointing began to take shape some years later), it hit the "Latter Rain" (movement) in '50 and '51… (*Eye of the Eagle II*, 05/12/2000).

Even as a young boy William Branham claimed to have visions, with his first occurring at the age of two. At the age of seven Branham claimed to have his first encounter with what he called "the voice"; later in life he claimed "the voice" was his angel who gave him his supernatural powers. Indeed, a conversation between Branham and an interpreter at one of his healing meetings is recorded in *William Branham: The Man and His Message* (by Carl Dyck) in which the interpreter asked Branham, "Do you think your power to heal people comes from the Holy Spirit?" Branham replied, "No, my angel does it". Try finding justification for that in the Word of God.

Branham was not raised in a Christian family; his parents were in fact known to be fortune-tellers, meaning he grew up in an environment where practice of the occult was commonplace. When Branham met other fortune-tellers they told him they could discern he was powerfully influenced by the supernatural world. Branham himself is quoted in his autobiography, *Footprints on the Sands of Time – My life story*, as saying:

> … one day my cousins and I was going down through a carnival ground, and we was just boys, walking along. So there was a little old fortune teller sitting out there in one of those tents… She said, "Say, you, come here a minute!" And the three of us boys turned around. And she said, "You with the striped sweater" (that was me) … and I walked up, I said, "Yes, ma'am, what could I do for you?" and she said, "Say, did you know there's a Light that follows you? You were born under a certain sign." I said, "What do you mean?" She said, "Well, you were born under a certain sign. There's a Light that follows you. You were born for a Divine call."

When Branham was born, it was said that a one-foot in diameter halo shone above his head, and continued to appear over his head from time to time throughout his ministry, such as the one captured in the photo below, which was taken during a meeting in Houston attended by over 8,000 people.

The photo was captured by a professional photographer hired to expose Branham as a fraud and false prophet, but instead convinced him of Branham's genuine supernatural abilities.

At a public baptism administered by Branham (who became a Baptist minister – imagine how Spurgeon would have responded!), it was claimed that some 4,000 people witnessed a light shining down on him like a halo, with some even claiming to hear a voice declaring that Branham would be as John the Baptist, a forerunner of the Second Coming of Jesus Christ (reminiscent of Dowie's bizarre claims). According to the account, many of those who witnessed this ran in fear, but many others worshipped in the belief they had witnessed a miraculous sign from God confirming Branham's authority as a true prophet of God. This is in spite of halos being completely unbiblical and pagan in origin, dating back to the Hellenists three centuries before the birth of Christ (and of course featuring heavily in Roman Catholic imagery).

Branham himself testifies to this event during a recorded sermon given at the Lane Tech High School in Chicago on 17th January 1955:

> I was baptising down on the river, my first converts, at the Ohio River… And just then a whirl come from the heavens above, and here come that light, shining down… And it hung right over where I was at. A voice spoke from there, and said, "As John the Baptist was sent for the forerunner of the first coming of Christ, you've got a message that will bring forth the forerunning of the second coming of Christ". And it liked to a - scared me to death.

> And I went back, and all the people there… they asked me, said, "What did that light mean?" A big group of coloured people from the – the Gilead Age Baptist Church and the Lone Star Church down there, and many of those was down there, they began screaming when they saw what happen, people fainted.

Very tellingly, Branham admitted in the same sermon that he was often disturbed and scared by the power his angel had over his life. Speaking of a conversation he had with his wife, Meda, he said:

> I said, 'honey, I can't go on like this, I'm a prisoner'. I said, 'All the time, when this thing keeps happening, and things like that, and these visions a-coming, and so forth like that, or whatever it is'. I said, 'Them trances like', I said, 'I don't know what it is. And, honey, I-I-I I don't want to fool with it, they – they tell me it's the Devil. And I love the Lord Jesus.

He clearly felt a prisoner to the angel and the supernatural manifestations he experienced often disturbed him, but at the same time he was sufficiently seduced by the supernatural powers to ignore the warnings of people who were rightly discerning the origin of the power.

What Branham then goes on to describe in some detail is how he reached a point where he determined to lock himself away in a small cabin in the woods he had used as a boy until the supernatural manifestations stopped. However, his account of what occurred in the cabin sounds more like the script for a supernatural horror movie than an encounter with anything holy and truly divine. Until his experience in the cabin, Branham's angel had manifest itself to him through a light or an audible voice, but now the angel revealed itself in physical form as well:

> And, all at once, I seen a light flicker in the room. And I thought somebody was come up with a flashlight. And I looked around, and I thought, 'Well…' And here it was, right in front of me… a light on the floor… I looked around. And here it was above me, hanging right like that. Circling round like a fire, kind of an emerald colour, going, 'Whoosh, whoosh, whoosh!' like that, just above it, like that. And I looked at that, and I thought, 'What is that? Now, it scared me.

> And I heard somebody coming, just walking, only it was barefooted. And I seen the foot of a man come in. Dark in the room, all but right here where it was shining right down. And when he come into the room, walked on up, he was a man about… looked to weigh about two hundred pounds [Branham also described him as having a dark complexion and shoulder length hair]. He had his hands folded like this.

> Now I had seen it in a whirlwind, I had heard it talk to me, and seen it in the form of a light, but for the first time I ever seen the image of it. It walked up to me, real close. Well, honest friends I-I thought my heart would fail me… cause of hundreds and hundreds of times of visitations, it paralyses me when he comes near… I almost completely pass out, just so weak when I leave the platform many times. If I stay too long, I'll go completely out. I've had them ride me round for hours, not even know where I was at. And I can't explain it.

> So I was sitting there and looking at him. I-I kind of had my hand up like that. He was looking right at me, just as pleasant. But he had a real deep voice, and he said, 'Do not fear. I am sent from the presence of Almighty God'. And when he spoke, that voice, that was the same voice that spoke to me when I was two years old, all the way up. I knowed that was him.

> He said, 'I am sent from the presence of Almighty God, to tell you that your peculiar birth' (as you know what my birth was up there; that same light hung over me when I was first born). And he said, 'Your peculiar birth and misunderstood life has been to indicate that you're to go to all the world and pray for the sick people'. And said, 'And regardless of what they have… if you

get the people to believe you, and be sincere when you pray, nothing shall stand before your prayers, not even cancer'.

And he said, 'As the prophet Moses was given two gifts, signs to vindicate his ministry, so will you be given two'. He said, 'One of them will be that you'll take the person that you're praying for by the hand, with your left hand and their right', and said, 'then just stand quiet, and there'll be a physical effect that'll happen on your body. Then you pray. And if it leaves, the disease is gone from the people. If it doesn't leave, just ask a blessing and walk away'.

He said, 'And the next thing will be, if they won't hear that, then they will hear this. Then it'll come to pass that you'll know the very secret of their heart. This they will hear'. He said, 'You were born in this world for that purpose'.

Because of the "signs and wonders" Branham could perform, thousands of people a night flocked to wherever he held meetings. He travelled from city to city creating astonishment wherever he went and building a reputation for being able to perform the supernatural that spread all over the world; a reputation that remains strong today within much of the Pentecostal and Charismatic church. One notable example is a series of healing meetings he held in Kansas which attracted thousands of people every night, hungry to witness Branham's supernatural powers, including a young Oral Roberts, who was deeply influenced by Branham.

In 1950 Branham took his ministry to Europe. 7,000 people packed in to Finland's largest auditorium not just for one night, but night after night, with hundreds, sometimes thousands standing outside. This was repeated time and time again in cities all over Europe. After traveling to Africa in 1952 (where his influence remains strong to this day), he returned to Europe in 1955 to continue the spread of his influence.

Whilst I have read many accounts from people who personally worked closely with Branham during his healing crusades testifying to fake healings (including many accounts of people dying after Branham had declared them healed), there are also countless recorded personal testimonies and accounts of Branham's supernatural powers being manifest in very real and undeniable ways. He would call out words of knowledge and prophecy that were incredibly detailed and accurate. Just as his angel said he would be able to, he would take hold of a person's hand, tell them their name and the illness they were suffering from and would then heal them from it. Kurt E. Koch (1913-1987), respected evangelical scholar who specialised in the study of the occult and demonic possession, provides in his 1967 book, *Between Christ and Satan*, an example of Branham's power in action in a meeting held in Zurich:

He called a young man to the platform. He then asked the young man, "Do we know each other?" "No" was the reply. Branham went on to say, "Have you got a letter in your pocket from a young lady?" This time the answer was, "Yes". "There is a picture with the letter". "That's right". "Will you show me the picture?" The young man pulled it out and Branham held it out for all… to see. "Am I not a prophet?" he called out. There was an enthusiastic response from the people together with cries of "Hallelujah!" and "Praise the Lord!" But we ask, is a piece of fortune telling proof of one's prophetic ability? There should be no confusion here, as the Bible points out, fortune telling is of the Devil (Acts 16:16).

He further comments in the same book:

> He [Branham] not only exhibits abilities of fortune telling, mesmerism [hypnotism], and magic, but he also has certain Christian characteristics. His whole work is hidden behind a screen of Christian words and phrases. Both his parents believed in fortune telling and he was burdened with occultism at an early age. He once told an audience… that he had visionary experiences since childhood… My comment is that the gifts of the Spirit are not imparted to a person at birth, but they receive them after their spiritual rebirth.

Branham was an enthusiastic follower of John Alexander Dowie and actively promoted his teachings in his *Voice of Healing* magazine, which was started in 1948 by Gordon Lindsay, a close associate of Branham's. Lindsay was born in Dowie's Zion City in 1906 and was directly influenced by him and John G. Lake; he was converted under the ministry of Charles Parham. Circulation of the magazine continued to grow long after Branham retired from ministry (if you can call it that), thus keeping the influence of his false doctrine alive. By the early 1970s it was reported to have a circulation of 250,000 worldwide.

Branham had **real** power, but what he preached was very plainly occult; so much so that many Pentecostal churches discouraged him from preaching when visiting and asked him to just stick to performing the miracles. Branham believed that Dowie's "mantle" had been passed to him and that he was now both Elijah the prophet and the angel (messenger) of the seventh church of the book of Revelation, Laodicea.

Branham denied that Eve ate the fruit from the tree, but instead taught his "serpent seed" doctrine in which Eve had sex with Satan, which produced Cain, spawning a soulless race of people destined to be damned.; he taught men could divorce as often as they pleased, providing they married a virgin (women were not free to divorce); he denied hell was eternal and taught all disease was demonic; he taught healing could be lost if a person stopped believing; he taught the words he spoke would literally transform the bodies of his listeners into glorified bodies ready for the Rapture, which he prophesied would happen in 1977; he described the doctrine of the Trinity as a "doctrine of demons"; he claimed he could not perform any miracles until his angel turned up and he believed in three Bibles: the Scriptures, the Zodiac and the pyramids – he preached (when given the opportunity) that all three were equal revelations from God. Branham even has a pyramid on his tombstone in Indiana, USA, as does Charles Taze Russell, the founder of the Jehovah's Witness false religion, who also believed God communicated through the pyramids.

People were scared of what Branham preached, so many asked him to stop, but they could not get enough of his miraculous "signs and wonders", failing to understanding that his doctrine exposed the source of his supernatural power. Supporters of William Branham need to ask themselves a very simple and honest question: why would God give such supernatural power to such an obvious heretic? Branham's bondage to his angel, the voices that tormented him, the vibrations in his hands, the lights that followed him around, his clairvoyant ability to tell people their darkest secrets and the way in which he was left completely exhausted by manifestation of his supernatural "gift", all these are commonplace in the occult, not Biblical Christianity.

A man called Ern Baxter (1914-1993) travelled with William Branham for a number of years (from 1947 to approx. 1953), often doing the speaking for him (particularly when gatherings asked Branham to just perform his miracles, but not preach his heresy). Also, Baxter's personal secretary, George Warnock, was not only one of the North Battlefield brethren, but in 1951 wrote the *Feast of Tabernacles* during his four year stint at *Sharon Bible School* in the capacity of "deacon". Warnock's book laid out a formalised doctrine for the *Latter Rain Movement* and became extremely influential. Branham preached about the coming Latter Rain and Manifest Sons of God. For example, in a message titled "Adoption" accessible on www.williambranham.com, he declares:

> Tell me, my brother, tell me, my sister, when was the time that the sons of God was ever to be manifested outside of this time now?…Nature, the nature itself is groaning, waiting for the time of the manifestation….Now, all things has been brought, coming, shaping up to a headstone, to the manifestation of sons of God coming back, and the Spirit of God coming into these men, so perfectly, until their ministry will be so close like Christ's, till it'll join Him and His church together….Now, the world and nature is groaning, crying; everything's a moving what? For the manifestation of the sons of God, when true sons, born sons, filled sons speak and their word is backed. I believe we're on the border of it right now.

He went on to claim in the same recorded message:

> Oh, waiting for the manifestations of the sons of God (Hallelujah), when God will make Hisself known, when they'll stop sickness, they'll stop cancer, they'll stop diseases.

In response to a question, Branham made reference to the coming of Joel's Army:

> Yes, Brother Copp, I am sure that you are referring to Joel's prophecy in the Old Testament, Joel 2:28, how that he prophesied that in the last days he would pour out his spirit upon all flesh, the sons and daughters would prophesy, the old man would dream dreams and the young men would see visions.

Branham was badly injured in a car crash on the way to Arizona, and died from his injuries six days later on the Christmas Eve of 1965, age 56. Many of his followers at the time of his death were convinced he would rise from the dead, but he did not and his body remains in the grave where he was buried, under a tombstone in the shape of a pyramid. Nevertheless, his occult methodology continues to this day to be regarded by many Pentecostal and Charismatic churches as genuine works of God to be revered and imitated.

THE LATTER RAIN MOVEMENT

The *Latter Rain Movement* began in the 1940s through some in the Pentecostal churches embracing William Branham as a true prophet and man of God, instead of the dangerous demonically empowered deceiver he really was; the church had indeed received a *"different spirit"* as Paul had warned about in 2 Corinthians 11:4.

Based **very** loosely on Ephesians 4:11-13, Branham instigated his *Fivefold Ministry*, with the purpose of restoring the "office" of "apostle" and "prophet" to the church in order for it to be able to fulfil its mission in accordance with the prophecy given at the *Sharon Bible School*. This doctrine quickly became central to the *Latter Rain Movement* and continues to be so today in the modern-day *Prophetic Movement* it spawned and so heavily dominates today's charismatic/evangelical church. From where did the *Latter Rain Movement* derive its name? Hosea 6:3; Joel 2:23 and James 5:7 all refer to the former and latter rains. Taken in their literal sense they refer to the Jewish agricultural calendar where the former rain was essential for the preparation of the soil so seed could be sown, and the latter rain was essential for the perfecting of the crop for harvest. The spiritual application of the former rain is the Law of Moses, which does to people's hearts what the former rain did: prepare the soil for the seed to be sown. Spiritually speaking, the latter rain corresponds to the giving of the Holy Spirit at Pentecost. However, the *Latter Rain Movement* reinterpreted this long-established orthodox understanding so the former rain became the outpouring of the Holy Spirit at Pentecost (some even believing the former rain was Azusa Street) and the latter rain being something even greater than Pentecost; a great End-Time world revival they would be instrumental in bringing forth that would "Christianise" the world in preparation for inviting Jesus to return. This expectation is what has driven this movement's enthusiasm for every false revival you could care to think of, such as Toronto, Pensacola, John Wimber's Signs and Wonders movement and Lakeland with Todd Bentley [see Appendix 3].

The *Latter Rain Movement* claimed a firm belief in the first "fundamental" of the faith as set out by the General Assembly of the Presbyterian Church: the inspiration of Scripture[8], but in practice the prophetic "revelations" and "words" they allegedly received direct from God via these new "apostles" and "prophets" were treated as if they superseded God's written Word, even when the "revelation" or "word" contradicted the Bible. They would never deny the inerrancy of Scripture, but in practice they denied the **sufficiency** of Scripture, because their "revelations" and "words" allegedly received from God were giving them more than Scripture provided.

Ephesians 4:11-13 says:

> *11 And He Himself gave some to be **apostles**, some **prophets**, some evangelists, and some pastors and teachers, 12 for the equipping of the saints for the work of*

ministry, for the edifying of the body of Christ, [13] *till we all come to the unity of the faith and of the knowledge of the Son of God, to a perfect man, to the measure of the stature of the fullness of Christ* (emphasis added).

The new self-proclaimed "apostles" and "prophets" of the *Latter Rain Movement* deemed themselves to be restoring the office of apostle and prophet (whilst giving little attention to the other ministries mentioned in Ephesians 4:11-13 of evangelism, teaching and pastoring) and called this a new restoration of what happened in the church during the first century, and this continues to be a central doctrine of the modern-day *Prophetic Movement* that dominates much of the charismatic/evangelical church today. Influential modern-day "apostle", Bill Haman, provides a clear chronology for how the movement sees its development throughout church history spanning back even to the days of Martin Luther:

> And men of God like that was progressed, and we had the Protestant Movement in the 1500s, the Evangelical Movement in the 1600s, Holiness Movement in the 1700s, Divine Healing Movement, 1800s, Pentecostal Movement, 1900s, then the Latter Rain Charismatic Movement in the 50s and then the Charismatic Renewal in the 60s, then Faith in the 70s. But now the Prophetic in the 80s, Apostle in the 90s, and now we have all five, Apostle, Prophet, Evangelist, Pastor and Teacher, who are going to equip the saints, and then the saints are going to demonstrate the Kingdom (*Trinity Broadcasting Network*, 12/1/2004).

APOSTLES

The following statement by self-appointed "apostle", Chuck Pierce, is representative of the view held by today's *Prophetic Movement* when he writes:

> The apostle John was probably the last of the original apostles who walked on the earth. These apostles were responsible to pass their mantle of revelation from generation to generation (*The Worship Warrior: How Your Prayer and Worship Can Protect Your Home and Community*, pages 117-118).

Pierce of course provides neither any Biblical nor historical evidence to support his claim that the 12 apostles were responsible for passing on to succeeding generations their mantle of revelation, but that is because there is **no** Biblical or historical evidence for him to present. With the exception of Matthias, who was chosen to replace Judas as a member of the original 12, the apostles made no effort to replace their number as they passed away.

The New Testament is clear that the role of apostle was **temporary**, since they were chosen to give **eyewitness** testimony of the risen Christ (Acts 1:21-26; 5:32; Luke 1:1-4; 1 Corinthians 1:9). Paul indicates that he was the last person to see the risen Christ and receive an apostolic commission (1 Corinthians 15:8). The epistles of 2 Peter and Jude, among the very last New Testament writings, exhort the reader to avoid false doctrines by recalling the teachings of the apostles (2 Peter 1:12-15; 2:1; 3:2; 14-16: Jude 3-4; 17). Peter and Jude did not instruct the believer to listen to the apostles living today, but instead urged believers to **remember** what the apostles **had** said.

To be clear, apostolic authority does still exist in the church today, but how this is exercised, and by whom, needs to be properly understood in light of Scripture. Apostolic authority is exercised in the church today in two **Biblical** ways. Firstly, and most importantly, Jesus remains **the** Apostle, with all other apostolic authority within the church deriving from him. Hebrews 3:1 describes Jesus as "***the*** *Apostle of our confession*"; the definite article. Ephesians 2:20 makes clear that the foundations of the church are built on the Biblical apostles and prophets, with Jesus being the "*chief cornerstone*". Nowhere in Scripture does it say the foundation of the church needs building over and over again by new apostles and prophets; there is **no** Biblical mandate for that anywhere.

Secondly, apostolic authority continues in the church today by Peter, Paul, James and John through their New Testament writings that were inspired by the Holy Spirit. No other writings or revelation are even equal to either Jesus the Apostle or the original apostles.

Apostolic authority in the church today is exercised doctrinally and is concerned with defending the truth from error; exactly the kind of error spouted by these new self-appointed "apostles" and "prophets". Their multiple claims of "God has revealed to me…" are bogus and should be treated with the contempt they deserve.

As mentioned earlier, the evidence that the authority of these new "apostles" and "prophets" is self-proclaimed and not Biblical is the fruit it has produced in the lives of the people who have been under their authority. People who have placed themselves under their authority have fallen victim to terrible heavy shepherding that has shipwrecked faiths, broken up families and left multitudes emotionally scarred and disillusioned with what they thought was Christianity. This is what the prophet Ezekiel predicted:

> The weak you have not strengthened, nor have you healed those who were sick, nor bound up the broken, nor brought back what was driven away, nor sought what was lost; but with force and cruelty you have ruled them (Ezekiel 34:4).

In spite of the Biblical definition of an apostle clearly being someone who had been an eyewitness to the risen Christ, and therefore was a temporary role as far as it being held by a person is concerned, an expansive description of what a modern "apostle" is can be found on the *International Coalition of Apostles* website. The following is just a small fragment of that description:

> An apostle is a Christian leader gifted, taught, commissioned and sent by God with the authority to establish the foundational government of the church within an assigned sphere of ministry by hearing what the Spirit is saying to the churches and by setting things in order accordingly for the extension of the kingdom of God.

It then goes on to describe nuclear church apostles, marketplace apostles, territorial apostles, vertical apostles, horizontal apostles and philanthropic apostles.

Returning to the first of the seven letters which Jesus wrote to the seven churches of Asia Minor, Jesus commended the church at Ephesus because they had *"tested those who say they are apostles and are not, and have found them liars"* (Revelation 2:2). The self-appointed "apostles" of the *Prophetic Movement* are demonstrable liars.

In response to the teaching that the role of apostle had been restored to the church, the Assemblies of God published a position paper in 2000, which stated:

> The leadership of the local church, according to the Pastoral Epistles, is in the hands of elders/presbyters and deacons. These are the last of Paul's epistles. There is no indication in these last writings of continuing offices of apostles and prophets, though the ministry functions still continue.

The teaching of a continuation or restoration of the role of apostle and prophet in the church today is dangerously similar to the teaching of the Mormon Church, which claims to have living apostles, without which the Mormon Church cannot function. Without their "apostles" and "prophets" the *Prophetic Movement* cannot function.

PROPHETS

As for restoring the position of prophet, whilst we are no longer called to stone false prophets, the individuals involved in this crazy movement have made so many false prophecies and predictions you would be forgiven for thinking they were stoned in another way when making them!

For example, on 31/12/1997 Rick Joyner and Bob Jones prophesied that within nine months of giving the prophecy, California would be destroyed by earthquakes and nuclear bombs and the Mississippi River would be 35 miles wide. Obviously none of this came to pass, but those who did believe the prophecy were thrown into panic and sold houses and left jobs in response, and were then left to pick up the pieces of their lives when it did not happen.

Consider the following prophecy given by Kim Clement on TBN on 12/1/2004 about the imminent capture of Osama bin Laden:

> Osama bin Laden said that in 35 days, America, he was prophesying, predicting, that this country would be abolished basically, wiped out, because he has a plan for 35 days. **And the word of the Lord came to me… the spirit of the Lord said to me**, "You prophesy that the very thing that he said and predicted for this nation, tell him, prophesy, that that is reversed, and I'm going to bring him out in 35 days! (emphasis added).

In spite of Clement claiming he was told to give the prophecy by "the spirit of the Lord", when American Special Forces did finally catch up with bin Laden, it was **seven years** later, not 35 days, and he was shot dead, **not** captured.

Consider also the following prophecy declared by Bill Yount, a man whose prophecies are regularly published in the "Elijah List" online newsletter (more on this later); a prophecy so obviously idiotic that it would be funny had he not claimed to speak directly on behalf of the Lord by ending his prediction with the words, "earth, earth… hear the word of the Lord":

> I sense the Father saying, 'I will begin to meddle in the candy industry.' I sense the Lord is going to begin to name some new candy bars. When these are named they will release a prophetic anointing every time the name of the candy is mentioned. These names will have the power to call forth life and salvation. I am sure this prophetic candy is bound to have a heavenly

taste to it that will be out of this world! People will end up tasting and seeing that the Lord is good! I saw angels anointing candy bar wrappers like God anointing prayer cloths of the apostle Paul. Names on popular candy wrappers will speak prophetically to whomever reads or speaks their names. Candy wrappers will become like anointed prayer cloths throughout the land.

Anointed candy bars? I guess God must have been using a whisper, because I have never heard of Yount's prophecy coming to pass...

As if the above prophecy was not lunacy enough, he went on to predict that Levi's jeans were going to receive a prophetic anointing to call forth the spiritual Levites of this hour and that Wrangler clothing would be anointed to tame the tongue and give people the "tongue of the learned to speak a word to those who are weary".

It would be all too easy to make a joke out of such blatantly ridiculous prophecies and simply dismiss Yount as nothing more than a harmless crackpot, but the reality is that Yount is an influential and regular contributor to the "Elijah List", who claims to speak these things in the name of the Lord, and is never brought to task by others on the "Elijah List" for predicting such rubbish in the name of the Lord.

Another example was the following prophecy given by Catherine Brown on 27/3/2007:

> There will be a seven-year period of plenty, followed by a seven-year period of famine. From 2007-2014, I am granting a window of grace and mercy to prepare for the seven years of famine.

What actually happened was that on 15/9/2008, one of the worst financial crashes in history occurred with the Dow Jones plummeting 500 points in just one day, resulting in hundreds of billions of dollars being wiped off the value of the American Stock Market, thousands of jobs being lost, and an unprecedented government bailout to prevent the financial system from collapsing completely; a financial crisis that the whole world has still not recovered from and exactly the opposite of what Catherine Brown prophesied!

But inaccuracy is perfectly acceptable according to these new "prophets". For example, in *Prophets and Personal Prophecy*, modern-day "apostle" Bill Haman claims:

> The prophet who misses it occasionally in his prophecies may be ignorant, immature, or presumptuous, or he may be ministering with too much zeal and too little wisdom and anointing. But this does not prove him a false prophet… It is certainly possible for a true prophet to be inaccurate.

Not according to God!

In a teaching tape titled *Shepherds Rod*, Kansas City (false) Prophet, Bob Jones, rationalises his (and his associates) false predictions by claiming the spoken word of God (*rhema* – more on this later) would be two-thirds accurate in the days to come, as the new "prophets" practice their gift and calling. Even if Jones and his fellow "prophets" did ever get close to being two-thirds accurate they would still be a full one-third short of God's standard for a true prophet.

In spite of Peter declaring, *"No prophecy of Scripture is of any private interpretation"* (2 Peter 1:20), Bob Jones claimed to have a standing appointment with the Lord; every year on Yom Kippur (the Day of Atonement) Jones claimed the Lord came to "stand before" him to give him personal and private revelation; yes, you read that right, Jones claimed that God stood before him! On the same Shepherds Rod teaching tape Jones described how he inaugurated an annual day of judgment where everyone in his fellowship had to literally pass under **his** shepherd's rod for inspection of the fruit in their lives! Who was checking his fruit when he was exposed for committing serious and prolonged sexual immorality?[9] Bob Jones was an immoral and wicked deceiver who was under the direct influence of demonic spirits, and I challenge anyone to refute that.

In spite of neither of the newly restored "offices" being in the Biblical model, these new "apostles" and "prophets" were, and have continued to be embraced, believed and revered by so many charismatic/evangelical Christians who refuse to judge their leaders by the standards set out in Scripture. For example, in a YouTube video titled "False Prophets" posted 7/9/2010, Kris Vallotton, a leader at Bill Johnson's *Bethel Church*, made the following statements, which typify the attitude of people within this movement today:

> There's a difference between a bad prophetic word and a false prophet.

> You can get the [prophetic] word wrong, and not be a false prophet.

> Because you give words that aren't completely accurate, it doesn't mean you're a false prophet. It just means that you have prophetic words that need help.

I can tell you that there are people who've been wrong for thirty years. I'm not saying they're false prophets. I'm just saying they are bad ones.

There's a difference between a false prophet and a bad prophet. A false prophet has an evil heart. A bad prophet just gets everything wrong.

Vallotton's double-talk is no better than trying to make a distinction between a scoundrel and a rogue, or a liar and a fibber. Compare Vallotton's statements against the Biblical definition of a true and false prophet and you quickly see how deeply unbiblical his statements are. Consider for example how Samuel is described in the Old Testament:

> *[19] So Samuel grew, and the Lord was with him and let none of his words fall to the ground. [20] And all Israel from Dan to Beersheba knew that Samuel had been established as a prophet of the Lord* (1 Samuel 3:19-20).

Why would people like Vallotton go to such effort to justify blatantly false prophets? I believe Jeremiah 5:31 provides the answer:

> *The prophets prophesy falsely, and the priests rule by their own power, **and My people love to have it so*** (emphasis added).

But he is far from alone in the way he ignores what the Word of God says about the accuracy of prophets in order to justify why the people he follows are still in ministry. For example, in an interview with *Charisma* magazine in April 2001, Francis Frangipane defended the false prophecy about California given by Rick Joyner and Bob Jones by claiming:

> The idea that a prophet should never make a mistake assumes that teachers, evangelists and pastors also never make mistakes… All are speaking for the Lord, yet who has not admitted that they either taught something wrong or at least publicly repeated wrong information.

Frangipane's claim completely ignores the fact that the Bible **never** makes the same distinction he does; even though the Bible says teachers will receive a *"stricter judgment"* (James 3:1), it clearly applies a higher level of accountability to those who claim to speak and prophesy directly in the name of the Lord than it does to those in the ministries of teaching or evangelism. Just read Jeremiah 23:25-32 to understand the Lord's view of those who prophesy falsely in His name.

In an even more dishonest handling of the Word of God in an attempt to justify false prophets, Frangipane uses Jonah as an example of a man who gave a false prophecy, but was still regarded by God as a true prophet. He quotes Jonah 3:4 in which Jonah declared in the city of Nineveh, *"Yet forty days, and Nineveh shall be overthrown"*, but of course Nineveh was not overthrown. Is this therefore a Biblical example of a false prophecy from a true prophet of God as Frangipane claims?

No.

First of all, (and most importantly) Jonah 3:1 makes clear that Jonah said exactly what God wanted him to say; unlike the false prophets Frangipane tries to defend, Jonah **did** speak directly for God.

Secondly, Jonah did not give a false prophecy because implied within the prophecy was a condition under which the predicted judgment would not take place. The people of Nineveh clearly understood the judgment prophesied by Jonah would be avoided if they repented, and that is exactly what they did (Jonah 3:5-9).

Thirdly, because Jonah **was** a true prophet, and knew God's merciful nature, he knew the Ninevites would repent and therefore avoid the judgment he was warning of; **that** is precisely why he did not want to go to Nineveh in the first place:

> *But it displeased Jonah exceedingly, and he became angry. So he prayed to the Lord, and said, "Ah, Lord, was not this what I said when I was still in my country? Therefore I fled previously to Tarshish; for I know you are a gracious and merciful God, slow to anger and abundant in lovingkindness, One who relents from doing harm* (Jonah 4:1-2).

The lengths people like Francis Frangipane will go to in order to defend a lie is far greater than most Christians will go to in order to defend **the** truth. Apologists like Frangipane will go to ridiculous lengths to try to convince us that genuine prophets can give false prophecies when in reality Deuteronomy 18 very clearly says they cannot. But then the new "apostles" and "prophets" of the modern-day *Prophetic Movement* that dominate so much of today's charismatic/evangelical church do not accept they are subject to the Deuteronomy 18 test. For example, Rick Joyner claims:

> One of the greatest hazards affecting maturing prophets is the erroneous interpretation of the Old Testament exhortation that if a prophet ever predicted something which did not come to pass he was no longer considered a true prophet… The warning was that if this happened, the prophet has been presumptuous and the people were not to fear him. If one predicts something in the name of the Lord and it does not come to pass, he probably has spoken presumptuously and needs to be repented of, but that does not make him a false prophet. No one could step out in the faith required to

walk in his calling if he knew that a single mistake could ruin him for life (*Morningstar Prophetic Newsletter*, Vol. 3, No. 2, Page 2).

Joyner gives no explanation of **how** it is erroneous to interpret Deuteronomy 18 as meaning we are supposed to reject inaccurate prophets. If we are to believe Joyner and not subject their "prophets" to the God-given Deuteronomy 18 test, just how **should** we test the authenticity of a prophecy? Influential *New Apostolic Reformation* (NAR) "prophet", Bill Haman promotes the "inner witness test", which he describes the following way:

> The inner witness of the [Holy] Spirit with our spirits is one way of determining that a prophetic utterance is of the Lord (*Prophets, Pitfalls and Principles*).

This "inner witness" is said to manifest itself through physical sensations in the "upper stomach or lower chest area" that let believers know if a prophecy is true or not. In *Prophets, Pitfalls and Principles*, Haman describes the sensations that indicate a false prophecy:

> A negative spirit-witness with a message of either "No", or "Be careful", or "Something's not right", usually manifests itself with a nervous, jumpy, or uneasy feeling, a deep, almost unintelligible sensation that something is not right.

Alternatively, if a prophecy is true, Haman describes the sensation as follows:

> There is a deep, unexplainable peace and joy, a warm, loving feeling, or even a sense of our spirit jumping up and down with excitement.

Not only are these physical sensations utterly subjective and never described in the Word of God, they are in fact very disturbingly similar to the "burning in the bosom" experienced by Mormons as a way of confirming the truth of the Mormon faith to them.

So what does Deuteronomy 18 say about identifying a true and false prophet?

Deuteronomy 18:22 states:

> *When a prophet speaks in the name of the Lord, if the thing does not happen or come to pass, that is the thing which the Lord has not spoken; the prophet has spoken it presumptuously; you shall not be afraid of him.*

In spite of Kris Valloton's double-talk and Bill Haman's "burning in the bosom", the Bible provides a crystal clear definition of a false prophet: if what is predicted does not happen, he/she is a false prophet; no room for an acceptable percentage of error, or left to a "gut feeling", the Bible is very clear, and whilst we are no longer called to put false prophets to death, there is absolutely **nothing** provided in the New Testament to supersede the God-given Deuteronomy 18 definition of a false prophet.

But what if the prophecy/prediction comes true?

Do we then automatically assume the prophet is of God?

Just as we recognise a false prophet by the false prophecy, do we therefore recognise a true prophet by a true prophecy?

Absolutely **not**.

Let us use William Branham as an example because he **passed** the Deuteronomy 18 test with flying colours, because the prophecies and words of knowledge he was able to give were **very** accurate. Deuteronomy 13:1-5 therefore provides a further test to establish whether or not the person who made an accurate prophecy/prediction is genuinely from God:

> *If there arises among you a prophet or a dreamer of dreams, and he gives you a sign or a wonder, ² and the sign or the wonder comes to pass, of which he spoke to you, saying, 'Let us go after other gods'—which you have not known—'and let us serve them,' ³ you shall not listen to the words of that prophet or that dreamer of dreams, for the Lord your God is testing you to know whether you love the Lord your God with all your heart and with all your soul. ⁴ You shall walk after the Lord your God and fear Him, and keep His commandments and obey His voice; you shall serve Him and hold fast to Him.⁵ But that prophet or that dreamer of dreams shall be put to death, because he has spoken in order to turn you away from the Lord your God, who brought you out of the land of Egypt and redeemed you from the house of bondage, to entice you from the way in which the Lord your God commanded you to walk. So you shall put away the evil from your midst.*

Deuteronomy 13 clearly tells us that even if what is prophesied/predicted comes true, we should **not** judge the authenticity of the prophet just by the fact that it has come true, we should also judge that persons authenticity by what he **teaches**, and what William Branham taught was plainly heretical and **occult**. In spite of this Branham was used as the model for what occurred at the *Sharon Bible School* "revival", the model for the development of the *Latter Rain Movement* by those in the Pentecostal church wanting a "new thing", and continues to be the model used by almost every modern-day prophetic and healing ministry since; hardly a sound Biblical foundation.

Most of those who continue to use Branham as the spiritual model for their ministries refuse to acknowledge the heresy he preached, and even the few people who do acknowledge what he preached try to play-down his heresy, or suggest it was just towards the end of his life. For example, in his book, The *Reality of the Supernatural*, Todd Bentley writes, "…a great deal of controversy surrounded the final days of Branham's ministry" (page 81). In addition, Bill Johnson, a prominent member of the modern-day *Prophetic Movement* said:

> William Branham – If I mention the name, William Branham, in certain circles, I mean, they almost want to, you know, stone me, because William Branham is known for heresy towards the end of his life. And yet there are few men that have ever lived, and perhaps no one that has ever lived that carried the anointing and the power that this particular man had.

Johnson's quote clearly demonstrates his admiration for William Branham as a true and powerful man of God, which should be reason enough for members of his church to be stampeding for the exit door, but also illustrates how dishonest he (and Bentley) is in trying to play-down Branham's heresy because, as mentioned earlier, he was most certainly **not** just known for it towards the end of his life; his life was identified with occult manifestations from early childhood and he preached his occult heresy right from the beginning of his ministry; Branham's miraculous "signs and wonders" were the result of his heretical and occult beliefs, not in spite of them. Christians both during Branham's lifetime and since have wrongly used his "signs and wonders" as the test of his authority and authenticity as a man of God, instead of what he preached; they ignore the God-given Deuteronomy 13 test.

But I hear people cry:

> Why would God allow a false prophet to prophesy something that comes true?

This is the question I am always asked by people who have been taught William Branham was a true man of God. Deuteronomy 13:3 provides the answer to that question:

> *You shall not listen to the words of that prophet or that dreamer of dreams, for the Lord your God is testing you to know whether you love the Lord your God with all your heart and with all your soul.*

God uses false prophets to test His people's love for Him, to test their obedience to His Word; a test that is continued in the New Testament:

> *He who has My commandments and keeps them, it is he who loves Me. And he who loves Me will be loved by My Father, and I will love him and manifest Myself to him* (John 14:21).

Jesus answered and said to him, "If anyone loves Me, he will keep My word; and My Father will love him (John 14:23).

This is love, that we walk according to His commandments. This is the commandment, that as you have heard from the beginning, you should walk in it (2 John 1:6).

Of those who claimed to follow Him, but did not obey His commands, Jesus said:

But why do you call Me 'Lord, Lord,' and not do the things which I say? (Luke 6:46).

1 John 2:3 states:

³ Now by this we know that we know Him, if we keep His commandments. ⁴ He who says, "I know Him," and does not keep His commandments, is a liar, and the truth is not in him. ⁵ But whoever keeps His word, truly the love of God is perfected in him. By this we know that we are in Him. ⁶ He who says he abides in Him ought himself also to walk just as He walked.

Jesus even said there would be no salvation without obedience:

Not everyone who says to Me, 'Lord, Lord,' shall enter the kingdom of heaven, but he who does the will of My Father in heaven (Matthew 7:21).

Serous stuff.

FRUITS

The above passage in Matthew 7 brings me nicely to what the New Testament says about identifying a false prophet, from the mouth of Jesus Himself:

¹⁵ "Beware of false prophets, who come to you in sheep's clothing, but inwardly they are ravenous wolves. ¹⁶ You will know them by their fruits. Do men gather grapes from thornbushes or figs from thistles? ¹⁷ Even so, every good tree bears good fruit, but a bad tree bears bad fruit. ¹⁸ A good tree cannot bear bad fruit, nor can a bad tree bear good fruit. ¹⁹ Every tree that does not bear good fruit is cut down and thrown into the fire. ²⁰ Therefore by their fruits you will know them (Matthew 7:15-20).

Most Christians will be familiar with Jesus' statement that we would know false prophets *"by their fruits"*, but far fewer really seem to have a proper understanding of its application, because too many Christians assume the *"fruits"* of a ministry include only things like temporal or material success and size, or whether or not the people involved subjectively seem sincere, happy and peaceful, or perceive them to be closer to God. Supernatural manifestations are often interpreted as *"fruits"* and blessing from God, whilst others see good works as *"fruits"*, such as giving to the poor. Whilst some of these things can be *"fruits"*, it should also be noted that such things are also used to justify entirely false religions and cults. For example, Mormons do a lot of charitable work and often come across as being happy, peaceful, sincere and very moral; their founder, Joseph Smith, made prophecies and performed healings that were far more impressive than today's so-called new "apostles" and "prophets" perform. *"Fruits"* mean more than most Christians recognise it to mean; **doctrine** is an important *"fruit"*. The teaching of a man or ministry must be examined in the light of Scripture, because no matter how closer to God someone may feel through someone's teaching and ministry, false doctrine can in reality do nothing other than take someone further away from God.

Another *"fruit"* that is rarely considered is the impact on the lives of those who have been damaged by false prophecy; the people who have responded to a prophecy by perhaps uprooting families, selling homes, or giving money away to a man or ministry, only to find the prophecy that prompted them to do so turned out to be false. What about the impact on the lives of those who received a word of prophecy about the healing of a loved one, only to see their loved one die? How many false prophets have returned to the scene of their "crime" in order to apologise and/or help rebuild the life and faith that their false prophecy has shattered?

Returning to the previously mentioned issue of the supernatural, in Matthew 7 Jesus gives a sober warning that the manifestation of the miraculous does not necessarily indicate the Lord is present in it, and to those who held up their own miraculous activities as proof of their discipleship He said, *"I never knew you"*. Supernatural activity from someone claiming to be a disciple of Jesus is not the final proof. Another passage along the same lines is Matthew 24:24 where Jesus declares:

> *For false christs and false prophets will rise and show great signs and wonders to deceive, if possible, even the elect.*

Here we have again Jesus warning that false prophets will arise who will be able to perform the supernatural, thus demonstrating further that, contrary to what many Christians believe, **power** is not the test. The overwhelming emphasis of the New Testament is on testing the message (doctrine) of the prophet, but this was wilfully ignored by followers of William Branham during his ministry, and continues to be wilfully ignored by those within the modern-day Prophetic Movement who still hold up William Branham as the ultimate model and benchmark for their ministries. For example:

Bill Johnson has described Branham as having an "anointing and power" like "no one that has ever lived" (www.youtube.com/watch?v=VbTCDk2CGNo).

Paul Cain called Branham "the greatest prophet that ever lived in any of my generations or any of the generations of revival I've lived through".

In *The Coming Revival*, Rodney Howard Browne (the man acknowledged as being responsible for originally "imparting" the so-called "blessing" to Toronto Airport Vineyard Fellowship) called Branham "a true prophet of God" and "a great man of God".

In his book, *The Reality of the Supernatural World*, Todd Bentley lavishes praise on Branham and claims he "moved in more accurate realms of revelation than almost anyone else in his time did. Some say his gifting was 100 percent accurate (page 82).

On www.elijahlist.com, Paul Keith Davies lavishes the following praise on Branham:

> During the 1930s an extraordinarily gifted prophet began to emerge as a spiritual leader of a new ministry model... God wonderfully graced thus humble man with a revolutionary gift and supernatural power not seen since the early church... In this experience God gave William Branham a forerunner message for his life and ministry. **I believe he was a token or prototype of an entire body of people who will emerge as Jesus' bridal company** (emphasis in the original).

In *Early Supernatural Models*, Paul Keith Davies states:

> Branham had several supernatural experiences for which he had no frame of reference or ability to understand.

Allow me to interpret what Davies actually meant:

> There was absolutely no Biblical precedent or justification for Branham's supernatural experiences, but they were nevertheless powerful and real so we will embrace them and pursue them for ourselves.

Whilst "prophesying" over Todd Bentley, Che Ahn (a key figure in the "Toronto Blessing") declared:

> There's a Branham anointing on you, a double portion of it.

Very shortly afterwards of course, Bentley's extra-marital affair with a member of his ministry team was exposed. Bentley said he was unable to perform any miracles until his "healing angel" turned up, claiming it was the same angel that gave Branham his power. For example, Bentley writes in *Discerning the Call of God*:

> An angel appeared to me, the angel said, "I am the angel that has been assigned to your life. I am the healing angel... You are going to take miracles,

signs and wonders around the world. I was with William Branham". He told me about William Branham's angelic encounter in 1946.

In *Growing in the Prophetic*, Mike Bickle writes:

> Throughout church history there have been a lot of anointed people who have wound up with strange doctrines. Their constituency bought into the false assumption that a person whom God uses in a genuine prophetic or healing ministry *must* be 100 percent doctrinally correct. The most notable example in recent history is William Branham (italics in original).

Bickle creates a straw man argument about someone having to be 100 percent correct in their doctrine before God can use them, because no one is claiming that. However, William Branham was a full card-carrying **heretic**. Men like Bickle within the modern-day *Prophetic Movement* use Branham's power as the test of his authenticity instead of his heretical and demonically inspired doctrine; with his doctrine so obviously being demonically inspired, surely it is obvious that his power was demonically empowered. How would the apostle Paul have responded to William Branham? Would he have accepted his "signs and wonders" as evidence of his authority as a true man of God? Would he have over-looked Branham's doctrine as nothing more than minor theological differences of opinion between believers?

> *But even if we, or an angel from heaven, preach any other gospel to you than what we have preached to you, let him be accursed. ⁹ As we have said before, so now I say again, if anyone preaches any other gospel to you than what you have received, let him be accursed* (Galatians 1:8-9).

Is not Branham's "serpent seed" doctrine, or his denial of the Trinity preaching another gospel?

If not, what **is?**

Branham preached doctrine contrary to Biblical truth. Would Paul have embraced Branham for the sake of unity within the Body of Christ?

> *Now I urge you, brethren, note those who cause divisions and offenses, contrary to the doctrine which you learned, and avoid them* (Romans 16:17).

God does not magnify unity above His name, as so many Christians seem to think; God magnifies His **Word** above His name (Psalm 138:2). This is how important God's Word is to Him, yet far too many prominent and influential Christians today use Branham as the model and benchmark for their ministries. Welcome to the apostasy…

Fortunately, during the 1940s, the majority of (but sadly not all) Pentecostals were more Biblically literate and obedient than Mike Bickle or Paul Keith Davies, and **did** test William Branham and the *Latter Rain Movement* in accordance with the Deuteronomy 18 and 13 tests, and recognise the *"fruit"* he was producing in accordance with the words of Jesus in Matthew 7. They therefore rejected Branham and the *Latter Rain Movement* accordingly; they **noted** him and **avoided** him in accordance with Paul's instruction in Romans 16:17. William Branham and the *Latter Rain Movement's* influence within mainstream Pentecostalism had seemingly therefore withered by the end of the 1960s. However, it most certainly did not wither enough to die off; it just moved underground for a time, waiting for the opportunity to surface again, and that is exactly what it did initially on the fringes of the *Charismatic Renewal Movement* of the 1970s, but then gaining more significant influence in the 1980s through John Wimber and the Vineyard Churches, the Promise Keepers[10], the Spiritual Warfare Movement and the Kansas City Prophets, which came out of the Kansas City Fellowship run by Mike Bickle. In fact, Paul Cain, one of the Kansas City (false) Prophets, directly participated in the *Voice of Healing Revival* initiated by William Branham in the 1950s, and was regarded at the time by those within the *Latter Rain Movement* as Branham's protégé; it was claimed by some that Cain had the same "anointing" as Branham. Paul Cain was later exposed (in 2004) as a homosexual alcoholic. This is the same Paul Cain who spoke at the Toronto Airport Vineyard Fellowship in 1992 and declared:

> What is happening here in Toronto is nothing more than what was predicted in the Latter Rain teachings in 1948. It went underground for a number of years, because it was kind of embarrassing to talk about it because so many were against it, but I'm not embarrassed anymore and I am going to proclaim that the Latter Rain is being fulfilled.

Whilst in the 1940s *Latter Rain* doctrine was viewed as a relatively small distraction to the church at large, it was to evolve into a mainstream deception from the 1980s onwards, thanks in no small part to John Wimber.

JOHN WIMBER

John Wimber's role and influence in promoting both unbiblical "signs and wonders" and Latter Rain teaching cannot be overstated. We must therefore take a closer look at this man and his ministry that has left such a legacy within mainstream charismatic/evangelical circles.

John Wimber (1934-1997) first visited the UK in the early 1980s and found the mainstream charismatic/evangelical church fully primed and ready to accept his "signs and wonders" as an authentic move of the Holy Spirit; in spite of the manifestations being characterised by a complete lack of self-control and Galatians 5:23 clearly stating the fruit of the spirit is self-control. He was introduced to the UK through Anglican clergymen David Pytches of St. Andrew's in Chorley Wood (founder of New Wine) and David Watson of St. Michael le Belfrey in York (who left St. Michael's for London in 1982). St. Andrew's in particular played a key role in the development of the Vineyard movement in the UK, especially through the New Wine Christian festivals that enthusiastically promoted Wimber and his teaching. These initial connections with the UK led Wimber to develop a close and long-lasting association with St. Thomas' Church in Crookes, Sheffield.

Prior to being saved in 1962, John Wimber enjoyed the kind of success in the music industry that most people can only dream of. He managed the *Righteous Brothers* (whose music enjoyed somewhat of a renaissance with people my age through some of their songs being featured in blockbuster movies such as Top Gun and Ghost during the 1980s and 1990s). However, when he (and his wife) got saved, Wimber gave up the secular success, took up a job in a factory and entered into discipleship. By 1970, he was pastor of a Quaker church.

Wimber's influence on the broader body of Christ began in the mid 1970's when he left the Quaker church he was pastoring in California to become a lecturer at the

Fuller Institute of Evangelism and Church Growth at Fuller Theological Seminary in Pasadena, California. This travelling ministry gave him the opportunity to get a broad view of the church in America, across denominational lines. He served more or less as a consultant to local churches on church growth and related issues and quickly became a highly sought after lecturer.

In was through his position at Fuller Church Growth Institute that he came into contact with a fellow professor called C. Peter Wagner, a key leader in the "church growth" movement, founder of Global Harvest Ministries and the man who would eventually head up the emergence of the *New Apostolic Reformation* in the late 1990s.

Wagner was responsible for introducing terms to the church that were previously unknown, such as territorial spirits, Spiritual Warfare Network (of which he was the leader), ground-level spiritual warfare, occult-level spiritual warfare, strategic-level warfare, cosmic-level spiritual warfare, praise marches, prayer walking, prayer journeys and spiritual mapping; the practice of discovering the exact location of a demon's domain. In fact, from 1991 to 1999, Wagner taught a class on spiritual mapping as a critical element for effective missions in his MC551 course at Fuller Theological Seminary. In spite of this being taught at a theological seminary, it certainly was not derived from the word of God, because there is nothing in the Word of God about identifying and naming regional demons. Spiritual warfare evangelism is deeply rooted in *Latter Rain* teaching, with Wagner first obtaining this teaching from John Dawson of YWAM (*Youth With A Mission*). Wagner describes Dawson's book, *Taking Our Cities For God: How to Break Spiritual Strongholds*, as "the most important book on the subject ever written". Dawson would consult shamans in order to ascertain the names of demons.

SPIRITUAL WARFARE

Introducing a book he edited called *Breaking Strongholds in Your City: How to Use Spiritual Mapping to Make Your Prayers More Strategic, Effective and Targeted,* Wagner writes:

> This book uncovers the wiles of the devil and exposes the prayer targets that will force the enemy to release millions of unsaved souls now held captive. I am excited that God has given us a marvellous new tool for effective spiritual warfare.

A new tool? How on earth did the Christian church cope evangelising for the last 2,000 years without this tool for spiritual warfare?

In *Engaging the Enemy: How to Fight and Defeat Territorial Spirits*, he explains:

> Spying out the land is essential when warring for a city… Christians should walk or drive every major freeway, avenue and road of their cities, praying and coming against demonic strongholds over every neighbourhood… Even if you don't see instant results, keep the trumpets blowing…always remember God is not slack concerning His promise; the walls will come down!

Nowhere in the Bible does it even remotely suggest that naming local spiritual entities, binding and attacking them and defeating them is a part of reaching people with the gospel of Jesus Christ. The *"pulling down strongholds"* of 2 Corinthians 10:4-5 often quoted by advocates of this lunacy is in reality referring to arguments and imaginations that challenge the knowledge of God, not the territories of demons.

Mark 5 is often appealed to as Biblical evidence of territorial spirits, because in verse 10 the demons beg Jesus not to *"send them out of the country"*. Surely this proves demons are territorial? Scripture interprets Scripture, so let us allow it to do just that by looking at the same account in Luke 8:31 where it is clear that the demons begged Jesus not to *"send them out of the country"* **not** because it would banish them **from** their territory, but because they were afraid Jesus would send them in **to** the abyss. Furthermore, even though Jesus did not banish them from the country, Luke 8:40 tells us that when Jesus returned to the area the demons had absolutely no power or authority in the way advocates of spiritual warfare claim, because the people of the region welcomed Jesus; they didn't need binding for Jesus' message to be welcomed.

Daniel 10:13, 20 is also commonly appealed to by advocates of spiritual warfare, which tells us of the battle between the Prince of Persia and the archangel Michael. It is claimed that the Prince of Persia is an example of a territorial spirit which can be defeated by Christians through the techniques of strategic-level spiritual warfare. In *Warfare Prayer*, Wagner writes:

> This story leaves no doubt that territorial spirits greatly influence human life in all its socio-political aspects (page 66).

However, a proper examination of Daniel 10 makes clear that:

1. The battle was fought in heaven, not earth.

2. The battle was between two angels and a demon; no human was involved.

3. The battle was directed by God in heaven (and by Michael), not by humans on earth.

4. Daniel was not asked to bind a demon.

5. Daniel was not even asked to pray!

Whilst Ephesians 6:12 implies the Devil's minions are highly organised, nowhere does Scripture tell us the Devil has assigned them to every geopolitical area. Only God is omnipresent, so there is no doubt that when demons are on earth they have a locality by definition of only being able to be in one place at a time. But that does not mean (and the Bible does not teach) that the Devil has assigned demons to every geopolitical area.

Nowhere does Scripture provide an example of a believer rebuking or even confronting geographical demons. Nowhere in Scripture does it tell us we are to command demons to relinquish territory. We **are** told in Ephesians 6 to oppose the Devil through putting on our spiritual armour, but the context is one of the believer taking a defensive stance in the power of God and praying always with all prayer.

At the end of the day, advocates of this lunatic teaching do not need to justify it from the Word of God, because they validate it by the experience itself. Wagner writes:

> One fundamental thesis will control this discussion…of us coming to grips with some of the relatively new and at times somewhat radical ideas surrounding strategic-level spiritual warfare, spiritual mapping…and other such issues…the thesis that ministry [experience] precedes and produces theology, not the reverse (*Confronting*, page 43).

Part of Wagner's far-reaching legacy on the charismatic/evangelical church is that experience does indeed precede and produce theology in the area of spiritual warfare for millions of Christians; so much so that most charismatic Christians who were saved within the last 20 to 30 years accept unquestioningly Wagner's unbiblical methods on spiritual warfare as wholeheartedly as they do the doctrine of the virgin birth!

When it comes to spiritual issues, Christians can all too easily fall in to one of two camps of extreme error. They can either naively and ignorantly underestimate the influence and power of the Devil, or be far **too** focused on the Devil and assume they are in a spiritual battle with him and his minions all the time. C. Peter Wagner's teaching on spiritual warfare has been the cause of a whole generation of Christians unwittingly falling into the latter error; the extent of which can be demonstrated by the sheer number of Christian books on the subject of spiritual warfare and deliverance on sale in Christian bookstores that have absolutely no foundation in the Word of God. A good example of this is a book called *Self Deliverance* by Kirt Schneider, an instruction manual on how Christians should wage war on the Devil and evil spirits.

The opening sentence of the book sets out the whole premise for what follows on every page. The author claims that as deliverance (from evil spirits) was such a significant part of Jesus' ministry (one third of His ministry he claims), it should also be a significant part of every Christian's ministry. Whilst it is true that deliverance from evil spirits was a significant part of Jesus' ministry, Schneider misses the crucial point that it was always directed at people **before** they believed on Him; **nowhere** in the New Testament is there an example of Jesus casting out a demon from someone who had believed on Him as their Lord and Saviour and been born again. The very foundation of the author's theology on spiritual warfare is therefore dangerously flawed from the beginning, because he uses how Jesus deals with the spiritual problems of unregenerate people as a blueprint for how Christians should deal with fellow-believers in Jesus Christ; this fundamental error is at the root of so many Christian "deliverance" ministries.

Like so many similar books available in Christian bookstores, *Self Deliverance* is full of accounts of when the author "discerned" Christians he knew were "struggling with demons" without ever explaining **how** he discerned such things. This is of course reminiscent of how (I described earlier in this book) the IHOP leadership "discerned" Stephanie had a demon. Schneider seems to attribute every human emotion as evidence of demonic oppression. For example, on page 101 of his book Schneider writes:

> If you think about people who are angry, oftentimes they are angry because they are afraid. This means two spirits are at work.

Who says? Where does the Word of God tell us such rubbish? It does not. The Bible tells us we contend with the world, the flesh and the Devil and the sad legacy of C. Peter Wagner's teaching is that it has left Christians with no ability to discern which one of the three we are dealing with at any given time. Our struggles are not always the work of the Devil. For example, James 1:14 says:

> *But each one is tempted when he is drawn away by his **own desires** and enticed* (emphasis added).

James 4:1 says:

> *Where do wars and fights come from among you? Do they not come from **your desires for pleasure** that war in your members?* (emphasis added).

Most charismatic Christians have embraced a central tenet of the Word of Faith heresy that attributes every trial and struggle they experience to demonic spiritual powers that need fighting and defeating; this even often extends to struggles with poverty and sickness, meaning any Christian struggling with financial difficulties or illness is viewed as being under demonic attack (because of their lack of faith) and needs deliverance from it. This is a dreadful heresy that completely distorts what the Bible says about the spiritual walk of the New Testament believer and leads to charismatics refusing to create a theology that allows for sickness or financial difficulty (see Appendix 1). In contrast, James 1:1 says:

> *Consider it all joy when you fall into various trials, knowing that the testing of your faith produces patience.*

Trials, hardships, suffering and even sickness are not always demonically inspired, nor are they just experienced by Christians who do not trust God enough. It is undeniable that God Himself sometimes intentionally allows, or even causes trials, hardship, suffering and even sickness to accomplish His sovereign purposes. Just consider Job who declared:

> *Though He [God] slay me, yet will I trust Him* (Job 13:15).

Hebrews 12:5-11 describes God disciplining those He loves (verse 6) to *"produce a harvest of righteousness"* (verse 11). Psalm 23:4 speaks of the Shepherd (God) using both the rod and the staff with the flock. The rod is used to discipline and the staff is used to guide.

Being in a relationship with God is not all about us demanding blessing from Him; we work out our salvation *"with fear and trembling"* (Philippians 2:12). Trials, hardships, suffering and even sickness and poverty can be a means of God's loving discipline. It is difficult for us to comprehend why God would work in this manner, but it is nevertheless clear from Scripture that He can and does. One of the clearest illustrations of this in Scripture is found is Psalm 119. Notice the progression through verses 67, 71, and 75:

> *Before I was afflicted I went astray, but now I obey your word...It was good for me to be afflicted so that I might learn your decrees...I know, O LORD, that your laws are righteous, and in faithfulness you have afflicted me.*

The author of Psalm 119 does what Word of Faith proponents fail to do: he looks at suffering from God's perspective. It was good for the Psalmist to be afflicted. It was faithfulness that caused God to afflict him. The result of the affliction was so that he could learn God's decrees and obey His Word.

Schneider explains in *Self Deliverance* that he trained a team to minister deliverance. Again, this is reminiscent of the "rehabilitation facility" the IHOP leaders wanted to send Stephanie to; a place that was specially equipped for delivering Stephanie from her demon. Of course Schneider leaves out of his book **how** he trained his team to minister deliverance, because there is absolutely nothing in the Word of

God about how to do such a thing. One therefore has to conclude that he based his techniques on something other than the Bible, and this is confirmed on page 19 where he explains how God gave him understanding on the issue of spiritual warfare in a "vivid dream".

Extra revelation divinely provided in a dream?

How convenient.

The fact is that God does not provide extra revelation through a dream; He has told us everything He wants us to know through His written word, but unfortunately that is not enough for a growing number of professing Christians. Dreams are completely subjective and because they are impossible to objectively test they leave the believer wide open to spiritual deception; ironically, the very thing the author of *Self Deliverance* warns against!

When proponents of these kinds of methods of spiritual warfare do actually try to provide a Biblical basis for them they go to the Old Testament rather than the New. This is evidenced time and time again by Kirt Schneider who constantly creates a pretext for his false teaching by taking an Old Testament passage out of context and applying a spiritual meaning to it for the New Testament believer. This is as dishonest as it is dangerous. If a doctrine for the New Testament Christian cannot be established from the New Testament, it cannot be a true doctrine. It is perfectly acceptable to use Old Testament passages to illustrate, illuminate and demonstrate a New Testament doctrine, but Christians need to be very suspicious of a teacher "proving" their doctrine by only using Old Testament passages. For example, on page 21 of his book, Schneider gives Exodus 23:31 a spiritual application for how a New Testament believer should "drive out our spiritual enemies". He repeats this error on the following page in the way he wrongly applies 2 Samuel 22:35 and Psalm 144:1. Schneider quotes King David declaring *"God trains my hands for battle..."* and *"Blessed be the Lord, my rock, who trains my hands for war"* as justification for how New Testament believers should be ready to wage war against demonic powers, when in reality neither passage has any meaning other than David praising God for giving him the physical abilities to wage war against his physical enemies.

Another more subtle example of Schneider applying Old Testament principles to New Testament believers is his reference to "familiar spirits" and "generational sins". These terms have become part of the common vocabulary for the modern Christian, particularly in the pseudo-Christian *Inner Healing Movement*, which I address later in the book. Schneider states:

> The iniquities of our ancestors, called "generational sins", can open the door to demons (page 30)... Familiar spirits are demonic personalities that have been living in our families for generations (page 31).

Where does the New Testament say anything like that? It does not, but the teaching of "familiar spirits" and "generational sins" has been the cause of so much unnecessary burden and condemnation for millions of Christians.

The word "familiar" is derived from the Latin for "household servant", and is intended to express the idea that sorcerers had spirits as their servants ready to obey their commands. It is an Old Testament term used to describe sorcerers and mediums who had spirit guides they believed could be trusted. Schneider's application of this term to describe how New Testament believers can be affected by "familiar spirits" is simply not justified. Schneider even gives a list of "familiar spirits" that affect Christians, including the "familiar spirit" of poverty! This is completely in line with the teaching of Word of Faith heretics like Benny Hinn, who claims God showed him that poverty is a demon. This has nothing to do with Biblical Christianity.

As justification for his claims about "generational sins" and their spiritual consequences, on page 32 of his book Schneider appeals to Exodus 20:4-6; an Old Testament passage yet again wrongly applied to the New Testament believer. Exodus 20:4-6 speaks about the sins of the fathers being visited on the sons. The context is the consequence of the sin, not leaving the son open to spiritual oppression or possession. In addition, this is a principle that God did away with even before Christ's First Coming. We read in Ezekiel 18:

> *The son shall not bear the guilt of the father, nor the father bear the guilt of the son. The righteousness of the righteous shall be upon himself, and the wickedness of the wicked shall be upon himself* (Ezekiel 18:20).

In the New Testament we read in John 9:1-3:

> *Now as Jesus passed by, He saw a man who was blind from birth. 2 And His disciples asked Him, saying, "Rabbi, who sinned, this man or his parents, that he was born blind?" 3 Jesus answered, "Neither this man nor his parents sinned, but that the works of God should be revealed in him.*

2 Corinthians 5:7 makes clear that once we give our lives to Christ we are a new creation, the old has passed away.

Schneider reveals further his sympathies for Word of Faith teaching on page 36 when he refers to "word curses" put on us by others, such as when a parent or teacher has said we are lazy, or stupid. This Word of Faith heresy that is so common in charismatic circles attributes power – both positive and negative - to the words we speak. Good things spoken by a person, or by a person over someone else are regarded as "positive confession", where the words themselves have creative power; the speaker brings into existence the things they confess. Schneider's belief in this nonsense is further evidenced on page 80:

It is only after what is in the heart is confessed in words, whether through our inner man or out loud with our physical mouths, that the transaction is completed in the spirit realm.

Alleged "word curses" is the term given by followers of the Word of Faith heresy to describe when someone speaks something negatively into someone's life, thus giving birth to the negativity in reality. This is utter rubbish and not grounded in Scripture. Whatever reaction we may have to the words someone speaks to us (either positive or negative) is completely on an emotional level and nothing more; their words do not do anything more than hurt us on an emotional level. We find release from this emotional hurt through our identification in Christ, not by combatting non-existent spirits.

In-keeping with Wagner's teaching that Christians should be on the offensive in taking the battle **to** the Devil, Schneider teaches that the believer needs to employ a kind of aggressive spiritual militancy in their strategic spiritual warfare. On page 125 of his book, Schneider says Christians need to "grasp the concept of holy violence". Where is that in Scripture? That has more in common with the Islamic doctrine of *Jihad* than anything found in the Bible. As justification for this outrageous claim he cites Deuteronomy 7:1-2 (yet another Old Testament verse) in which God told the Israelites to destroy the tribes before them. This has **nothing** to do with how New Testament believers should approach spiritual warfare, let alone deal with the Devil himself. Again, the author has to spiritualise and misapply an Old Testament passage to justify his theology on spiritual warfare because it cannot be justified from the New Testament.

On page 135 he states:

> If you fail to have an aggressive spirit against darkness, you are going to miss many of your kingdom blessings (page 135).

This is simply not found in Scripture. The Biblical way to defeat the Devil is not to be aggressive by taking the fight to him. James 4:7 tells us to:

> *...submit to God. Resist the devil and he will flee from you.*

We resist the Devil, not get aggressive with him, and we resist him only by first submitting to God, because we resist the Devil in God's strength and authority, not our own (Ephesians 6:10). Even the archangel Michael, one of the most powerful of the angels, did not dare to accuse Satan, but rather said, *"The **Lord** rebuke you"* (Jude 1:9). In response to the Devil's attacks (assuming we are **ever** directly attacked by Satan, who is **not** omnipresent), the Christian should appeal **to** Christ instead of focusing on the Devil. In stark contrast, on page 141 of *Self Deliverance* the author recounts when he dealt with a possessed woman by simply shouting "Shut up Satan!"

The New Testament believer in Jesus Christ is to put on the whole armour of God so that we may *"be able to **stand** against the wiles of the devil"* (Ephesians 6:11). Ephesians 6:13 declares:

> *Therefore take up the whole armour of God, that you may be able to **withstand** in the evil day, and done all, to **stand.***

Verse 14 then begins, *"**Stand** therefore, having girded your waist with truth........"* Schneider's approach typifies the way in which millions of Christians have widely missed the target by taking an aggressive and militant strategy against the Devil. Ephesians 6:13-18 describes the spiritual armour God gives the New Testament believer. We are to stand firm with:

The belt of truth,

The breastplate of righteousness,

The gospel of peace,

The shield of faith,

The helmet of salvation,

The sword of the Spirit,

And by praying in the Spirit.

It is important to understand that of the six pieces of armour listed, only one is an offensive (aggressive) weapon, with the other six being defensive. The only offensive weapon is the sword of the Spirit, *"which is the Word of God"* (verse 17). Sadly, thanks to Wagner's false teaching on the issue of spiritual warfare, millions of charismatic Christians do not know how to wield this weapon properly or effectively.

How should we really defeat the powers of darkness? Start by asking God for His wisdom to be able to discern between the world, the flesh and the Devil, so you know which power you are fighting against; that is as close as you will get to naming your opponent! In contrast, on page 84-85 of his book, Schneider echoes Wagner's teaching about commanding demons to identify themselves.

GROWTH THROUGH SIGNS AND WONDERS

Wagner took what could only be described as a very pragmatic approach to church growth, in that he applied modern-day secular marketing techniques to canvas a broad spectrum of churches that were experiencing growth to find out what was working for them. Rick Warren was taught by Wagner at Fuller and regarded Wagner as his mentor, wholeheartedly applying his church growth techniques. In his 1984 book, *Leading Your Church To Growth*, Wagner featured everyone from the Southern Baptist Convention to Robert Schuller, from John Wimber to John MacArthur. I mention this because understanding Wagner is crucial to understanding Wimber, because he was greatly influenced by Wagner and vice versa. As we shall see, Wimber developed a very pragmatic approach to ministry, healing, spiritual growth, etc. He consistently showed a willingness to put into practice in his ministry (particularly in the area of healing) whatever seemed to work, without much consideration for how Biblical it was or was not; the important thing was it worked and was successful.

Prior to his position at Fuller Church Growth institute, Wagner had been a missionary in Bolivia, and he fascinated Wimber with stories of supernatural confrontations, miracles, healings, demonic oppressions, and deliverances, and how churches would grow wherever the power of God was demonstrated. These stories had a massive influence on Wimber and his views on evangelism, healing and spiritual warfare.

Wimber left Fuller Church Growth Institute in 1977 to start a local church and put into practice the ideas he had formulated about evangelism and church growth. The church started as a small Bible study in his home, but began to grow quickly. The fellowship was initially affiliated with Chuck Smith's Calvary Chapels, but due to a growing number of Calvary Chapel pastors expressing concern over reports of Wimber's theology and practice heading in a different direction to theirs, Wimber was asked to leave Calvary Chapel, but was recommended to associate with the Vineyard Church, another former Calvary group of seven churches that was moving in the direction Wimber was heading, i.e. allegedly manifesting moves of the Holy Spirit. In 1982 Wimber's fellowship became a Vineyard Church. In fact, he became the head of the Vineyard churches as a result of its leader, Ken Gullickson turning the leadership over to Wimber.

Whilst a focus and interest in "signs and wonders" was definitely growing in Wimber's fellowship (and is why it eventually went its separate way from Calvary Chapel), it was not necessarily the overriding focus until Mother's Day in 1981, when something happened during a service at Wimber's church (which at the time was still a Calvary Chapel); an event that has remarkable similarities with what happened at the so-called "revivals" at Azusa Street and the *Sharon Bible School*, and what happened some years later at the "Toronto Blessing" and so-called revivals that followed. The following account is narrated by Carol Wimber, John's wife:

> On Mother's Day of 1981 we had a watershed experience that launched us into what today is called, "Power Evangelism." At this time, John [Wimber] invited a young man who had been attending our church to preach one Sunday evening. By now we had grown to over 700 participants. The young man shared his testimony, which was beautiful and stirring; then asked for all the people under the age of 25 to come forward. None of us had a clue as to what was going to happen. When they got to the front, the speaker said, "For years now, the Holy Spirit has been grieved by the church, but He's getting over it. Come, Holy Spirit." And He came. Most of the young people had grown up around our home. We had four children between the ages of 15-21. We knew the young people well. One fellow, Tim, started bouncing. His arms flung out and he fell over, but one of his hands accidentally hit a mike stand and he took it down with him. He was tangled up in the cord with the mike next to his mouth. Then he began speaking in tongues, so the sound went throughout the gymnasium. We had never considered ourselves Charismatics, and certainly had never placed emphasis on the gift of tongues. We had seen a few people tremble and fall over before, and we had seen many healings. But, this was different. The majority of the young people were shaking and falling over. At one point it looked like a battlefield scene, bodies everywhere, people weeping, wailing, speaking in tongues. And Tim in the middle of it all, babbling into the microphone. There was much shouting and loud behaviour!
>
> John sat by quietly playing the piano and wide eyed! Members of our staff were fearful and angry. Several people got up and walked out...But I knew God was visiting us. I was so thrilled because I had been praying for power for so long. This might not have been the way I wanted to see it come, but this was how God gave it to us...I asked one boy, who was on the floor, "What's happening to you right now?" He said, "It's like electricity. I can't move." I was amazed by the effect of God's power on the human body. I suppose I thought that it would be all inward work, such as conviction or repentance. I never imagined there would be strong physical manifestations (Carol Wimber, *A Hunger for God*. Kevin Springer, ed. Power Encounters. Harper and Row. 1988).

When I read the above account by Carol Wimber, my first thought was: who was the "young man" Wimber had invited to preach? It was Lonnie Frisbee (1949-

1993), a self-described "nudist, vegan, hippie preacher" and "seeing prophet", who had LSD-induced visions of Jesus (before and after his conversion), struggled with homosexuality and eventually died of AIDS at the age of 43. In the 2005 documentary film about Frisbee called *The Life and Death of a Hippie Preacher*, writer, director and producer, David Di Sabatino observes:

> One of the ironic twists of the 60s was that many openly stated that drugs – LSD in particular – played a large part of their experience in Christian salvation.

Just like William Seymour of Azusa Street fame, Frisbee believed that a Christian must be baptised in the Holy Spirit, with the initial evidence of that being speaking in tongues. His "ministry" was therefore based around "anointing" converts in order for them to speak in tongues and manifest all sorts of supernatural experiences, such as uncontrollable bouncing, shaking, falling over, wailing and the sensation of electricity shooting through their bodies. He preached with conviction that Protestant Christianity had lost its mystics, and was the worse for it, but God had raised him up to restore mysticism to the church; he identified himself with the Catholic mystics whose spiritual practices had **nothing** to do with Biblical Christianity and everything to do with the Eastern mystery religions of Buddhism and Hinduism. Bearing that in mind, it should surprise no one that Lonnie Frisbee is popular today with proponents of the *Emergent Church*.

In spite of all this, many believed Frisbee to be gifted with great power from God, but of course this is because they judged him not on what he preached, but on the manifestations he could produce. Frisbee was an influential figure in the development and growth of first Chuck Smith's Calvary Chapels and then later John Wimber's Vineyard Fellowship Movement. Regarding  the former, Chuck Smith was first introduced to Frisbee through his daughter's boyfriend at the time, John Higgins. By Frisbee's own admission (recorded on tape) he was pastoring at Chuck Smith's Calvary Chapel at the age of 19; between 1968 and 1971 he was leader of the Jesus Movement, and it was through this connection that he swelled the congregation of Calvary Chapel with thousands of hippies. It has to be said that whilst Frisbee was responsible for bringing these young people to Smith's fellowship, it was Smith's Bible teaching that kept them there, made disciples of them and changed their lives; in reality, much more so than Frisbee's life was changed.

Frisbees drug-taking and homosexual practices were regarded as an "open secret" within Calvary Chapel, but were conveniently ignored for quite some time. I have listened to the testimonies of people who were members of Calvary Chapel at the time Lonnie Frisbee was there, who became very disillusioned because of the way Frisbee's habitual immorality was known, but overlooked by the leadership, including Chuck Smith himself; it was well-known that on a Saturday night Frisbee would often be out partying, dropping acid and engaging in homosexual acts, but then preaching on Sunday morning and imparting his "anointing" on the congregation.

Frisbee was divorced in 1973. *In The Life and Death of a Hippie Preacher*, his ex-wife, Connie admits:

> At the end of the marriage he [Frisbee] told me that he had been staying late in some gay bars.

Whilst Chuck Smith and John Wimber were eventually forced to distance themselves from Frisbee because his habitual immorality became too widely known to ignore, neither of them ever stopped believing Frisbee had a special "anointing" from God, with Smith even making reference to Frisbee's "anointing" at his memorial service in 1993 (which was held at Robert Schuller's Crystal Cathedral), likening him to Samson, a man anointed by God, but plagued by his human flaws. By the time both men had eventually been forced to distance themselves from Frisbee, he had become an integral and important part of the histories of both their ministries; Frisbee is the dirty little secret that both Calvary Chapel and the Vineyard Fellowship Movement have subsequently tried to write out of their histories.

Bearing in mind the meeting at which Wimber invited Frisbee to speak and minister his "anointing" was in 1981, over a decade before things began happening at the Toronto Airport Fellowship, consider carefully the startling similarities between the two:

1. It happened in a Vineyard Church.

2. There was a prophecy in the name of the Holy Ghost.

3. There was a prayer **to** the Holy Ghost (something we are never told to do in Scripture).

4. There were similar manifestations, bouncing, shaking, violently falling, weeping, electricity.

Wimber's first mistake as a pastor was to give Lonnie Frisbee the platform at his church. The Greek word translated in the New Testament as "pastor" is *poimen*, meaning shepherd; "pastor" is in fact a Latinisation of *poimen*. A New Testament pastor is a shepherd and has a responsibility to protect the flock from wolves. Wimber did exactly the opposite and **invited** a wolf on to the platform of his church.

Wimber was said to be initially quite troubled by what had happened. However, something changed Wimber's view, which his wife recounts;

> John wasn't as happy as I. He had never seen large numbers of people sprawled out over the floor...He spent that night reading scripture and historical accounts of revival from the lives of people like Whitefield and Wesley...But, his study did not yield the conclusive answers to questions raised from the previous evenings events. By 5 am, John was desperate, he cried out to God, "Lord, if this is you please tell me." A moment later the phone rang and a pastor friend of ours from Denver, Colorado was on the line. "John," he said, "I'm sorry I'm calling so early, but I have something really strange to tell you. I don't know what it means, but God wants me to say, "It's Me John" (*A Hunger for God*).

This account told by Carol Wimber actually contradicts her husband's own account of the same event, which I have seen for myself on video. John Wimber states on video his friend (Tommy) from Denver did call out of the blue, but that was nothing unusual because they called each other every few weeks to catch up. Instead of his friend just cryptically calling to tell Wimber, "It's Me John", Wimber admits that he spent some time on the phone telling his friend everything that had happened in the meeting led by Frisbee, and in response his friend told Wimber it was a move of the Holy Spirit. Wimber asked his friend how he knew that for certain, to which his friend replied because he had been to meetings led by Frisbee and seen it for himself.

It is important to note what Carol Wimber said, because she said that her husband could not find Biblical justification for what they had experienced during that service, nor did he find justification in church history. It was left to his friend to confirm it was from God. How did his friend know it was from God? Because he had **experienced** it too! Just like with the "Toronto Blessing" that followed and the "revivals" it spawned, and the so-called "revivals" that occurred earlier in history, it was not the Word of God (or even church history) that provided justification for what was experienced at Wimber's church, it was the **experience** itself that affirmed it, with further affirmation being provided by a friends **experience** of the same.

In the early 1980's, Wimber was invited back to Fuller again to lecture. The course he taught was entitled, *MC510, Signs, Wonders, and Church Growth*, but was later renamed, *The Miraculous and Church Growth*. C. Peter Wagner recounts in his book, *On the Crest of the Wave*:

> One of our adjunct professors, John Wimber, who is a pastor of Vineyard Christian Fellowship of Yorba Linda, California, came to us recently with a

suggestion that we offer a course in Signs, Wonders and Church Growth. I agreed to cosponsor the course with him, and early in 1982 we experimented with it (page 131-132).

When Branhamite Paul Cain heard about what Wimber and Wagner were teaching at Fuller, he visited them, told them what they were doing was from God and anointed them "apostles" in accordance with William Branham's *Fivefold Ministry*. As if that does not make the *Latter Rain* connection glaringly obvious, the official Franklin Hall website states:

> The ministry of Dr. C. Franklin Hall was lectured on in C. Peter Wagner's and John Wimber's Signs and Wonders course at Fuller Theological Seminary. Such was the influence and effectiveness of Dr. C. Franklin Hall.

The course proved hugely popular. It consisted of ten consecutive Monday evenings, for four hours each night. The first three hours consisted of a lecture, including questions, answers, and discussion. The last hour was a "lab" in which the gifts of the Spirit were demonstrated by Wimber and the class. Words of knowledge, healings, and deliverances were reported to have occurred, as Wimber and his students ministered one to another. This idea that gifts of the Spirit can be taught remains alive and well today within the charismatic/evangelical church, with churches like Bill Johnson's Bethel having their own *School of Supernatural Ministry*, which in reality has more in common with *Hogwarts School of Witchcraft and Wizardry* than anything that could be described as Biblical, but that should surprise no one when its roots go back to John Wimber, C. Peter Wagner and ultimately Franklin Hall and William Branham.

In his Healing Seminar Syllabus, Wimber taught thousands of different healing techniques. In teaching his students to recognise the "anointing" that ministered healing, they were told to look for:

> …sensations of warmth (flowing out of hands), tingling feelings, trembling of hands, and a sense of anointing… These spiritual phenomena are manifestations of the Spirit's presence on the person. By observing them you can begin to see what the Spirit is doing in and through the person (Healing Seminar Syllabus II Observations A. Spiritual Phenomena. Pages 74-75).

The signs and manifestations Wimber taught his students to recognise as evidence of the "anointing" being present cannot be found anywhere in Scripture, but are commonplace in the occult and Eastern mystery religions.

Wimber's course gained nationwide attention when Robert Walker, the editor of *Christian Life Magazine* devoted the October 1982 issue - now known as the "sold out" issue - to "Signs, Wonders, and Church Growth." That issue was subsequently reprinted as a book by C. Peter Wagner in 1986 titled, *Signs and Wonders Today* and, according to Wagner:

> It is currently being read as a study guide in churches and other Christian groups across the country (*The Third Wave of the Holy Spirit*, page 25).

Many of the terms and concepts presented by the teaching have become common terminology since then in charismatic/evangelical churches. Terms like "Power Encounter," "Divine Appointment," "Power Evangelism," "Proclamation and Demonstration Evangelism," and "Paradigm Shift", with most Christians nowadays not even being aware of their origins (or indeed whether or not they are even Biblical).

Wimber published a hugely influential book in 1985 called *Power Evangelism*, the basic premise of which was that the preaching of the gospel must be accompanied with "signs and wonders" in order for people to respond in faith. This was a belief firmly held by Smith Wigglesworth many years before Wimber. In contrast, consider John 12:37 in which we are told that *"although He [Jesus] had done so many signs before them, they did not believe in Him"*. Paul declares in Romans 1:16 it is the **gospel** that is *"the power of god to salvation for everyone who believes"*, and *"it pleased God through the foolishness of the message preached to save those who believe"* (1 Corinthians 1:21). No mention of "signs and wonders" being required, or the naming, binding and defeating of demonic strongholds.

Furthermore, in practice the "signs and wonders" were given pre-eminence in Wimber's ministry and the preaching of the gospel was increasingly non-existent; people flocked to see Wimber for the manifestations, not the preaching. The fruit of this can clearly be seen today at the previously mentioned *School of Supernatural Ministry*, which teaches their students to go out on the streets and evangelise **not** by preaching the gospel (most of the students clearly still need to hear the gospel themselves), but by performing "signs and wonders" in front of non-believers. Multiple examples of this can be found on YouTube where  young people from *Bethel* perform what can only be described as a cheap "magic trick" in front of an unwitting non-believer on the street that is far less impressive than tricks performed by people like David Blaine, Derren Brown or Dynamo. At no time is any gospel message presented, just a "sign and wonder". No one attends churches like Bethel for the teaching; they go because that is where the "power" is deemed to be.

An appendix in Wimber's *Power Evangelism*, tried to legitimise his "signs and wonders" by suggesting they have appeared throughout church history, and he cites an eclectic catalogue of individuals and movements, both orthodox and heretical, as evidence. Included in these are Hilarion (a fourth century hermit), Augustine, Pope Gregory I (The Great), Francis of Assisi, The Waldenes (who opposed the Pope and were persecuted by the Dominicans), Vincent Ferrer (who was himself a Dominican), Martin Luther, Ignatius Loyola (founder of the Catholic Jesuit order which was formed for the express purpose of reversing the Reformation), John Wesley, and the Jausenists (a Catholic sect). In a booklet published by *The Vineyard*, Wimber adds The Shakers (a cult that demanded celibacy), Edward Irving (discredited leader of the Irvingite sect in 19th century England), and the supposed miracles and healings worked by an apparition of the Virgin Mary at Lourdes, France. Talk about clutching at straws.

C. Peter Wagner also looked to extra-Biblical sources for justification for the signs and wonders being manifested in the name of the Holy Spirit. For example, in his book, *The Third Wave of Holy Spirit*, he appeals to supernatural events recorded in the Apocrypha[11].

Wimber's book set the tone for a movement named by C. Peter Wagner as the "Third Wave". This "Third Wave" described the move of the Holy Spirit that people like Wimber, Wagner and the Kansas City prophets believed would usher in a global revival through the manifestation of "signs and wonders" and (based on his faulty interpretation of Joel 2) the emergence of a triumphant church generation. Just what constituted the first, second and all-important "Third Wave" has, even from the start, been something of a moveable feast. For example, many within the movement initially considered Pentecost as the first wave, the *Azusa Street Revival* as the second and an immanent global revival as the third (using the manifestations experienced at Azusa Street as the blueprint for their anticipated "Third Wave"). Even Wagner himself would flip-flop on what exactly he considered to be the so-called waves. For example, he was known to consider the Pentecostal Movement (not Pentecost itself) to be the first wave, the Charismatic Movement to be the second, and what they were bringing into the church as the "Third Wave". But then he claimed to receive a prophecy in 1989 regarding a three-strand cord not easily broken, which comprised of conscientious liberals, evangelicals and charismatic Pentecostals. According to Wagner, this cord was the Third "Wave".

Just what constitutes each wave (and in particular the "Third Wave") has conveniently also been changed by others as and when a proclaimed revival has proven to be nothing of the sort. For example, in 2008 Bob Jones claimed God Himself had revealed to him that the "Toronto Blessing" was the first wave (therefore implying it was greater even than Pentecost), Pensacola (which made John Kilpatrick famous) was the second wave, and Lakeland (with Todd Bentley) was the "Third Wave" that would usher in global revival. You have to ask: how many times can these false teachers get this wrong before their followers see them for what they are?

In a further demonstration of his utter lack of spiritual discernment, in the mid to late 1980's Wimber became enamoured by the ministry team of the *Kansas City Fellowship*, or as they came to be more commonly known as The Kansas City Prophets. At an August 1989 conference in Denver, Colorado, Wimber called on Vineyard pastors to receive their ministry. Wimber is recorded as saying the following on an audio tape titled *Unpacking Your Bags*:

> I think you'll find that the prophets are pretty nice people by and large, I've come to know several of them here, I think maybe five or six, that are from Kansas City Fellowship. And then we have Paul Cain that lives in Dallas and has had quite a relationship with Kansas City for a number of years, but is not evidently technically considered a Kansas City Prophet. You'll hear from them, some this week, although they won't be largely behind the scenes. They've already ministered significantly this weekend. And, it's my hope that every one of you, if you've not today had the occasion of sitting down with one or two of them and having them minister to you, that that will happen before the week is over. Because I believe that in God's providence you'll be blessed and you'll go home with your pockets full and you're heart singing, if they do so.

In 1990, A Kansas City pastor named Ernie Gruen published a lengthy report exposing some of the teachings and practices at Mike Bickle's *Kansas City Fellowship*. His report was distributed nationwide and such was the extent of what he exposed, it could and should have meant the extinction of the movement. However, their extinction was averted by the intervention of Wimber, who offered his services for guiding their "correction". In spite of all that was exposed by Gruen's report about the Kansas City Prophets, Wimber never stopped promoting the erroneous teachings of Paul Cain, Mike Bickle, Bob Jones or John Paul Jackson. He did eventually stop promoting Bob Jones in 1991, but not because of heresy, but because of immorality. The problem is that such was the broad influence of Wimber on the charismatic/ evangelical church that his public acceptance of demonstrably false prophets made this acceptable for so many others to follow his lead. Wimber is responsible for so much of what is wrong today in the charismatic/evangelical church.

The link between the Kansas City Prophets and William Branham is undeniable not only through the false prophet Paul Cain, but also Ern Baxter, who (like Cain) travelled with William Branham, spoke at the Shepherds Conference in Kansas in 1975 attended by between 40,000 and 50,000 men. In fact, Baxter closed the conference by preaching what was possibly his most famous sermon: "Thy Kingdom

Come!" It could hardly be regarded as a coincidence that only a few years later in 1982 the *Kansas City Fellowship* was founded by Mike Bickle after he heard an audible voice from God declaring:

> I will change the understanding and expression of Christianity in the earth in one generation (*Growing in the Prophetic*, Page 30-31).

Wimber's pragmatic (but unbiblical) attitude of "if it works, do it" is demonstrated by the way in which he incorporated both secular and mystical practices in to his ministry. For a secular example, consider the fact that he recruited Sam Thompson, a licensed psychologist [see Appendix 4], as an assistant pastor in charge of counselling. Thompson developed the ministerial aspects of the Vineyard, combining psychological theory with charismatic practices. He taught how to look for signs of spiritual and physical problems, and how to deal with them. The emphasis was, and still is, on attaining spiritual power. The congregation would stand in circles, holding hands and command demons to manifest themselves in order to cast them out.

Wimber's mystical influences were well documented, but all too often ignored by his supporters. For example, Morton T. Kelsey's name popped up frequently in Wimber's teachings; Wimber even dedicated a seminar series to him. Morton T. Kelsey (1917-2001) was an Episcopal priest who trained at the *C. G. Jung Institute* near Zurich, Switzerland, and became a Jungian psychologist [see Appendix 4 for information on the occult origins of Carl Jung's philosophies and practices]. Christian apologist Bob DeWaay described Kelsey in his 2004 article, *Contemporary Christian Divination*, as "the most prolific writer among twentieth century Christian mystics".

Kelsey introduced much occult practice into the church. For example, in his 1976 book, *The Christian and the Supernatural*, Kelsey equates gifts of the Holy Spirit with shamanistic powers and declared that a shaman or witch doctor is "one in whom the power of God is concentrated and can thus flow out to others" (page 93). This is no different to the philosophies of Franklin Hall! Kelsey writes:

> There is nothing intrinsically evil about …psi [psychic power] or its use… Psi experiences…are simply natural experiences of the human psyche… Clairvoyance, telepathy, precognition, psychokinesis, and healing have been observed in and around the lives of many religious leaders and nearly all Christian saints (page 109, 113, 142).

Even more disturbingly, he asserts:

> My students began to see the role Jesus was fulfilling when they read Mircea Eliade's Shamanism and Carlos Castaneda's Journey to Ixtlan [glorifying shamanistic powers] (page 93).

Kelsey equated the ministry of Jesus with that of a shaman – a witch doctor.

There were many other significant influences whom Wimber cited in his teachings:

AGNES SANFORD (1897-1982)

Agnes Sanford was one of the principal founders of the *Inner Healing Movement* (also called Theophostic healing); her pastor and mentor was none other than Morton T. Kelsey. In spite of Sanford being a pantheist[12], a number of her books can still be readily found in Christian book shops, including *The Healing Light*, which is endorsed by the *Theosophical Society*[13]. John Wimber promoted Sanford's books.

In her book, *The Healing Gifts of the Spirit*, Sanford called God "the very life-force existing in a radiation of an energy…from which all things evolved" (page 22) and declared that "God…made everything out of Himself and somehow He put a part of Himself into everything" (page 27). This is not Biblical Christianity, this is pure pantheism. But Sanford knew that, so in order to justify her heresy, instead of appealing to Scripture, she turned to people like Pierre Teilhard de Chardin, a Catholic Jesuit priest who was even denounced as a heretic by the Roman Catholic Church; he is re-garded as the "father" of the *New Age Movement*. Hardly an authority for a professing Christian to appeal to.

Agnes Sanford taught the occult philosophy that everything was a matter of thought vibrations, with negative thought vibrations causing illness and positive thought vibrations causing healing. She went as far as teaching that positive thought vibrations projected at an unsaved person could turn them into a Christian. In *The Healing Light*, she wrote:

> A new age is born…when love-power [projected] at the command of ministers [and others] is sufficient to change hearts... We [have] an inner source of power that can be tapped at will (page 21-22, 60, 75).

Sanford wrote:

> God's love was blacked out from man by negative thought-vibration of this sinful…world… So our Lord…lowered His thought-vibrations to the thought –vibrations of humanity…[and] cleansed the thought-vibrations that surround this globe… Therefore since He became a very part of the collective unconscious of the race, when He died upon the cross a part of humanity died with Him…[and] an invisible and personalised energy of our spirits has already ascended with Him into the heavens…

His blood, that mysterious life-essence…remains upon this earth, plasma form, blown by the winds…to every land…exploding in a chain reaction of spiritual power…

We direct this great flow of life into a closed mind…by doing penance for the sins of the world, or for [a] particular [person]… And by taking that one [by visualisation] to the cross of Christ and there receiving for him forgiveness, healing and life…

I have learned to combine the sacramental with the metaphysical approach… the metaphysical methods (*The Healing Light*, page 125-126, 165 and *The Healing Gifts of the Spirit*, page 140-141).

Try finding Biblical justification for any of that. Sanford grew up in China and drew many of her ideas from Taoism, rather than the Word of God.

For Sanford, anything that enabled her to tap into the "inner source of power" was acceptable. In *The Healing Gifts of the Spirit*, she referred to it as "this flow of energy" (page 48), and in *The Healing Light*, referred to it as the "high voltage of God's creativity" (page 146) and claimed "we are part of God" (page 10, 34-35). She even referred to God as "primal energy" (page 30) and taught Christians could forgive another's sins through visualisation (page 63-64, 68, 112).

Just in case some reading this book think that Sanford's *New Age* and occult influence is far removed from today's mainstream charismatic/evangelical Christianity, think again. Consider for example the 2012 book released by *Bethel* titled, *The Physics of Heaven – Exploring God's Mysteries of Sound, Light, Energy, Vibrations, and Quantum Physics*, with contributions from both Bill and Beni Johnson and the forward written by *Bethel* Senior Associate pastor, Kris Vallotton. The content of this book is so deeply *New Age* and occult it could have been written by Agnes Sanford herself. Just consider a few of the chapter titles and headings of the book:

Vibrating in harmony with God (by none other than Bob Jones)

The God Vibration

Good vibrations

Healing Energy

Human Body Frequencies

Quantum Mysticism

The book has its own website which states:

We want to hear about any revelations or experiences you've had with sound, light, energy, vibrations, frequencies, and quantum physics principles.

Ellyn Davis, assistant to Bill Johnson and author of the chapter titled, Good Vibrations, states, "In recent years, God has been opening the eyes of some of His people to the mysteries of sound, colour and light, and of "vibrations" and "energy." Let me be very clear, it is Satan, not God who has been opening the eyes of His people to the mysteries of sound, colour and light, and of "vibrations" and "energy". Ellyn Davis and *Bethel* are practicing and promoting the occult, and even the most cursory review of *New Age* and occult literature will make clear the origins of the very concepts *Bethel* is promoting as being acceptable for Christians. The concept of "energy" for example is a central theme in *New Age* and occult literature, but found nowhere in the Word of God. It is part of the pantheistic worldview that God is everything and everyone and that everyone and everything is God. This is not what the Bible teaches about God. He is everywhere (omnipresent), but He is not all and in all; He is separate from His creation and the Holy Spirit (the third person of the triune Godhead) indwells **only** those who have repented of their sins and have given their life to Jesus. For example, in Ephesians 4:6 Paul states:

> One God and Father of all, who is above all, and through all, and in you all.

Paul is not just making a general statement about God being "in all" in the pantheistic sense, but is declaring this truth specifically to **believers** in Christ in the church at Ephesus who are indwelt by the Holy Spirit.

The God of pantheism is an impersonal "energy" force that can be used and manipulated through certain practices. This is what is at the root of all the Eastern mystery religions (and the philosophy behind "the Force" in *Star Wars*); a belief that "energy" (often referred to as Chi in the Eastern mystery religions) travels through the body in channels called *meridians* (or *chakras* in Hinduism) and can be used, channelled and brought into balance through meditation, ritual, breathing techniques and physical practices, such as Reiki, acupuncture, acupressure, Tai Chi and Yoga. Reiki for example, literally means "spiritually guided life force energy." The Reiki practitioner allegedly removes obstructions to the flow of life force energy (called *Ki*) throughout the body and allows it to "vibrate" in balance, thus promoting physical and spiritual wellbeing. In acupuncture, needles are inserted into the "energy" channels in order to balance its "vibration", and in acupressure the "energy" is balanced through the application of pressure on to the channels. In Yoga, the special positions and postures (known as *asanas*) and breathing exercises (known as *pranayama*) are the means by which the "energy" (called *prana* in Hinduism) is balanced. The physical practice of Yoga has a spiritual application and one cannot be separated from the other. This is demonstrated by the following Hindu saying:

> There is no Hinduism without Yoga and no Yoga without Hinduism.

How tragic it is to see so many Christians participating in Yoga in the naïve belief they can separate the physical aspect of it from its spiritual application.

Obstruction to the "energy" being able to "vibrate" in balance is said to be caused by negative thoughts, actions, or feelings, which some believe are the fundamental cause of illness. I have even heard it claimed that balancing the "energy" was how Jesus obtained His healing power, rather than attributing His power to the fact that He is God. There is **nothing** in the Word of God to suggest we have "energy channels" running through our bodies filled with an impersonal "life force". The Bible tells us that God created human-beings with a body, soul and spirit.

The concept of "energy channels" is occult and is found throughout *New Age* and occult teaching. For example, Alice Bailey (1880-1949) was an influential writer on the occult who is credited as being instrumental in the development of the *New Age Movement*. She references "energy" over 1,000 times in her book the *Rays and the Initiations*. On page seven of her book, *Externalization of the Hierarchy*, she states:

> **The inflow of this energy** has brought many hundreds of people into a new and deeper spiritual realisation;…**Thus is the New Age dawning**…**This is the occult law** (emphasis added).

Make no mistake, *Bethel* is dabbling in the occult when it promotes the *New Age* concepts of "vibrations" and "energy".

In her song, *A Bottle of Red*, singer song writer, *New Ager* and **Satanist**, Tori Amos, defines the *New Age* "energy" as Lucifer:

> **To visit Father Lucifer**, to have a moment to dance… to go down in the dark, to visit with the dude! Not these little "Princes of Darkness" wannabees… some of them are cute, but to visit **the real energy force** that has held the darkness: you go there with honour (emphasis added).

Alice Bailey also wrote extensively on the *New Age* concept of "light". For example, on page 58 of *The Reappearance of the Christ*, she declares:

> **This light** will irradiate (in a fashion unknown before) not only the Father's house, which is the source of all our **planetary light**. **This light** will now flood the world of men, bringing **illumination** to men's minds and light into the dark places of human living. **It is light and – above all else**… (emphasis added).

In another of Bailey's many disturbingly Christian sounding books, *From Bethlehem to Calvary*, she says on page 153:

> To **this light** the mystics testify, and it is **this light** into which they enter, and which enters into them, revealing **the light** which is latent and drawing it forth to potency. "In **thy light shall we see light**." **This is the outstanding fact of scientific mysticism. God is light** (emphasis added).

The guiding light of the *New Age Movement* is Lucifer. Lucifer is a Latin word derived from *lucem ferre*, meaning "light-bearer". Hence why *New Agers* proudly call themselves "light-bearers".

It is not that the occult has stolen these concepts from Christianity; it is Christianity that has stolen these concepts from the occult. Thanks to the diabolical groundwork laid by people like Alice Bailey and Helena Blavatsky (founder of the aforementioned *Theosophical Society* that promoted Agnes Sanford's books – see end-note 13) occult Eastern practices were first widely and openly embraced by *New Agers* in the West in the 1960s, but when (particularly) Hindu's saw how the Western *New Agers* were embracing their doctrines and practices, the call went out to "evangelise" the West with the vision of "Vedanta" (the philosophical traditions concerned with self-realisation and reaching *Brahman*). It may surprise many to learn that the largest missionary organisation in the world is not Christian, but Hindu – India's *Vishva Hindu* Parishad (VHP). Thanks to the incredible success of VHP since its inception in 1964, the occult has become commonplace both in the world and in the church, which is precisely the fulfilment of Alice Bailey's vision.

JOHN AND PAULA SANDFORD

Pantheists, founders of Elijah House Ministries, disciples of Agnes Sanford and pioneers of the *Inner Healing Movement*. John and Paula Sandford openly confess that Agnes Sanford was "for all of us the forerunner in the field of inner healing… [and] our own first mentor in the Lord, our friend and advisor". Yet incredibly, John Sandford claimed to have cast out a demon from Agnes Sanford and led her to Christ, **AFTER** she had mentored him and other inner healers!

In keeping with Word of Faith heresy, John and Paula Sandford believed they had discovered the "laws of miracles" which God must always follow to perform a miracle. Their God is not the transcendent Creator who exists outside His physical creation, but a God who is **in** all His creation, is tied to the physical universe and bound by its laws. This is well documented in their writing. For example, in their 1977 book, *The Elijah Task*, they state:

> Miracles happen by the cooperation, union, and interplay of spirit and matter together… Confused….men have thought…there had to be a violation of principles for miracles to happen… What rot and bunk! Miracles happen by releasing power within matter according to God's principles… Nature, being filled with the Spirit of God, has immeasurable power, locked within its tiniest cells… Miracles happen by the operation of the Holy Spirit within principles far beyond our ability to comprehend but nonetheless scientific…

I have sometimes been called a Christian scientist when lecturing on these subjects (page 142-143).

RUTH CARTER STAPLETON (1929-1983)

Sister of former American President Jimmy Carter, and well-known as a charismatic Christian in America. She was a disciple of Agnes Sanford, who claimed that one could be "born again" by listening to greater music or gazing upon certain works of art.

DENNIS (1917-1991) AND RITA BENNETT

Disciples of Agnes Sanford, and early pioneers of the *Charismatic Movement*.

FRANCIS MACNUTT

Roman Catholic charismatic priest, trained by Agnes Sanford, and proponent of Inner Healing methodologies.

MICHAEL SCANLAN (1931-2017)

Roman Catholic charismatic priest, disciple of Agnes Sanford, and proponent of Inner Healing methodologies.

KENNETH E. HAGIN (1917-2003)

Regarded as the "father" of the Word of Faith movement, Hagin was a disciple of E.W. Kenyon, whose theology was based not on the Word of God, but on the metaphysical *New Thought* (mind science) teachings of Phineas Quimby. Kenyon claimed Jesus did not defeat Satan on the cross, but instead in hell, when he allegedly became one with Satan.

Hagin was mentor to many Word of Faith heretics who are also part of the *Prophetic Movement* and widely accepted by the charismatic/evangelical church. One such notable disciple of Hagin is Kenneth Copeland, a man at the forefront of promoting the "Toronto Blessing"; a man with such extensive heretical beliefs that it would require a book larger than this to even begin to address them properly. However, just one tiny example is his heretical claim that we are all little gods. When speaking of this he famously said, "When God said 'I AM', I say that's great so am I".

The dangerous and heretical inner healing teaching remains alive and strong today in charismatic/evangelical circles, with the most prominent and successful being *Bethel's Sozo Ministry*, which is used by churches all over the world. Sozo is also promoted by *The Freedom Resource* (TFR), headed by author and executive director Andy Reese. On the *Bethel* website *Sozo* is claimed to mean:

> Saved, healed and delivered – *Sozo* contains the whole package of being made whole or well.

Sozo actually more accurately means "to save, keep safe and sound, to rescue from danger or destruction". It is derived from an obsolete Greek word *saos* that simply meant "safe". It is a verb that is translated as "to save" and the noun form, *soteria*, is translated "salvation". The foundation of this 21st century so-called "Christian healing ministry" is the heresy of Inner Healing, which involves a "Christianised" form of Regression Therapy; a practice that had been used by secular Psychotherapists for decades, but for all intents and purposes died out in the 1990s as a result of a number of patients suing their therapists over false recovered memories. I guess this is why in spite of the *Bethel Sozo* website banner stating, "[A] Ministry of Bethel Church", the FAQ section has the disclaimer, "The Sozo staff are independent contractors and are not Bethel Church staff". They do not like to call it "counselling" or "therapy", but rather refer to it has "healing prayer", and all recipients are required to sign a waiver (TFR brands their version of *Sozo* as "Freedom Prayer").

In Regression Therapy, secular Psychotherapists used hypnosis to "regress" their patient into a state where they would allegedly recall events in their life that they had repressed memory of because of its disturbing or traumatic nature. Regression Therapy would allegedly bring out into the open these traumatic memories so the therapist could "counsel" the patient to come to terms with them. The problem was that many of the memories brought forth turned out to be completely false and caused untold damage to the patient and their families.

The Regression Therapy used within *Sozo* is given a "Christian" veneer by claiming it is the Holy Spirit, rather than hypnosis that brings forth the regressed memory (often through the practice of contemplative prayer techniques), and the Holy Spirit who brings the inner healing, thus releasing the individual into a closer relationship with God. The problem is that the results are no better than those achieved by the secular Psychotherapists, and there are many testimonies of how dangerous and destructive *Sozo* has been. For example, I read the tragic testimony of the father of a girl who had gone through *Sozo* therapy and had experienced a "recovered memory" of her father molesting her from the age of three to 13. In spite of the girl's mother and siblings testifying to this "recovered memory" being completely untrue, the girl had been convinced by the *Sozo* therapist that it must be true because it was the Holy Spirit at work. It completely destroyed the girl's relationship with her family. The father tried to contact Bill Johnson regarding this, but Johnson would not communicate with him. He therefore contacted two lawyers with experience in dealing with cases of "false recovered memory", both of whom were shocked that Regressive Therapy was still being practiced.

I can testify that Inner Healing is a doctrine of demons by both comparing it to the Word of God and from my own personal experience, because when I was younger I accepted the counsel of a close and trusted family friend who had a ministry in "Christian counselling" and was an elder at a local church. I did not know then what I know now, so did not recognise it as Inner Healing, but I did know it was blatantly unbiblical. I therefore never went back after the first session, but the result of that one single "counselling" session directly opened me up to have the only truly demonic experience I have ever had.

CATHOLIC CONNECTION

Wimber was not just influenced by heretical Roman Catholic proponents of inner healing, he also had a fascination with the healing power of Catholic relics. On a 1981 Healing Seminar tape Wimber said:

> In the Catholic Church for over a 1,200 year period people were healed as a result of touching the relics of the saints. We Protestants have difficulty with that...but we healers shouldn't because there's nothing theologically out of line with that.

John Goodwin, former Vineyard pastor and close associate of Wimber confirmed his fascination and acceptance of such things:

> Wimber talked about the use of relics to heal people. He believed that is legitimate… relics are things the saints have either touched or owned, their bones, a lock of hair, having been imbued with the healing power of the saint and someone comes into contact with that relic and they get healed. [Wimber] encouraged that (*Testing*, tape 2).

Goodman also made very clear Wimber's affection for the Roman Catholic Church:

> John actively promotes the reunification of Protestants and Catholics. I was there at a seminar, a pastor's conference in Anaheim [where approx. 5,000 pastors attended]. The archbishop of the archdiocese was attending, sitting up in front with his robes on… John asked him to stand up and said to him, "I want to apologise to you on behalf of all Protestants for leaving the Catholic Church and for the things we've said about you and the Church (*Testing the Fruit*, tape 2).

Wimber even wrote an article for the Catholic charismatic publication, New Covenant (June 1988) titled, Why I Love Mary. Whilst the article did not affirm Roman Catholic dogmas of Mary's sinlessness, her perpetual virginity, or her assumption into heaven, neither did it offer any refutation of them. Knowing the Catholic belief in Mary as "the Mother of God," and the unbiblical doctrines that attend her veneration, such an article left the impression that Wimber had no problem with the Roman Catholic veneration of Mary.

EXPERIENCE DICTATING DOCTRINE

Wimber knew the "signs and wonders" being manifested in his ministry could not be justified by Scripture, but the reality is he did not care; he merely mirrored the attitude of C. Peter Wagner of being absolutely fine with experience preceding and producing theology. This is illustrated by how he removed the Toronto Airport Vineyard church from the Vineyard movement **not** because of the bizarre manifestations taking place, but because some within the Vineyard movement were actually trying to test the authenticity of the manifestations against the Word of God, and Wimber regarded this as neither necessary nor helpful for the promotion of what he believed to be a genuine move of the Holy Spirit. Only nine months before the Toronto Vineyard Church was removed, Wimber stated in a February 1995 edition of *Charisma* Magazine:

> There's nothing in Scripture that supports these kinds of phenomena that I can see, and I can't think of anything throughout the church age that would. So I feel no obligation to try to explain it. It's just phenomena. It's just people responding to God.

Upon Toronto being removed in December 1995, the Vineyard Association's statement concluded:

> OUR ACTION DOES NOT MEAN THAT WE HAVE REJECTED THE CURRENT RENEWAL. Many of our churches have benefited greatly from

this current renewal and have incorporated it into their church life within the healthy and biblical guidelines reflected in the articles and policies published over the past two years. WE HOPE THAT THEY WILL CONTINUE TO PURSUE RENEWAL IN THIS WAY.

Wimber took the view that if it worked, it must be from God; he famously declared:

> We are cataloguing all our experiences so we can develop a theology.

Does this not simply mirror the words of C. Peter Wagner?

In his healing seminar series he even unapologetically admitted:

> We don't have an explanation for all the various manifestations.

In a 1985 audio tape titled, *Healing, An Introduction*, he called for Christians to:

> …know more personally the God who exists both beyond and within the boundaries of well-defined doctrinal systems (tape 5).

In his book, *Power Evangelism*, Wimber explains,

> God uses our experiences to show us more fully what He teaches us in scripture, many times toppling or altering elements of our theology and world view (page 89).

As far as Wimber was concerned, experience trumped doctrine every time; experience dictated the doctrine.

Before giving his life to Christ and becoming a pastor of a Vineyard church and a prominent leader within the movement, close associate of Wimber, John Goodwin, had been heavily into drugs and Eastern mysticism. He eventually came to the startling realisation that through Wimber's Vineyard church movement he was involved in the very same occult practices he had abandoned when he gave his life to Christ. He says:

> I was a Vineyard pastor, and according to John Wimber, in his words, I "could do stuff… anywhere and any time…" I was tuned in… I was in lock-step with what John was teaching… I have literally been to hundreds of Vineyard conferences… I'm here to [explain] that this is part of the last days heresy that's bringing the church into the New Age… (*The Bulletin*, Bend, Oregon, 31/8/1997).

The widespread acceptance of the obviously unbiblical manifestations of Wimber's *Signs and Wonders Movement* was mainly due to the spiritual state of the *Charismatic Renewal Movement* that had started in the late 1960s, grown through the 1970s and was in full swing in the 1980s. I have no doubt the *Charismatic Renewal Movement* did start as a genuine move of the Holy Spirit, but deteriorated as it progressively looked inward instead of outward and used the spiritual gifts God had bestowed on His church to empower it to fulfil its commission, for self-fulfilment and self-gratification; instead of being the channel of God's gifts and blessings as He had intended, the movement instead became a consumer, with its focus on the gifts themselves (the so-called "signs and wonders") rather than the giver of the gifts, just like it did at Azusa Street, and just like it has at every false revival since. This can be seen today in churches that still look to Azusa Street and John Wimber's "signs and wonders" as their "model" for manifestations of the supernatural in church; churches such as *Bethel Church* in Redding, California, pastored by Bill Johnson, a man who (as referred to earlier) has described William Branham as having an "anointing and power" like "no one that has ever lived". As part of their worship service, *Bethel Church* regularly experiences supernatural manifestations such as white feathers, "angel" dust and "jewels" appearing, or people claiming to supernaturally receive gold fillings; all standard manifestations for churches who trace their roots back to Azusa Street and *Latter Rain* teaching. Signs that make you wonder. In an interview I watched with Bill Johnson, he conceded that he could find no Biblical justification for the bizarre supernatural manifestations occurring at his *Bethel Church*, so just concluded that God must just "enjoy messing with our head" by giving us "signs that make us wonder". It is precisely this dangerously unbiblical attitude toward supernatural manifestations that seriously makes me wonder; they should make every Bible-believing Christian wonder.

Johnson's reckless attitude toward supernatural manifestations completely flies in the face of Scripture, which tells us to *"test all things"* (1 Thessalonians 5:21) and *"do not believe every spirit, but test the spirits, whether they are of God"* (1 John 4:1). If Christians cannot be deceived by false spirits and false supernatural experiences, why would the Word of God warn us to test all things and not to believe every spirit? The Bible tells us to test **all** things, not just those things we may subjectively think are questionable. Johnson's books are filled with examples of his unbiblical and reckless attitude towards spiritual experiences. For example, in his book, *When Heaven Invades Earth*, he described a supernatural experience that I can't find **any** Biblical justification for:

> For months I had been asking God to give me more of Him. I wasn't sure of the correct way to pray, nor did I understand the doctrine behind my request (page 113).

What a staggering statement for a Christian teacher and pastor to make. Based on the experience that followed (which Johnson describes in his book), I would suggest that he did not understand the doctrine behind his request because what he was asking for, and the way in which he asked, cannot be found within the pages of Scripture. The experience he describes **can** however be found at any "Toronto Blessing" or "Lakeland Revival" type meeting.

Too many within the charismatic/evangelical church seem so desperate so receive "more of God" (as it is so often described) that they jettison God's Word which tells us how we should ask God for more of Him, how we should experience Him and how we should worship Him. In 1 Corinthians 4:6, Paul warns us to not go beyond what is written, and I am absolutely convinced that when a Christian does just that in the way they pursue experience of the Almighty, they open themselves up to deceiving spirits. On page 116 of *When heaven Invaded Earth*, Johnson writes:

> For decades the Church has been guilty of creating doctrine to justify their lack of power…

I would suggest the exact opposite is in fact true for much of the charismatic/evangelical church, in that it has been guilty of creating doctrine to justify the extra-Biblical manifestations it experiences; the experience dictating the doctrine.

I am firmly convinced that at least some of these "miracles" experienced at churches like *Bethel* **are** genuinely supernatural in nature, but are not from God. How can I be so sure they are real but **not** from God? Because these "miracles" ultimately do not point to Jesus. True miracles and "signs and wonders" will always point to Jesus; that is the whole **Biblical** point of them. True Biblical "signs and wonders" are performed by the Holy Spirit for the purpose of glorifying Jesus. The promise of John 16:14 – *"He will glorify Me"* – was fulfilled after the Holy Spirit came upon the disciples at Pentecost, and everything the Holy Spirit does is intended to glorify Jesus, not the Holy Spirit, and certainly not those receiving the Holy Spirit. If the Holy Spirit glorified the person receiving Him, that would make Christianity an eccentric and egocentric religion – off centre. If the Holy Spirit glorified Himself in what He did it would make Christianity spirit-centred rather than Christ-centred.

Do the supernatural manifestations even make those experiencing them read the Word of God more? Based on the general low regard for the written Word of God expressed by the leaders of the modern-day *Prophetic Movement* (as we will see later) and the general level of Biblical illiteracy within the charismatic/evangelical church, I think the answer is self-evident. A. W. Tozer put it like this:

> If this new experience does not make us read the Word more, it is not of God. If it does not make us meditate on the truth more, it is not of God. I do not care how good we feel. If we feel so good we feel brand new, we are still not being blessed by God (*The Christ-Centred Church*, page 213).

A perfect example of such a supernatural experience can be found by viewing video footage on YouTube of the so-called "glory cloud" being manifested at Bill Johnson's

Bethel Church. Members of the church claim this is a physical manifestation of the Shekinah Glory[14] no less, but if that really is the case, why are people not falling on their faces in awe, reverence and fear instead of casually filming it on their iPhones? Signs that make you wonder…

The "signs and wonders" experienced by much of the charismatic/evangelical church do not make Christ bigger, sweeter and more indispensably beautiful in their lives than He was before the "miraculous manifestation". In fact, the exact opposite is true, because the manifestations leave the person focused on the experience and how it can be repeated and even bettered, rather than wanting more of Christ in their lives. This was the problem at Azusa Street, this was the problem at the *Sharon Bible School*, this was the problem with William Branham, this was the problem with John Wimber, this was the problem with Toronto, Pensacola and Lakeland, and continues to be the problem at places like *Bethel* and IHOP. The yearning for the gift instead of the gift giver is what allows a *"different spirit"* into the church. Based on the manifestations catalogued at so-called "revivals" I would strongly suggest the *"different spirit"* allowed in is the demonic kundalini spirit of Hinduism. Mike Bickle provides a helpful list of the kind of manifestations experienced and witnessed; a list that accurately records the type of manifestations experienced at meetings both pre and post Azusa Street:

> Shaking, jerking, loss of bodily strength, heavy breathing, eyes fluttering, lips trembling, oil on body, changes in skin color (sic)… drunkenness… visions, hearing audibly into the spirit realm… jumping, violent rolling, screaming, nausea as discernment of evil, smelling or tasting good or evil presence… feeling heavy weight or lightness, trances… disruption into the natural realm, i.e. [electric] circuits blown (*God's Manifest Presence: Understanding the Phenomena that Accompany the Spirit's Ministry*, Metro Vineyard Fellowship, 1995).

Many of the aforementioned experiences continue to manifest themselves in day-to-day life long after the meeting has ended. For example, within the testimony I read of someone who was saved **out** of what they described as the *Bethel* **cult**, they describe how it was almost impossible to "communicate with people even about simple matters like the weather or a basketball game without them jerking or convulsing… these convulsions were so profuse within the [Bethel] cult… Another idiosyncrasy was the constant belting out of the phrase… 'WHOA' or 'WOE'. This is heard constantly". He goes on to say that during his time at *Bethel* "never once did I hear salvation, repentance, holiness, righteousness, judgment, or wrath preached, neither from the pulpit nor when I'd travel the streets with them. The whole business plan (because it's NOT a ministry) is to focus on LYING signs and wonders… impotent magic tricks".

KUNDALINI

Millions of people all around the world involved in the ancient Eastern mystery religions and the *New Age Movement* (which is nothing more than the ancient Eastern mystery religions repackaged for the gullible Western world) experience powerful spiritual manifestations that are identical to the manifestations many charismatic/evangelical churches attribute to the Holy Spirit. Practitioners in the ancient mystery religions experience a powerful "kundalini awakening". Kundalini (meaning "coiled one" in Sanskrit) refers to the dormant power or energy that is said to be lying like a coiled serpent at the base of the spine.

Who is described as the serpent in Scripture?

Interestingly, people Like Todd Bentley say when they feel their "anointing" come upon them, they feel it at the base of their spine, and when they (allegedly) "impart" the Holy Spirit on to people, the recipient very often testifies to feeling the "impartation" in the base of their spine. This experience has absolutely no validity in Scripture.

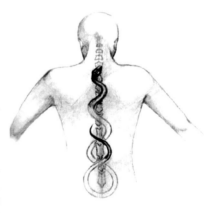

In Hinduism, the guru imparts spiritual energy on the devotee by touching them on the forehead with his open palm in what is known as the *shaktipat* or divine touch. Is that not disturbingly similar to the way in which people receive the "impartation" of the Holy Spirit by the "laying on of hands" on their foreheads at many charismatic/evangelical churches today.

After a period of spiritual preparation, which usually involves the use of repetitive music for hours on end (and can also involve meditation and yoga), the Hindu devotee reaches a "kundalini awakening" that is evidenced by the fact that they begin to shake, jerk, or hop or squirm uncontrollably, sometimes breaking into uncontrolled animal noises or laughter as they reach an ecstatic high. These manifestations are called "kriyas" – the outward physical expression of awakened kundalini. During "kundalini awakening" devotees sometimes roar like lions and show all kinds of physical signs. Often devotees move on to higher states of spiritual consciousness and become motionless physically and appear to slip into a trance of unconsciousness.

Hindu guru Shri Yogānandji Mahārāja describes the effect of the "kundalini wakening":

> ... your body begins trembling, hair stands on roots, you laugh or begin to weep without your wishing, your tongue begins to utter deformed sounds, you are filled with fear or see frightening visions. The kundalini shakti has become active.

There are literally countless testimonies from people who have experienced the effects of "kundalini awakening", and the more of them you read the more you become disturbed by the startling similarities between them and the testimonies from professing Christians who have had an alleged encounter with the Holy Spirit. Here is just one testimony of a "kundalini awakening" from the 1978 book, *Dance Your Way to God* by Bhagwan Shree Rajneesh:

> Suddenly her body was shaking, she was screaming. Somendra [the guru] was moving around her – touching her on the back of her neck, on the chest, on the belly. As he'd touch her, his hands vibrating with energy, the part of her body where he touched her would begin shaking more violently. Shaking, screaming, crying – she became a dynamo of energy... she was on fire, from the opposite corner [of the room] they could feel her energy (page 149).

Replace the name of the guru with just about any "anointed" one in the charismatic/evangelical church today and you have the testimony of literally millions of Christians who believe this is what an encounter with the Holy Spirit feels like.

Consider for example chapter 14 of the 2012 Bethel book titled, *The Physics of Heaven – Exploring God's Mysteries of Sound, Light, Energy, Vibrations, and Quantum Physics*, in which we read:

> Many men and women of God have experienced physical shaking and "vibrating" and seen bright light when undergoing a deep spiritual transformation. Others have described sensations like electric shocks when encountering God's presence. This chapter shares experiences by contributors Bill Johnson, Beni Johnson, Cal Pierce [who reopened John G. Lake's healing room on the original site], Ellyn Davis, and two other people [one of whom was Bob Jones] who have had transformative experiences that involved vibrating, electrical sensations, and light.

The *Physics of Heaven* website invites people to post accounts of their experiences from putting into practice the methods taught in the book, and the following is (very disturbingly) typical of the testimonies posted:

> In 1965 I was 15 and I got a book about meditation and to cover your body in vibrations. Well it took about a week and at the base of my spine I felt [a] burst of vibration it felt like electricity. I was thinking this is cool, I want more. So I daily would meditate and draw these vibrations into my life. Over months of doing this I could get the vibs [vibrations] to travel up my spine to my head then a new realm opened up and it flooded my whole body and boy was I stoned. This is better than drugs. In 1970 I get saved and filled, [and] never being in a church before I didn't know what to expect. Well talk about electricity I went down under power never seeing this or knowing anything about it in the church. I was out for 20 mins and Jesus verbally spoke to me and said Michael I Am the messiah. His presence, vibes, electricity was stronger than anything I ever felt before, it was the best high ever. I have been walking with The Lord ever since. The anointing is neither good or evil and both sides of the fence know about it they just call it life force Che [chi] or whatever… Because I already knew about the anointing before I got saved, when I went down under the power of God I understood what the electricity was about. I now activate people into the prophetic by passing my Mantle over them and they enter into His presence more easily. I just have to think about the Anointing now and it comes instantly to me. I have learned how to move it around to change this present reality so others may learn to enter into the presence of The Lord and I love anointing people and watch it increase in their lives and how they awaken more readily to the presence of The Lord. Our Father wants us to share in the Glory and spread it throughout the earth. To bring us back to the frequency Adam had when he walked and talked with The Lord.

The author of this testimony readily acknowledges that even before he was saved he had experienced this "anointing" through completely occult methods. As far as he is concerned there is no difference, because "…the anointing is neither good or evil and both sides of the fence know about it they just call it life force Che [chi] or whatever". This man has simply describe a "kundalini awakening". The occult has infiltrated the church. Welcome to the apostasy.

Time and time again I have watched video footage of professing Christians having "fire imparted" on them during a charismatic meeting by the laying on of hands, where the recipient actually screams, sobs and writhes around in agonising pain as if they are actually on fire. In spite of these poor people being in very obvious and severe physical pain and emotional distress from the experience, the person "imparting" the "anointing" just yells louder and louder, "THIS IS THE FIRE OF GOD. MORE! MORE! MORE!", and with every cry of "MORE" the recipient's pain and distress very clearly increases (sometimes to the point where they run out of the hall), but that does not stop the "imparter" from increasing the recipients "anointing". This is so obviously demonic it is painful and distressing to watch.

In the Old Testament, the outpouring of fire is synonymous with God's judgment, not blessing; so much so that it would require a separate Bible study on the subject to do it justice.

But what about the New Testament?

Has God changed the way He uses fire from judgment to blessing?

Does God now use fire as a way of imparting His Holy Spirit to the New Testament believer?

Most of the charismatic/evangelical church thinks so, which can be demonstrated by how many Christian ministries contain the word "fire". In their name. For example, following the "Toronto Blessing", the Toronto Airport Christian Fellowship changed its name to *Catch the Fire Toronto*; Todd Bentley's ministry is called *Fresh Fire*; *Bethel Church* even has the "fire tunnel" during services which people pass through to catch the fire of God.

So is there anything in the Bible to suggest God has changed how He uses fire for New Testament believers? Acts 2:2-4 is the verse always pointed to:

> *² And suddenly there came a sound from heaven, as of a rushing mighty wind, and it filled the whole house where they were sitting. ³ Then there appeared to them divided tongues, as of fire, and one sat upon each of them. ⁴ And they were all filled with the Holy Spirit and began to speak with other tongues, as the Spirit gave them utterance.*

It is important to actually look at the text, which states the tongues were *"as of fire"*, **not** literal fire; neither is there **any** indication the recipients actually felt like they were **on** fire. The sensation of being **on** fire is part experiencing the "kundalini awakening", not Biblical Christianity.

In the Gospels, Mark and John speak of the baptism of the Holy Spirit, but there is no mention of baptism with fire. Matthew and Luke **do** mention the baptism with fire, but the immediate context of both is clearly **judgment** and **not** something Christians should be calling down on themselves or others (Matthew 3:7-12; Luke 3:7-17). The passages in both Matthew and Luke recall John the Baptist declaring judgment on the Sadducees and Pharisees and has nothing to do with blessing; he calls both groups a *"brood of vipers"*! The Lord Jesus is coming in flaming fire to **judge** those who do **not** know God (2 Thessalonians 1:3-10; John 5:21-23; Revelation 20:11-15).

PENTECOST

A **true** move of the Holy Spirit is documented in Acts 2 at Pentecost. Do **any** of the manifestations described earlier by Mike Bickle have **anything** in common with what happened at Pentecost? Of course not, but they have everything in common with what was manifested at Azusa Street, the *Sharon Bible School*, the "Toronto Blessing", the Pensacola Outpouring, the Lakeland "Revival" and what takes place most weeks at *Bethel* and IHOP.

In addition to the issue of fire mentioned above, those who try to link what happened at Pentecost with the kind of manifestations experienced at many charismatic/ evangelical churches today **always** do so by claiming the manifestation of tongues at Pentecost is identical to what they experience and the apostles got drunk in the Spirit just in the way they experience today. However, they have not read the account in Acts properly, because first of all, the tongues spoken at Pentecost were **understood** by those listening; God used the gift of tongues to evangelise the people present in their own language; they were **not** talking unintelligible and self-indulgent gibberish.

Pentecost is significant in both the Old and New Testaments. "Pentecost" is actually the Greek name for a Jewish festival known in the Old Testament as the Feast of Weeks (Leviticus 23:15; Deuteronomy 16:9). The Greek word means "fifty" and refers to the fifty days that have elapsed since the wave offering of Passover. Jews from all over the known world would congregate in Jerusalem at the appropriate time of the year to celebrate the Feast of Weeks. Because these Jews were dispersed around the world, they did not all speak the same language, and certainly not Hebrew (Jesus spoke Aramaic). Therefore, God gave the gift of tongues to the apostles at Pentecost so they could minister and witness about Jesus Christ to these dispersed Jews in their own languages, who would then go back to their own Jewish communities and tell people what they had witnessed and heard; this is how the Gospel of Jesus Christ was first spread among the dispersed Jews before the apostles travelled far and wide; this would not have been achieved if those present at Pentecost had been speaking the unintelligible gibberish spoken at most charismatic/evangelical churches today.

Furthermore, regarding the alleged drunken state the apostles manifested under the power of the Holy Spirit, the actual text of Acts 2 does not support this in any way. Acts 2:13 states that some there **mocked** what they saw by saying, *"They are full of new wine"*, but in Acts 2:15 Peter flatly denies this accusation; the apostles were accused of being drunk by mockers who did not understand (or want to understand) what they were witnessing. There is absolutely no evidence from Scripture to suggest the apostles were "drunk" under the influence of the Holy Spirit. In fact, if they were drunk in the Spirit it would contradict what the rest of Scripture says firstly about the fruit of the Spirit being self-control (Galatians 5:23), and secondly about drunkenness. For example:

> *And do not be drunk with wine, in which is dissipation [debauchery]; but be filled with the Spirit* (Ephesians 5:18).

Paul says that getting drunk is akin to our old way of life with its worldly and self-serving desires and such behaviour is debased and leads to debauchery (compare Colossians 1:21; Romans 13:13). The word *debauchery* is a translation of a Greek word meaning "lawless insolence or unmanageable caprice." Instead of linking the indwelling of the Holy Spirit with a state of drunkenness like many in the charismatic/evangelical church do, Paul does exactly the opposite and purposely contrasts the state of drunkenness (a loss of self-control) with the indwelling of the Holy Spirit.

Additionally, and very importantly, Pentecost is not just defined by the supernatural manifestations recorded in Acts 2. Pentecost is also defined by Peter's bold and incisive preaching to those present, the effect of which was powerful, as listeners were *"cut to the heart"* (Acts 2:37) and instructed by Peter to *"repent, and let every one of you be baptised"* (Acts 2:38). The narrative concludes with three thousand souls being added to the fellowship. In stark contrast, preaching is non-existent at charismatic/evangelical meetings where these bizarre and unbiblical manifestations occur; preaching is conspicuous by its very absence! No one is *"cut to the heart"* by a call to repentance and no true converts are made; "signs and wonders" do not bring people to repentance and a saving faith in Jesus Christ. In fact, Jesus Himself declared:

> *An evil and adulterous generation seeks after a sign, and no sign will be given to it except the sign of the prophet Jonah* (Matthew 12:39, 16:4).

The sign of Jonah Jesus spoke of was His death and resurrection (Matthew 12:40-42).

I would implore the reader to prayerfully and carefully consider how the Word of God describes genuine encounters with the Holy Spirit and the manifestations experienced through "kundalini awakening", and then consider which description is closer to the list of manifestations provided by Mike Bickle. The answer is clear to all but those who are wilfully blind.

PROFANE FIRE

Christians who actively seek out the kind of experiences listed by Mike Bickle as part of their worship and experience of God should prayerfully consider a number of sobering incidents recorded in the Word of God. Firstly, there is Leviticus 10:1-3 where Aaron's sons, Nadab and Abihu, made a fire offering of worship to God, but not in the way prescribed by God; they were worshiping the one true God, but in a way unacceptable to God. Verse 1 describes their offering as *"profane fire"* and God judged Nadab and Abihu most severely for it. Whilst the original Hebrew literally translates as *"profane fire"*, the term is a Hebraic idiom for **idolatry**; YAHWEH regards as idolatry worship given to Him in a way not prescribed by Him. If God regards the spiritual practices that result in extra-Biblical manifestations as idolatry, just **whose** power is being manifested**?**

Just because people who participate in these activities no longer receive the same kind of punishment that Aaron's sons did, do not make the mistake of assuming that God regards it as any less of a sin today than He did in the Old Testament. God remains as holy today as He has always been and He regards the sin of idolatry no less serious today than He did in Old Testament times. God does not change, but His covenants do; we are now under the covenant of Grace instead of the Law and the only reason why we are under His covenant of Grace is because His wrath was poured out on His Son Jesus Christ in our place. The only reason why God does not pour out His righteous wrath on people today who commit idolatry by offering *"profane fire"* to Him is because His wrath has already been poured out on His Son. But God's covenant of Grace is intended to draw us to repentance, not be a licence to commit these sins of idolatry.

Consider Cain and Abel, who both offered worship sacrifices to the one true God, but only Abel's offering was acceptable to God. Cain decided **how** he wanted to offer his worship to God, and that was clearly not his choice to make.

Consider also Genesis 32 where we are told that while Moses was up the mountain receiving instruction from God, the Israelites got impatient and built a gold calf to worship. They worshiped the image as YAHWEH, but this was not how God had instructed them to worship Him; they were worshiping the right God, but in the wrong way.

Then there is Jeroboam and what he did when Israel split after the reign of King Solomon, with the ten Northern tribes following Jeroboam and the two Southern tribes (Judah and Benjamin) following King Solomon's son, Rehoboam. 1 Kings 12:28 tells us how Jeroboam built two gold calves to be worshiped (thus repeating the sin of the Israelites in Genesis 32) in order to prevent his subjects from travelling south to worship at the temple in Jerusalem (under the rule of Rehoboam). He also made shrines on the high places and made priests from every class of people, instead of from just the Levi tribe as God had instructed. All this was done in the name of worshiping YAHWEH, the one true God of Israel, and in their hearts and minds the ten tribes **were** worshiping the God of Israel, but that was not **how** the God of Israel had commanded them to worship Him. As a result of Jeroboam's actions he has the unenviable title of being known as the king who sinned and made Israel to sin (1 Kings 14:16).

We do not get to decide how we offer to God our prayers and worship, or experience Him; God does. God is righteous and holy and unchanging. Jesus Himself shows us in Matthew 6:9-13 how to pray to God the Father. Verse 1 starts with:

> *Our Father in heaven,* **hallowed** *be Your name. Your kingdom come,* **Your will be done**...

God's name is hallowed (holy) and we are to submit to His will in all things; especially how we pray to Him and worship Him. Jesus declared that we should worship God *"in spirit and truth"* (John 4:24), and the spiritual manifestations experienced within many charismatic/evangelical churches contain neither God's Spirit, nor His truth; they are demonstrably extra-Biblical and counter-Biblical; they go beyond what is written.

THE BEST LEFT UNTIL LAST

A key figure in the re-emergence of the *Latter Rain Movement* was Bill Haman (the man with the prophecy discerning "burning bosom"), who sponsored the first *National Prophets Conference* in 1987, which was attended by around 700 people and from which the "Elijah List" began. The "Elijah List" still flourishes today in the form of an email newsletter that publishes the "words" and "revelations" of the hundreds of so-called new "apostles" and "prophets", and is received daily by over 130,000 people. The "Elijah List" took inspiration for its name from a faulty understanding of how Elijah imparted his "anointing" onto Elisha, and how John the Baptist carried the Elijah "anointing". Bill Johnson of *Bethel Church* illustrates this belief in his book, *When Heaven Invades Earth*:

> We will carry the Elijah anointing in preparing for the return of the Lord in the same way that John the Baptist carried the Elijah anointing and prepared the people for the coming of the Lord (page 184).

John Alexander Dowie was the first to claim to have the "Elijah anointing", which William Branham then claimed to have received from him. This should tell you all you need to know about this false doctrine.

A group of around 500 new "apostles" gathered in Singapore in 1999 and called themselves the *International Coalition of Apostles* (ICA); it is these self-proclaimed new "apostles" who have the authority to nominate new "apostles" within the movement today. The ICA official definition states the following on www.apostlesnet.net:

> …an office, such as the office of apostle, is not given by grace alone, but given as a result of works that have demonstrated faithfulness in stewarding the gift.

Compare this to Paul, who stated:

> *For I am the least of the apostles, who am not worthy to be called an apostle, because I persecuted the church of God.* [10] *But by the grace of God I am what I am, and His grace toward me was not in vain; but I laboured more abundantly than they all, yet not I, but the grace of God which was with me* (1 Corinthians 15:9-10).

This new generation of "apostles" does not merely claim to be in the apostolic succession and guardians of the apostolic truth, they claim to be even **greater** than the former apostles. For example, Shawn Bolz, a "prophet" who claims angelic visitations that make the ones recorded in Scripture sound dull, writes the following in his book, *The Keys to Heaven's Economy*:

Just as in John 2:10, the Father has saved the best wine for last, and we are about to witness a generation whom God will use to bring the most intense manifestation of Heaven and Earth (page 43).

God is declaring our generation to be unlike any other generation on the face of the earth (page 102).

In *The Harvest*, Rick Joyner declares:

> In the near future we will not be looking back at the early church with envy because of the great exploits of those days, but all will be saying that He certainly did save the best wine for last. The most glorious times in all of history have not come upon us. You, who have dreamed of one day being able to talk with Peter, John and Paul, are going to be surprised to find that they have all been waiting to talk to you.

Bob Jones claimed this new generation was actually called out from the bloodline of Paul, David, Peter, James (who was the half-brother of Jesus) and John. Not only that, God has kept the best of the bloodlines to the end. Speaking on behalf of the Lord, Jones pronounced:

> From out of the sands of time, I [God] have called the best of every bloodline in the earth unto this generation… Even the bloodline of Paul. Even the bloodline of David, the bloodline of Peter, James, and John. The best of their seed is unto our generation. They will even be superior to them in heart, stature, and love for me.

In a recorded conversation with Mike Bickle, during one of his many alleged visits to the third heaven, Jones claimed he had a face-to-face meeting with the apostle Paul. Jones declared:

> Paul was anxious to talk to the End-Time apostles and prophets more than the End-Time apostles and prophets would have been to talk to Paul…and the saints in the New Testament would wait in line to greet the apostles coming from this generation.

Paul Cain proudly declared the following at the *Vineyard Prophecy School* in 1989:

> God has invited us to have a role in establishing this New Order of Christianity… God is offering to this generation something He has never offered to any generation before. He's giving us an open invitation to participate in something that will lead to the prize of all the ages… It's greater than anything He's ever done from Adam clear down through the millennium.

In *Engaging the Revelatory Realm of Heaven*, Paul Keith Davies declares:

> Our generation stands on the threshold of experiencing a spiritual restoration that will equate in prominence with the recovery of the Jewish people to the land of Israel (page 55).

And if that claim was not grand enough:

> This apostolic reformation will ignite the re-establishment and functioning of the Church in genuine spiritual power and authority. From this foundation, the Church will be able to soar to even greater places in God that await us – the Melchizedek Priesthood and a deeper apprehension of being sons and daughters who have overcome and discovered rest in God (page 56).

These new "apostles" and "Prophets" do not just think themselves important to the point of superseding Paul, David, Peter, James and John, they consider themselves **essential** for the church to be able to fulfil its End-Time purpose on earth. For example, in *Prophets and the Prophetic Movement*, Bill Haman states:

> …the Apostle is the covering and protecting cloud and the Prophet is the enlightening and directing fire. That is one reason why apostles and prophets must be restored before the Church can fulfil its predestined end-time purpose on earth (page 57).

In *The Prophetic Ministry*, Rick Joyner states:

> No ministry which rejects or avoids what is now happening in the restoration of the prophetic ministry will be able to truly fulfil its own calling and purpose in this hour (page 53).

Just what **is** the church's End-Time calling and purpose as far as these new "apostles" and prophets" are concerned? Bill Haman provides a clear answer on page 59 of *Prophets and the Prophetic Movement*:

> The full restoration of apostles and prophets back into the church will then bring divine order, unity, purity and maturity to the corporate Body of Christ… that will in turn bring about the end of this world system of humanity and Satan's rule. **The fulfilment of all these things will release Christ**, who has been seated at the right hand of the Father in heaven, to return literally and set up His everlasting kingdom over all the earth (emphasis added).

On page 28 of the same book, Haman claims:

> Christ cannot return until His ascension gift ministries have brought the church into full manhood. The Pastor, Evangelist and Teacher have been

the only ones acknowledged as being active in that role. But now, Christ is activating His prophets in the 1980s and His Apostles in the 1990s. Jesus is thrilled at the thought that His Prophets will soon be fully recognised by the church.

In *Prophets and Personal Prophecy*, Haman states:

> The prophets are being brought forth to fulfil their part in preparing the Bride-church for her day of presentation to her heavenly Bridegroom, Christ Jesus. Jesus is rejoicing with great joy over the part the prophets are playing in preparing His Bride. **When the prophets have finished their ministry, He will be released to descend from heaven** with a shout and be fully and eternally united with His Bride. **Twentieth-century prophets are very precious to Christ, for they are perfecting the Bride He died to purchase, the Church** (emphasis added).

According to these new "apostles" and "prophets", Jesus Christ **needs** them to not only release Him, but also to perfect His Bride, the church. There is only one word suitable to describe this teaching: **heresy**; it puts Christ under man; it credits man with power, authority, responsibility and prerogatives that are reserved for Christ alone! The basis for this belief that Jesus needs the help of the church is a heretical teaching popularised by Word of Faith teachers like Kenneth Hagin and Kenneth Copeland, which claims God lost his rule and authority over the earth when Adam fell. But of course the *Prophetic Movement* goes hand-in-hand with the Word of Faith heresy; so much so that it is regarded as orthodox Christian doctrine in the majority of charismatic/evangelical churches today. Adam is said to have been created as a "god-class" type of being who was given rule and authority over the earth. However, when he sinned, he forfeited his dominion over the earth to Satan and God was removed from the earth. God needed (and still needs) man to take dominion of the earth back from Satan so He can return. In fact, according to Ed Silvoso in his book, *That None Should Perish*, prior to Jesus' victory at Calvary:

> God would not become a trespasser by challenging Satan directly in matters related to man and the world under his control. If he did so Satan would have called God a trespasser (page 195).

Setting aside for a moment the utterly false premise that God ever lost dominion over man or the earth (e.g. Psalm 24:1-2), consider Silvoso's words in light of Jesus' ministry **before** His victory at Calvary, where He regularly demonstrated authority over demons and directly challenged Satan in matters relating to man; instead of screaming "Trespasser!" at Jesus, all the demons, without exception (and including the demons His disciples could not cast out of people) yielded to Jesus' authority. Not only that, we read in Matthew 9:6 Jesus declaring and demonstrating *"that the Son of Man has power on earth to forgive sins"*, **before** His victory at Calvary. Furthermore, Matthew 10:1 describes how Jesus gave His disciples power and authority over unclean spirits. How could Jesus give authority and power to others that He did not have Himself?

Should anyone doubt that members of the modern-day *Prophetic Movement* actually believe this heresy, consider a 2007 edition of *The Shepherd's Rod*, in which Paul Keith Davies and Bob Jones state:

> The Bible declares that the heaven of Heavens belongs to God, but the earth has been delegated into the hands of man. Dominion of the earth was first entrusted to Adam. Unfortunately, that heritage was lost in the Garden of Eden. The spirit of this world has usurped the true spiritual authority originally given to mankind.

Then further on in the same article, speaking of a future time when they believe the church will take dominion over the earth, they state:

> When this transpires, we will learn how to release God's dominion in the earth.

At the *National Man's Shepherds Conference* in Kansas City in 1975, Ern Baxter prophesied:

> God's people are going to start to exercise rule, and they're going to take dominion over the powers of Satan. They're going to bring diabolical princes down. The dark powers that hover over the parliament buildings of the nations are going to be paralyzed by the corporate prayer of an authoritative community. As the rod of His strength goes out of Zion, He'll change legislation. He'll chase the devil off the face of God's earth, and God's people together, doing the will of God, will bring about God's purposes and God's reign.

In a supposed heavenly conversation between Adam and "prophet" Rick Joyner recorded in Joyner's 1999 book, *The Call*, Adam told him:

> Those who live in your times will prepare the earth for Him to rule…. He will use them to release His judgments….What He is about to do, He will do through His people, and His people will stand as Elijah in the last days. Their words will shut up the heavens or bring rain; they will prophesy

earthquakes and famines, and they will come to pass; they will stop famines and earthquakes. When they release armies in the heavens, armies will march on the earth. When they hold back armies, there will be peace. They will decide where He shows mercy and where He shows His wrath.

At the *National School of the Prophets Conference* in 1999, Hamon had the nerve to give orders to the archangel Michael, resulting in a supposed flood of angels filling the room:

> God says 'From this day forward I give you authority. When you call for Michael, he will bring a legion of angels and they will fight and war and I give you comradeship and I give you cooperation, and I'm adjoining you to join angelic hosts and the army of the Lord of the saints to win My battle' and God's raising up angels, and we're going to call them in right now.... Jesus, Commander-in-Chief, I call for General Michael and the host of war angels, come and appoint yourself companions now, now, now! Whoosh! Yeah! Yeah, here they come! Here they come! Yeah. Accept them! Accept them.

If only the Lord **had** sent Michael, it would silence these heretical false "prophets" and "apostles".

NEW APOSTOLIC REFORMATION

The forming of the *International Coalition of Apostles* (ICA) in Singapore in 1999 led directly to the creation of the *New Apostolic Reformation* (NAR). C. Peter Wagner was made President of the ICA and subsequently became the head "apostle" of the NAR. Of all the branches of the NAR, the ICA is perhaps the most visible. In a NAR brochure Wagner declared:

> The New Apostolic Reformation is an extraordinary work of the Holy Spirit that is changing the shape of Christianity globally...

Based on the number of charismatic/evangelical churches today with recognised connections or affiliations with the NAR, you could say Wagner was right! For example, it is estimated to directly influence a staggering **369 million** professing Christians around the world; this is no fringe organisation. Wagner went on to claim in the same brochure:

> The Lord is establishing the foundations of the Church for the new millennium. This foundation is built upon apostles and prophets. Apostles execute and establish God's plan on earth.

As we have already established from Scripture, God has **already** established the foundations of the church on the apostles and prophets. He is not doing it again!

The NAR is directly built on, and still follows, the heresies of the original *Latter Rain Movement* of the 1940s, such as the impartation of an "anointing", which has more in common with the Hindu practice of *shaktipat* than Biblical Christianity. The Holy Spirit comes when He wills, when God the Father wills, not when we demand.

ANOINTING

The unbiblical teaching of being able to "impart" an "anointing" of the Holy Spirit on someone by the laying on of hands which underpins almost all of today's charismatic/evangelical Christianity, is the same heresy that formed the foundation of William Branham's demonically empowered ministry in the 1940s.

The New Testament Greek words for "anoint" are:

1. *Chrio*, meaning "to smear or rub with oil, and by implication to consecrate for office or religious service".

2. *Aleipho*, meaning "to anoint".

In Bible times, people were anointed with oil to signify God's blessing, or call on that person's life (Exodus 29:7; Exodus 40:9; 2 Kings 9:6; Ecclesiastes 9:8), as a precurser to the Holy Spirit anointing people in the New Testament. A person was anointed for a special purpose – to be a king, a prophet, a priest or even a builder etc.

Another meaning for the word "anointed" is "chosen one" and this is where people within many charismatic/evangelical churches today have been turned away from New Testament Biblical truth about true anointing and teach that certain special people (like William Branham, Todd Bentley et al) have a special "anointing". This is dangerous and must be exposed as such, because it is the fuel that drives the engine of the modern-day *Prophetic Movement*. The Bible tells us that Jesus was anointed by God with the Holy Spirit to spread the good news and set free those who have been held captive by sin (Luke 4:18-19; Acts 10:38). After Christ departed from the earth, He left us the gift of the Holy Spirit (John 14:16) and as a result, now **all** Christians are anointed, chosen for the specific purpose of furthering God's Kingdom:

> *But you have an anointing from the Holy One, and you know all things* (1 John 2:20).

> *Now He who establishes us with you in Christ and has anointed us is God, who also has sealed us and given us the Spirit in our hearts as a guarantee* (1 Corinthians 1:21-22).

Every believer has the anointing of the Holy Spirit. There is **no** "special anointing" in the way people within the *Prophetic Movement* claim, such as Bill Johnson for example:

> He [the Holy Spirit] lives in all believers, but the glory of His presence comes to rest on only a few (*When Heaven Invades Earth*, page 149).

The extent to how this false teaching about special "anointing" has contaminated mainstream charismatic/evangelical Christianity simply cannot be understated. For example, members of Bill Johnson's *Bethel Church* (which is probably the most prominent and influential church in the NAR having been led out of the Assemblies of God in 2006 by Johnson), including Bill Johnson's wife, Beni (real name Brenda – see first picture below) participate in "grave soaking" where they visit the graves of dead Christians to be "soaked" in their "anointing". This is precisely how Benny Hinn claims to have received Kathryn Kuhlman's "anointing" and regularly returns to her grave for a "top-up". This has **nothing** to do with Biblical Christianity, but is a practice commonplace within witchcraft.

In spite of Beni Johnson's open participation in the activity, and the fact that there have been "grave soaking" trips arranged by the *Bethel School of Supernatural Ministry* (BSSM) for its students, both Bill Johnson and Senior Associate Leader, Kris Vallotton, have very dishonestly denied *Bethel's* involvement in the practice. Their denials have been somewhat undermined by students at BSSM posting pictures of their exploits on social media (and video on YouTube). Here are just a few examples, starting with a photo of second year BSSM students soaking up the "anointing" from the grave of Welsh revivalist Evan Roberts (1878-1951):

The photo on the right was posted with the caption, "…soaked at the grave site" [of Maria Woodworth-Etter]:

Other students posted the picture below of "soaking" at the same grave:

The following picture was posted by someone from *Bethel* sat on top of the grave of Smith Wigglesworth's wife with the caption, "In Bradford soaking up Smith's anointing..."

Just to prove the visit to Wigglesworth's grave **was** a *Bethel* trip, here is Bill Johnson himself posing for a photo at the same gravestone:

The following photo was posted of BSSM students "soaking" up Aimee McPherson's "anointing":

The photo below is of a BSSM student "soaking" up the "anointing" at the grave of John Alexander Dowie:

A video on YouTube is readily accessible of the heretical mystic John Crowder (of "toking the Holy Ghost" fame) kneeling at the same grave and declaring:

> And we've just come to the grave [of Dowie] today to release to you an impartation of healing revival, of city building, restoration city-taking anointing, master-building apostolic anointing, and so we just rip it right out of the ground, we just suck it right off his dead bones, in Jesus name, and loose it to you, a healing-revival-glory-master-building-apostolic anointing glory.

John Crowder and his ministry is supported by Bill Johnson and *Bethel*, and Crowder has been a regular speaker at *Bethel*. Johnson himself has very tellingly declared:

> There are anointings, mantles, revelations, and mysteries that have lain unclaimed, literally where they were left because the generation that walked in them never passed them on. I believe it's possible for us to recover realms of anointing, realms of insight, realms of God that have been untended for decades simply by choosing to reclaim them and perpetuate them for future generations.

Johnson openly tells the story of the time he knelt at the feet of Oral Roberts[15] and asked him to "impart" on him his "healing anointing" (www.youtube.com/watch?v=rOtI2H59vto). Johnson even has the audacity to "anoint" others using a sword as if he is the Queen of England knighting people! The photo below (taken at *Bethel Church*) shows Johnson personally "anointing" two very close friends of mine who I lost to his pseudo-Christian *Bethel* cult:

My friend with the sword on his shoulder, gazing dreamily into Johnson's eyes, is now an "ordained" *Bethel* pastor; he proudly posted this photo on social media for the whole world to see.

The extra-Biblical teaching that only certain people have a special "anointing" is the very thing that allows false prophets to spread their poison throughout an ignorant church that is hooked on experience rather than truth; they are told to "touch not the Lord's anointed" and not to question them when they are found to be doing things they should not.

INTERNATIONAL HOUSE OF PRAYER

Mike Bickle's *International House of Prayer* (IHOP) was also formed in 1999 and continues to this day to work hand in hand with the *New Apostolic Reformation*, sharing resources, personnel and doctrine and pushing the kind of extra-Biblical experiences listed earlier on church youth all around the world. Central to IHOP is the 24/7 prayer room where continuous and uninterrupted prayer has been going on around the clock 24-hours a day since Bickle opened it. A great idea, right? After all, the Bible tells us the *"pray without ceasing"* (1 Thessalonians 5:16). That all depends on what is being prayed for, because if the prayer being made is not in accordance with the will of God it is utterly pointless and without profit. Bickle set up his 24/7 prayer room based on his conviction that God cannot do anything without the prayers of saints; he firmly believes that God **needs** the prayers of Christians in order to establish His kingdom on earth. Whilst I would not necessarily regard Bickle as part of the Word of Faith movement, this misguided belief of Bickle's **is** nevertheless a central tenet of it, and is based on the (previously mentioned heretical) doctrine that God originally gave Adam dominion and authority over the earth, so a consequence of Adam's fall was that he relinquished his dominion and authority over the earth to Satan. It is therefore taught that Satan has **legal** right to the earth and God can do nothing to get it back, but must rely on the church to do so. Bickle and IHOP therefore pray continually because they believe God **needs** them to do that. This of course is proved to be utter rubbish when compared to what the Word of God says about who the earth belongs to (Deuteronomy 10:14; Psalm 24:1; Psalm 95:4-5; Exodus 9:29; Joshua 3:13; 1 Samuel 2:8; 1 Chronicles 29:11; Psalm 47:9; Psalm 89:11; 1 Corinthians 10:26). God never gave dominion of the earth to Adam, so it was never Adam's to relinquish to Satan; dominion and authority has always been God's. He gave Adam the responsibility of stewardship.

Bickle claims his life has been directed by a series of spiritual experiences triggered by a "prophet" called Augustine; experiences that include prophecies, miracles, signs and wonders, dreams, visions and revelations that by comparison make Jesus' own disciples look spiritually dull. Bickle says the "prophet" Augustine originally approached him in 1982 claiming an audible heavenly voice had instructed him to prophesy over Bickle's congregation in St. Louis. Naturally, being a mature and discerning good shepherd (pastor) of his church flock, Bickle completely ignored all the direction given in Scripture to protect the flock and first test what Augustine was claiming, and readily agreed to let him prophesy directly to his congregation. Big mistake.

In a short time, Augustine led Bickle to other "prophets" such as Bob Jones and Paul Cain, which in turn led to the founding of the Kansas City Fellowship. Through this newly formed fellowship attracting other like-minded "prophets", it quickly grew sufficiently in size and influence to be able to put into practice the heretical *Latter Rain* and Manifest Sons of God doctrine, including the restoration of the office of "apostle" and "prophet". In spite of the Kansas City (false) "prophets" having a long and well-documented track record of false teaching, false prophecies, immoral behaviour and the abusing of people (both inside and outside of their fellowship), Mike Bickle still to this day proudly regards them as the prophetic heritage of IHOP.

A former student and intern at IHOP wrote the following as part of a wider article titled "Why I Believe IHOP is a Cult":

> Every intern was required to listen to the 12 hours of IHOP's recorded history on CD footage. Much of this content was heavily edited before its publication. These tapes told of "prophetic words" and signs that were given to some of Mike's mentors (Bob Jones, Paul Cain, etc) – who were all naming him as the leader of the next "big thing" God was doing. Over and over and over again I've heard it said (both directly by Mike as well as from others) that he (Mike) would be the leader of a movement that "changed the nature and expression of Christianity in the earth". Every time, all recognition points to Mike. His "mission" to transform the church and capture the hearts of America's youth has been his declared goal since the early 1980's. One of the major dangers is that these grandiose sounding claims and "prophetic" words are laden with flattery, narcissism, elitism and are a perfect guise under which anything Mike introduces through IHOP can fall under the heading of being a "new thing" God is doing… When I was on staff, I heard people continually sing Mike's praises around the clock and quote more of what Mike says or thinks or teaches than actual Scripture… He teaches with passion and emotion rather than truth and it's that charisma that draws and hooks many to blindly follow (and defend) his message.

Similar testimonies from former IHOP students are almost limitless, and all combine to form a disturbing picture of cult-like activity and manipulation from an organisation hiding behind a thin veneer of Christianity. Consider the following testimony from a former student called Stephanie:

> I attended IHOP and Forerunner School of Ministry (FSM) and was heavily involved for over three years. I started feeling very weird about some things that were being done and said [at IHOP], so I took it to the Lord, as any Berean should. I began asking very genuine questions about where certain things are in Scripture and for certain things to be explained to me, such as deliverance ministry, false prophecy, manifestations and so on. [As a result] I noticed I had been "red flagged", so to speak, and I had certain people in leadership following me around. I was also moved out of my core group and into one with Sabrina Walsh, a former practicing witch and leader at FSM, to be monitored closer…. As I read more Scripture, I began to realise that much of what they were teaching and practicing is extremely unbiblical and even dangerous. We were constantly fasting and always in the prayer room, [but] after eating more and going to the prayer room less I felt my head start to clear up and I didn't like what I was seeing.
>
> About half way through my third year of school, I was brought into a room with several staff members including [Sabrina] Walsh who accused me of doing many things I hadn't even come close to doing. They said something to the effect of this: "We know that you have father issues that need to be resolved – I do not – and we can see that you are heavily oppressed by demons. However, we are incapable of this level of deliverance on someone. We just don't have the time or resources. So, we are going to send you to a wonderful place in Toronto, Canada. This rehabilitation facility is capable of handling your type of situation. We have sent many students here who have all come back completely delivered. We are going to send you there and you can't come back to IHOP or FSM until we have a written letter from them that you have been delivered [a part of IHOP's resources are spent on sending kids to re-education camps]. In the current state you are in, you're a danger to the other student's growth and spiritual well-being". So I told the leaders that I would go, but I had no intention of actually going. I was very much afraid and immediately called my dad, who told me not to talk to anyone, because he called IHOP a cult. He booked the first flight to Kansas City.
>
> My mom and I also owned a home and we were helping students of FSM by providing rooms for low rent. I had an excellent relationship with each and every person in the house, [but] within about two weeks of being pulled

into the office, ALL of my roommates and friends moved out of the house. When asked directly, they either had no response or told me that the school had told them it was an unsafe environment because me and my mom had a demon.

I was absolutely crushed. ALL I ever wanted was to know God and at the time I felt like it was God who rejected me. I was severely messed up for about two and a half years after that, [but] I thank God for my Calvary Chapel pastor back home who spent every minute being there for me… bringing me back to the Truth of the Word of God.

I grieve for the people who are stuck in the lie of IHOP, and for the many who are recruited daily. When looking back on those things [I did at IHOP] it's as though I was a mindless drone who just repeated everything I heard. It scares me to think so many people are deceived, so many families ripped apart, so many lives destroyed, and all in the name of Jesus… People have no idea how dangerous IHOP is.

Notice the IHOP leadership's ploy of trying to control and manipulate Stephanie by isolating her and claiming that she (and her mother) needed deliverance from a demon; and they knew of a special place which could administer the required level of deliverance. The source of this dangerous and unbiblical teaching on deliverance ministry and spiritual warfare is widespread within charismatic/evangelical circles and is addressed later in this book.

What started out as a small obscure church in the Kansas city area of America, on the fringes of the charismatic movement, has now grown to be a major movement of such size and strength that it threatens to engulf youth ministry in America with its methods and doctrines; it plays a leading role on American college campuses. Few parents who send their children to IHOP-sponsored events actually know what IHOP stands for theologically and what they are indoctrinating their children's hearts and minds with. However, just browsing the books on sale by IHOP provides a strong clue, as many of the same books are required reading for the *Emergent Church*. For example, an entire section is devoted to the works of Roman Catholic Mystics, such as Madame Guyon, Thomas Keating, Henri Nouwen and the (so-called) "Desert Fathers"[16]. **None** of these authors should have a place in a **Christian** bookstore. Allow me to take just one example to briefly explain why: Henri Nouwen.

In his book *Letters to a Young Evangelical, Emergent* leader Tony Campolo describes Henri Nouwen (1932-1996) as "one of the great Christians of our time." Henri Nouwen was a Roman Catholic priest who taught at the American universities of Harvard, Yale and Notre Dame. Nouwen's teachings have been a massive influence on the *Emergent Church* and he is just one of a number of Catholic mystics quoted by Rick Warren in his global best-seller, *The Purpose Driven Life* (page 108). Warren's website also has several positive references to Nouwen. Warren's wife, Kay, recommends one of Nouwen's books, *In the Name of Jesus*, and loved it so much she said, "I highlighted almost every word" (*Ministry Toolbox*, Issue#54, 6/5/2002). Nouwen is also mentioned by *Emergent Church* supremo Brian McLaren as an influence. Bearing in mind Nouwen is quoted and praised by such prominent (so-called) evangelical leaders, one would expect Nouwen to have evangelical views of Christianity, but this is not so. For example, in his book, *Sabbatical Journey*, Nouwen writes:

> Today I personally believe that while Jesus came to open the door to God's house, all human beings can walk through that door, whether they know about Jesus or not. I see it as my call to help every person claim his or her own way to God (page 51).

That all sounds very warm, cuddly and inclusive, but in reality is cold hard heresy that will damn to hell anyone believing it, because salvation is based exclusively on the person of Jesus Christ; both who He is and what He has done. For example, Jesus said, *"I am the way, the truth and the life. No one comes to the Father except through Me"* (John 14:6). Speaking of Jesus, Peter declared, *"...for there is no other name under heaven given among men by which we must be saved"* (Acts 4:12). Also speaking of Jesus, John declared, *"He who believes in the Son has everlasting life; and he who does not believe the Son shall not see life, but the wrath of God abides in him"* (John 3:36).

Instead of Nouwen helping "every person claim his or her own way to God", without pointing them exclusively to Jesus Christ, he merely helped people find their own way to hell.

In his book **Here and Now**, Nouwen states:

> The God who dwells in our inner sanctuary is also the God who dwells in the inner sanctuary of each human being (page 22).

This is the absolute lie at the heart of the *New Age Movement*. Scripture is clear that God (the Holy Spirit) dwells only within those who have been born again.

At the end of his life Nouwen declared all paths lead to God. Not according to Jesus (John 14:6). Nouwen did not regard Jesus as the only way; Jesus was merely regarded as a model for higher consciousness, rather than the unique Son of God, Emmanuel (God with us) who came die for our sins and reconcile us to the Father.

Nouwen openly promoted the works of a Trappist monk and *New Age* mystic called Thomas Merton, as well as the writings of the "Desert Fathers" and Tielhard de Chardin, a Catholic priest who believed Jesus would not return in person, but rather as a *New Age* cosmic Christ. John Lanagan, a former *New Ager* who has researched IHOP's spiritual practices extensively states:

> Much of the literature being sold through the International House of Prayer's online FORERUNNER Bookstore indicates a contemplative influence. Once such book being offered is *Fire Within*, written by [Catholic] Father Thomas Dubay. IHOP founder Bickle states, "I want this book to be the manual for IHOP-KC". That is high praise for this book from Mike Bickle. The full title of the book is *Fire Within: St. Teresa of Avila, St. John of the Cross, and the Gospel – On Prayer.*

In an audio message given by Bickle titled *Contemplative Prayer Part 1*, he states:

> The Protestant wing of the western church, which is a tiny percentage of the Body of Christ… is nearly completely (98%) unaware that the Holy Spirit is restoring contemplative prayer – centre stage – to the church… The Holy Spirit is restoring this precious jewel (contemplative prayer) to the Body of Christ. This is the God ordained means of attaining the fullness of God.

So just what is contemplative prayer? Is it Biblical? Is it a "precious jewel" being restored by the Holy Spirit?

Contemplative prayer (also known as Centering prayer) is a spiritual practice IHOP shares with the *Emergent Church Movement*. *Emergent* leader Tony Jones explains in his book, The *sacred Way*, how contemplative mystical silence is achieved by the same technique of focusing on the breath and using repetitive mantras used by Buddhists, Hindus and (Sufi) Muslims:

> Seated comfortably in a dimly lit room with the head bowed, attend to your breathing, and then begin the prayer in rhythm with your breathing. Breathe in: 'Lord Jesus Christ, Son of God' breathe out: 'have mercy on me a sinner.'

Guarding the mind against all distractions, the prayer focuses during every repetition on the meaning of the words, praying them from the heart and in the heart... in order to keep track of my repetitions, I use a prayer rope (page 17).

Jones elaborates further:

Like the Jesus prayer [described above], centering prayer grew out of the reflections and writings of the Desert Fathers... unlike the Jesus Prayer, a repetitive prayer is not used. The prayer is encouraged to choose a simple, monosyllabic word, "love" or "God" (page 70-71).

Emergent leader Tony Campolo teaches many forms of contemplative spirituality, including "centering prayer" with the use of mantras. For example, in *Letters to a Young Evangelical*, Campolo says:

In my case intimacy with Christ has developed gradually over the years, primarily through what Catholic mystics call "centering prayer". Each morning, as soon as I wake up, I take time – sometimes as much as half an hour – to center myself on Jesus. I say his name over and over again to drive back the 101 things that begin to clutter up my mind the minute I open my eyes. Jesus is my mantra, as some would say (page 26).

Former Archbishop of Canterbury, Rowan Williams, revealed in an interview with the *Daily Telegraph* that he spends up to 40 minutes a day in an intense early morning ritual that involves prostrating himself whilst reciting the "Jesus prayer". He stated in the interview:

Over the years increasing exposure to and engagement with the Buddhist world in particular has made me aware of practices not unlike the 'Jesus Prayer' and introduced me to disciplines that further enforce the stillness and physical focus that the prayer entails.

He went on to explain that those who perform such rituals regularly could reach "advanced states" and become aware of an "unbroken light". You will not find reference to "advanced states" and "unbroken light" in the Word of God, but you certainly will in occult *New Age* literature; such terms are part of the common vocabulary for those within the  *New Age Movement*. In fact, the last recorded words of Helena Blavatsky (see end note 13) before her death were, "Keep the light unbroken."

In her book P*raying the Bible: The Pathway to Spirituality: Seven Steps to a Deeper Connection with God*, Stacy Campbell, a prominent character during the "Toronto Blessing" and now a faculty member at the [Peter] *Wagner Leadership Institute*, and regarded as a "prophetess" within the *Prophetic Movement*, provides her readers with step by step instruction in how to practice mystical contemplative prayer through use of the "Jesus Prayer". As validation for her advice she gives an example of a nineteenth-century Russian peasant who said the "Jesus Prayer" 12,000 times a day in order to obey Paul's instruction in 1 Thessalonians 5 to *"pray without ceasing"*.

Contemplative/centering prayer (including the very popular "Jesus prayer") are **all** forms of meditation that have their origins in occult Eastern philosophies and religions that profess a "way" to godhood that the Bible does not teach. This kind of meditation must **not** be confused with what the Bible says about meditation. The Eastern definition of meditation that contemplative/centering prayer is based on requires the participant to intentionally empty their minds and focus on the inward, whereas the Biblical definition of meditation is to fill your mind with God's Word and focus outward toward Him, avoiding the kind of *"vain repetitions"* that Jesus warns about in Matthew 6:7; exactly the same vain repetition practiced through use of the "Jesus Prayer".

The word used in the Bible for meditation means "to ponder; to think on". It is an active engaging of the mind, not an emptying of it. The shutting down and emptying of the mind through repetition of words and phrases is pagan, not Biblical and is a total abdication of our God-given responsibility that Jesus Himself declared as the first and great commandment: to love Him with all our heart, soul and **mind** (Deuteronomy 6:5-6; Matthew 22:37). Therefore, the kind of meditation endorsed by *Emergent Church Movement* leaders, IHOP leader Mike Bickle and members of the *Prophetic Movement* violates one of God's most basic commandments. We are **never** told to empty our minds, but rather to meditate on:

God's Word (Psalm 119:148)

Law (Joshua 1:8; Psalm 1:2)

Mighty deeds (Psalm 77:12)

Work (Psalm 77:12)

Wonderful works (Psalm 119:27)

Precepts (Psalm 119:15 and 119:78)

Glorious splendour (Psalm 145:5)

Statutes (Psalm 119:23 and 119:48)

Our minds are **not** to be shaped by the world's way of thinking (Romans 12:2), and Eastern practices (on which Roman Catholic mysticism is based) are ways devised by sinful men under the power and influence of demonic spirits.

Set your minds on things above, not on things on the earth (Colossians 3:2).

Genuine mystical experiences are **never** initiated or achieved by man, but are always initiated by God. For example, when we read in the Old Testament about Ezekiel, Daniel and Isaiah having a vision, it was always God who initiated it; it was **never** initiated or achieved by the prophet (Ezekiel 1:1; Daniel 2:19; Isaiah 6:1). A New Testament example would be in Acts 11:5 where we read about God causing Peter to fall into a trance and see a vision; it was not initiated or achieved by Peter in any way. Another New Testament example is the vision given to John by God and recorded in the book of Revelation. John did nothing to initiate the visions, God did it all.

But it is not just the books on sale by IHOP that gives away its ecumenical ties with the Roman Catholic Church. IHOP is also happy to share fellowship and its stage with it, as is demonstrated by the recent participation of the Roman Catholic Church in IHOP's 2015 *Onething* Conference (28th-31st December). The Roman Catholic Church was in fact due to participate in the 2012 *Onething* Conference, but was cancelled. Interestingly, there was very little on the IHOP or Onething websites to advertise the Roman Catholic Church's participation in either the 2012 or 2015 conference, and one can only assume this is because Mike Bickle knows there are still many evangelicals who rightly do not recognise the Roman Catholic Church as a true expression of the Christian faith, and advertising its participation in the conference would adversely affect attendance and therefore valuable revenue; tickets to the 2016 *Onething Conference* cost $49 each. It was however openly and enthusiastically advertised on Roman Catholic sites such as *Majorchange.org*:

> …we would like to acknowledge this unprecedented event's historical and spiritual importance as we, by participating with the International House of Prayer, make a small step toward ecumenical unity… We are grateful to Mike Bickle and his leadership team for making it possible for us to gather ecumenically with fellow Christians.

As a demonstration of unity between Christians and Catholics in April 2016, *New Apostolic Reformation* affiliated false teacher Lou Engle, founder of *Azusa Now: The Call*, exchanged foot kisses with Roman Catholic leader Matteo Calisi live on stage in front of an audience of over 100,000 at the LA Coliseum. Calisi was appointed by Pope Benedict and is founder of *United in Christ*, an organisation committed to ecumenism between Christians and Catholics. He declared to the cheering audience that division between Christians and Catholics is a "diabolical sin" and that Jesus "doesn't care" that Christians and Catholics disagree on Biblical doctrine. God would beg to differ on both counts.

TAKE DOMINION

Both IHOP and the *New Apostolic Reformation*, with their new "prophets" and "apostles" believe in a "Dominion" theology (also known as "kingdom now" theology or "Restorationism") which, although can be traced back to William Branham and Franklin Hall in the 1940s, some of the doctrines actually predate Branham and can be found in the writings of early Pentecostal leader John G. Lake[17] who himself gleaned them from John Alexander Dowie during his time living in Zion.

C. Peter Wagner openly taught that "dominion mandate" was just another way of describing the "great commission" given by Jesus to His disciples, and when Jesus commanded His disciples to *"Go therefore and make disciples of all the nations"* (Matthew 28:19), He was commanding His disciples not to preach the gospel to individual people, but to take dominion of whole nations for God. If that is true, one has to wonder how the second part of Matthew 28:19 could be achieved, which says, *"…baptising them in the name of the Father and of the Son and of the Holy Spirit"*. How would you do that to a nation?

The following vision described by Rick Joyner on his Morningstar ministries prophetic bulletin in 2011 typifies the general prophetic teaching by today's "prophets" and "apostles":

> Not only were whole cities coming to Christ, but also entire nations were coming so that the state itself became like a large church.

"Dominion" theology teaches the "Manifest Sons of God" are going to bring about the kingdom of God here on earth through "signs and wonders" performed by a generation of latter-day "super-Christians", known as "over-comers", who will become perfected and sinless and will be "the man-child" of Revelation 12 before **releasing** (as Bill Haman describes it) Jesus to return to an already conquered earth as king[18]. Not surprisingly, the attitude held by "Dominionists" is typified by C. Peter Wagner, who declared:

> The Church is expected to war… Apostles are designated to lead the Church into war because it takes a government to overthrow a government (*Dominion!: How Kingdom Action Can Change the World Chosen*, Page 7).

"Dominionism" is not just bad theology, it is also blasphemous, because "the man-child" of Revelation 12 is Jesus the Messiah, but then "Dominion theology" teaches that Christ must be incarnated **within** the church before He can return; the church will literally become the fullness of Christ (*"the man-child"* of Revelation 12). Most Christians have been taught that the woman in Revelation 12 is the church, but if that is true, the church is in **serious** trouble because she is pregnant and the church is supposed to be the **virgin** Bride of Christ, i.e. betrothed but not yet married, with the marriage ceremony not taking place until Revelation 19:6-8. In contrast, Israel is described even back in the Old Testament as the **wife** of YAHWEH, i.e. already married. The woman described in Revelation 12 is Israel, not the church. She is:

Clothed with the sun, with the moon under her feet, and on her head a garland of twelve stars (Revelation 12:1).

This is an allusion to Joseph's dream in Genesis 37:9, where the sun represents Jacob, the moon represents Rachel (a symbol of Jewish motherhood) and the 11 stars represent the 11 sons of Jacob who bowed down to Joseph and who, including Joseph, fathered the 12 tribes of Israel. The child the woman gives birth to (that Satan tries to kill) is the Messiah; nowhere in Scripture does it suggest the church gives birth to the Messiah, but Scripture does consistently refer to Israel as being a woman in travail, and of course Israel did bring forth the Messiah. Understanding God's plans for Israel during the End-Times is essential for correctly understanding the book of Revelation and protects the reader from applying to the church passages intended for Israel; something the *Prophetic Movement* is guilty of time and time again.

Some early *Latter Rain* teachers went as far as to deny an actual physical Second Coming of Jesus in favour of the glorification of the church. Francis Frangipane writes of this glorified Bride Church in his book, *In The Presence of God*:

Secure this thought in your mind: when the Spirit of Christ comes into the physical world, He must enter through a physical body (page 154).

It is hard to know where to start with such a statement of error. First of all, the Spirit of Christ is used in Scripture to describe the Holy Spirit, and the Holy Spirit has always been active and present in the world since its creation. If Frangipane is using the term to describe Jesus Christ, he seems oblivious to the fact that He still has a physical body since His crucifixion and resurrection, and continues to have a glorified physical body in heaven at the right hand of the Father; he does not need a glorified church to return in **any** sense.

On page 157 of his same book Frangipane makes even clearer his reference to Revelation 12 when he declares:

Even now, hell trembles and the heavens watch in awe. For I say to you, once again, the 'virgin is with child'. Before Jesus Himself returns, the last virgin Church shall become pregnant with the promise of God. Out of her travail, the Body of Christ shall come forth, raised to the full stature of its Head, the Lord Jesus. Corporately manifested in holiness, power and love, the Bride of Christ shall arise clothed in white garments, bright and clean.

Notice what Frangipane is saying here: out of the larger church's travail, a *"man-child"* church will arise; the **true** Bride of Christ. According to Frangipane, not even all of the church belongs in this special Bride class. It must be understood where this rubbish originates from: William Branham:

> In them days it was God in a man, His Son, Jesus Christ... It was God in Christ, God, in a man, the fullness of the Godhead bodily in a man. God in a man; now, it's God in men. See? The fullness of God in the Godhead bodily in His entire Church, manifesting Himself, fulfilling His Word (*The Mighty God Unveiled Before Us*, page 20).

In a taped message, Paul Cain states:

> You know this army… is also in the New Testament. It's referred to as the manchild, Rev 12:5… the overcomers, Rev 2 and 3, the 144,000 servants, Rev 7:3[19], the Bride or Lamb's wife… the White Horse, Rev 6:2, the first fruits… the precious fruits… the wise virgins… the Manifested Sons of God… and it's really remarkable … that none of these names are expressions applied to the saints of God or at any other time in history… they belong to this generation… God's offering to the believers of this generation a greater privilege than was ever offered to any people of any generation at any time from Adam all the way down to the millennium.

In a teaching tape titled *Visions and Revelations*, Kansas City (false) prophet Bob Jones asserts:

> The Last Days church is being birthed out of the old church, and the old leadership is coming to an end and the new, young leadership is being raised up to reign over an end time church that will bring forth the bride.

Jones asserts the belief that not all the church belongs to the Bride class of believers.

Many within the modern *Prophetic Movement* preach an eschatology where the church is the **militant** bride of Christ, who must rise up to claim the earth **for** Christ. Manifestations of this dangerously unbiblical doctrine are numerous, but as a specific example, consider the following words of Mike Bickle:

> I've cared enough about that word "change" to study political and spiritual changes through history, and I'm telling you they are bloody, they are hurtful; it is not a pretty sight to the flesh. But the Lord says, 'I am changing', and the word "changing" is the scary part (*Kansas City Prophetic History*, Disc 2, track 2).

Bickle's words are wrong in so many ways, not least because the premise of what he claims is that God says He is changing, when God has declared:

For I am the Lord, I do not change (Malachi 3:6).

God's unchanging nature is further confirmed in the New Testament:

Every good gift and every perfect gift is from above, and comes down from the Father of lights, with whom there is no variation or shadow of turning (James 1:17).

Consider the astonishing words of Bill Haman in *Prophets and the Prophetic Movement*:

At that time the Sons of God will be fully manifested on the earth. Widespread spiritual warfare will result with the Sons of God doing battle with Satan and company, the non-Christian nations of this world will also be defeated. Once the earth has been subdued, Jesus will come back to earth and be given the kingdom that has been won for Him by this "manchild company". The Manifested Sons of God doctrine teaches that these sons will be equal to Jesus Christ: immortal, sinless, perfected sons who have partaken in the divine nature. They will have every right to be called gods and will be called gods.

There is so much error contained in the above quote that it is difficult to know where to start! The Sons of God doing battle with Satan? Non-Christian nations subdued by the Sons of God? Jesus **given** the kingdom by the Sons of God? The Sons of God being equal to Jesus Christ, and will be called gods themselves?

Haman also declared:

God is preparing His Church to become an invincible, unstoppable, unconquerable, overcoming Army of the Lord that subdues everything under Christ's feet (*Apostles, Prophets and the Coming Moves of God*, page 251).

In *The Eternal Church* Haman declares:

When the church has put under its feet all the enemies of Christ that he has ordained for them to subdue, then Christ can be released from heaven to return as the Manifested Head of His Physically Resurrected and Translated Church (page 333).

At a conference held at London Docklands in 1990 (attended by people like Paul Cain and Mike Bickle), John Wimber declared:

There is something higher than being a [denomination] and that is to be the

End-Time army and involved in this greater prize of bringing everything on earth and above the earth and below the earth to the feet of Jesus.

Consider also the words of Earl Paulk, who, until his death in 2009, was one of the most prominent NAR leaders and a major promoter of the Manifest Sons of God heresy, but whose ministry eventually collapsed under the weight of so many sex scandals. In his book, *The Wounded Body of Christ*, he claimed the church has:

> …been foreordained of God to become that people who will become so gloried [glorified] that we can bring Christ back to earth. This gloried [glorified] church must make the earth God's footstool before Jesus can come again.

Paulk also said:

> Jesus Christ has now done all He can do, and He waits at the right hand of His Father, until you and I as sons of God, become manifest and make this world His footstool. He is waiting for us to say, 'Jesus, we have made the kingdoms of this world the kingdom of God, and we are ruling and reigning in your world. Even so, come Lord Jesus'.

According to Paulk and Haman, it is the church that conquers this world **for** Christ and "subdues everything under Christ's feet". On page 267 of his same book, Haman states it is the church that "causes the kingdoms of this world to become the kingdoms of our Lord Jesus". These declarations are shown to be utter rubbish when examined in the light of what the Bible actually says, because in Matthew 22:44 Jesus (quoting Psalm 110:1) declares:

> *'The Lord said to my Lord, "Sit at My right hand, till I make Your enemies Your footstool".*

And in 1 Corinthians 15:25, Paul makes clear it is **Jesus** who puts His enemies under His feet:

> *For He [Jesus] must reign till He has put all enemies under His feet.*

Who should we believe, Jesus and the apostle Paul, or the likes of Earl Paulk and Bill Haman? Tragically, too many Christians in this age of apostasy are believing the latter, with the concept of a militant and victorious church rising up in dominion being widespread within affiliated ministries such as the *Jesus Culture* and *Bethel School of Supernatural Ministry* led by Bill Johnson, as well as Hillsong[20] (which is part of the NAR) which increasingly dominates the way in which charismatic/evangelical Christians worship. Why? Because their music has an eschatology; Christians need to understand what they are professing in the worship songs they sing. Through their music, through the so-called Joel's Army (also referred to as "omega Children", "overcoming Bride", "dread warriors" and of course "over-comers") of young, supernaturally empowered, militant believers, the youth of today's charismatic/evangelical churches are being taught they are going to take dominion of the world for Christ; it is them, not Jesus Christ who will establish His kingdom on earth. Todd Bentley has "Joel's Army" tattooed on his chest in the form of Armed Forces dog-tags (as a way of emphasising the militant nature of Joel's Army).

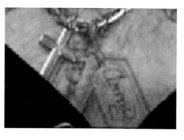

Dr Clifford Hill warned of this Joel's Army in *Prophecy Today* several decades ago:

> …the 'new breed' is an elite group of believers endowed with supernatural power that would enable them to be part of the army of 'dread warriors' that God was said to be raising up in our generation… According to John Wimber this is a type of Joel's Army, who will overcome all opposition to the gospel and eventually subdue the nations… The government of the nations will be upon their shoulders and when all the secular authorities, governments, princes and kings have finally submitted to them, Christ will return and they will present the kingdom to Him (Volume 7, Number 1).

According to Rick Joyner, Joel's Army will be completely without sin. In a conversation with none other than Adam, Joyner was told:

> During the times of the greatest darkness and evil that are about to come, His people will stand as a testimony for all time that He not only redeemed His people from sin, but He also removed sin from them. Through them, He will remove sin from the whole earth….He is returning for a people who are without stain from the world (*The Call*, page 78).

John Wimber stated:

> Those in this [Joel's] army will have the kind of anointing… his kind of power… anyone who wants to harm them must die.

Jack Deere, close friend of both John Wimber and Paul Cain, described what Joel's Army will be like in *It Sounds Like the Mother of All Battles*:

> This army is unique… when this army comes, it's large and mighty. It's so mighty that there has never been anything like it before. Not even when Moses, not even David, not even Paul. What's going to happen now will transcend what Paul did, what David did, what Moses did

The time frame for the ascendance of Joel's Army to power was given in a prophecy to C. Peter Wagner's Apostolic Council of Prophetic Elders. The prophecy declared:

> The church will be in key transition period between 2000-2003. During this period the youth in particular will be transitioning into revival.

Did this prophecy come true? Did we see revival, let alone the ascendance of Joel's Army? Of course not. The only thing we saw in ascendance within the church was further apostasy through the 75,000 young people who attended the conference being erroneously taught that they will take dominion of the earth for Christ through militant and supernatural means. But this is just one of many prophecies about when Joel's Army would come to prominence. For example, John Wimber very famously prophesied at his conference at Docklands in 1990 that it would emerge within two years of the conference and cause a great revival to sweep across Britain and Europe. Paul Cain confirmed Wimber's prophecy during the conference. In front of a large audience (recorded on video and later published in a magazine called *Equipping The Saints*), Cain declared:

> I don't care what anybody says [including God apparently]. You're going to see revival when you go out of here.

Did anyone notice this happen? Thought not.

The term "Joel's Army" is taken from Joel 2, but rather than it being a holy army, it is a reference to Nebuchadnezzar's army that God used to judge Judah and then destroyed. It is pictured as an army of locusts, and is referred to again in Revelation 9 as a demonic army used by God to judge the world (and carry out the fifth trumpet judgment). In neither case could it be interpreted as being an army of "super-Christians" raised up by God to take dominion of the earth, but who cares what the Bible really says when these new "apostles and "prophets" have authority to make Scripture mean what **they** want it to say?

Does the Bible say that **any** part of the End-Times church will subdue the nations and usher in the kingdom of God through "signs and wonders"?

No.

In fact, the exact **opposite** is found in Scripture. For example, in Matthew 24 Jesus warns that such "signs and wonders" at the end of the age would be a **deception**. Not only that, rather than the church getting stronger prior to Christ's return, the Bible warns that a massive *"falling away"* (*apostasy*) from the faith must take place before His Second Coming (2 Thessalonians 2:3). Returning to the words of Jesus in Matthew 24, Jesus warns that prior to His return *"the love of many will grow cold"* (Matthew 24:12). In the Greek language, there are several words with distinct meanings translated by the one English word "love". Three of these Greek words for "love" are found in the New Testament:

Philia, meaning friendship, or brotherly love.

Storge, meaning the kind of love a parent has for their child.

Agape, meaning selfless love, like the love God has for man.

The Greek word for "love" used in Matthew 24:12 is *agape*. The only people who can express the love of God are those who possess the love of God – born again believers in Jesus Christ. Matthew 24:12 is describing what will happen to many **believers** prior to Christ's return. Jesus Himself asked the rhetorical question:

> *When the Son of Man comes, will He really find faith on the earth?* (Luke 18:8).

And speaking of the Last Days Jesus also said:

> *And unless those days were shortened, no flesh would be saved; but for the elect's sake those days will be shortened* (Matthew 24:22).

All this hardly describes **any** part of the church taking dominion over the earth for Christ through victory and "signs and wonders".

If it is the church that is going to establish an End-Times kingdom **for** Christ, surely this would be explicit in the Word of God for **all** believers to see, so we would not have to rely on the extra-Biblical "revelations" and visions of these new "apostles" and "prophets" to tell us. But the truth is nowhere in Scripture are Christians instructed to build or prepare an earthly Kingdom of God for Christ's return. Christ will not be invited to return to a kingdom prepared **for** Him, but will bring His Kingdom **with Him** when He returns, because He said His kingdom was **not** of this world (John 18:36). He does not need our help in establishing His kingdom and I believe this point is perfectly demonstrated by examining what the Bible **does** tell us about the kingdoms of this world, past, present and future. The Bible tells us much about the End-Times, which is ignored by much of the church today, but let us start at the beginning.

THE BEGINNING

Genesis tells us that God created man on the **last** day of His Creation week (day six) after He had created everything else in preparation for man. At the beginning of history God prepared a place for man and then put him in it; God did not require the assistance of man to do it! So too in preparation for the end of history God is preparing a place for man (whether that be heaven or hell) ready for God to put man in, and He does not require the assistance of man to do it.

THE END

Chapter 2 of the book of Daniel tells us how Daniel interpreted King Nebuchadnezzar's dream of the statue, which was a prophetic picture of the global kingdoms that were to come throughout history, ending with the final kingdom before Christ's return[21]. In Nebuchadnezzar's dream that God gave Daniel the interpretation for, we have a **God-given** road-map of the future for humanity, leading right up to His return. Therefore, if the "Dominionist" view is correct, and they will take dominion over the world in preparation for inviting Jesus to return, then surely this future "Christian" kingdom would have been shown to Daniel.

THE INTERPRETATION

As we have the benefit of looking back at history we can see just how staggeringly accurate Daniel's prophesy was. Daniel's God-given interpretation of Nebuchadnezzar's dream depicted Babylon as the great head of gold, Medo-Persia as the chest and arms of silver, Greece as the thighs of bronze and Rome as the legs of iron; legs because the Roman Empire split in two between East and West (with the Eastern Roman Empire outlasting the Western Roman Empire by almost a thousand years).

Daniel's interpretation of Nebuchadnezzar's dream has thus far been fulfilled throughout history with 100% accuracy; the exact pass-mark for qualifying as a true prophet of the most high God, YAHWEH. The final kingdom Daniel saw was represented by the ten toes of the statue. These were made of a mixture of iron and clay, giving clear indication that the final empire in human history will be an extension of the Great Roman Empire, but mixed with something else represented by clay. As iron and clay does not mix (or adhere) together the final kingdom in human history will be partly strong and partly weak, thus compromising its integrity and strength.

All this was confirmed to Daniel in a vision God gave to him directly, which is recorded in Daniel 7. Daniel's vision began with the sea, which according to Isaiah 17:12-13; Matthew 13:47-51, Revelation 13:1 and 17:1, 15, represents the Gentile world. Four beasts arose from the sea. Verse four describes the first beast, which was lion-like and represented the Babylonian Empire. The lion is majestic and more powerful than all other creatures.

The second beast Daniel saw arising from the sea was bear-like and represented the Medo-Persian Empire. The bear Daniel saw was lop-sided being raised up on one side, which represented the fact that whilst the Medes and the Persians were joined together in power, the Persians were by far the dominant power of the two.

The bear had three ribs in its mouth, having devoured the flesh. This represented the three kingdoms the Medo-Persian Empire conquered in the process of attaining their empire: Lydia, Babylon and Egypt. The bear is less majestic than the lion; it is slower and more weighty, representing the fact that the Medo-Persian Empire conquered by sheer size and force of numbers.

The third beast revealed to Daniel was leopard-like, representing the Greek Empire. The leopard is less majestic than the lion and less impressive than the bear, but is far more swift. This represented the speed with which Alexander the Great conquered the Medo-Persian Empire and extended the Greek Empire. The four wings on the leopard-like creature represented how, after Alexander's death, the empire was split between his four generals: Ptolemy, Seleucus, Cassander and Lysimachus.

The fourth and final beast, representing the final empire in human history, is described in Daniel 7:7-8. Unlike the other beasts, the fourth beast is not described in terms of an animal. It is described as being *"dreadful and terrible, exceedingly strong"* and *"had huge iron teeth."* It is far more ferocious than the previous three beasts and breaks into pieces all that preceded it. The fourth beast in Daniel's vision had ten horns, but an eleventh horn arises (*"a little one"*), which uproots three of the ten other horns. In this horn, *"were eyes like the eyes of a man, and a mouth speaking pompous words."* These ten horns in Daniel's vision parallel the ten toes of iron and clay in Nebuchadnezzar's dream, and therefore provide more information to help us understand how the final empire in human history will work. The ten horns represent ten regions of government (or "kingdoms" as confirmed by Revelation 17:12) that the world will be divided into under a future one-world empire (government), with the *"little horn"* arising and initially taking over three of these regions (or "kingdoms"). Once the three horns have been overcome, the remaining seven horns will capitulate to the *"little horn's"* power, thus making the *"little horn"* ruler of the world and ruler of the last empire in history.

Scripture is clear that the *"little horn"* is the Antichrist and his empire will be defeated by the return of Jesus Christ as conquering King. So where is the "Dominionist" kingdom of Christian "overcomers" that **usher** in the return of Christ? Did Daniel predict the previous kingdoms absolutely right with breath-taking accuracy, only to completely miss the mark in his interpretation of the final kingdom? I do not think so. Daniel 2:44 tells us that God's kingdom will be established and will destroy all the previous kingdoms, so if anyone thinks the kingdom made of iron and clay is the Christian "Dominionist" kingdom, they need to explain why God has said He will destroy it along with the other kingdoms.

There are those who believe the *"stone cut out of the mountain without hands"* referred to in Daniel 2:45 is the Christian "Dominionist" kingdom prophesied by these modern-day false "prophets", but this is a very dangerous and flawed theology, because the *"stone cut out of the mountain without hands"* is a clear reference to Jesus Christ. Surely the best clue to it not being the man-made "Dominionist" kingdom is the very fact that the stone is *"cut out of the mountain **without hands**"* (emphasis added). Proponents of this view are therefore putting the church in place of Jesus Christ (again). But then why should this surprise us when people like Bill Haman claim the Manifest Sons of God "will be equal to Jesus Christ", who "have every right to be called gods and will be called gods".

Let us be clear, it is not "signs and wonders" that lead people to repentance, but the realisation that Jesus Christ is God. The evidence of this fact is found in Scripture, which records that not all who witnessed Jesus perform miracles repented. For example, we read in Matthew chapter 11 (from verse 20) how Jesus rebuked the cities in which He had performed *"most of His mighty works"*, because they did not repent; they had witnessed Jesus perform His most impressive "signs and wonders", but still refused to acknowledge Him as God. In 1 Corinthians 1, Paul actually criticises the Jews for demanding miraculous signs (and the Greeks for seeking worldly wisdom), and then goes on to say that he did not give in to the demands of the Jews (or the Greeks), but instead he preached the simple but powerful message of "Christ crucified".

These false doctrines that try to diminish Jesus' power and authority by elevating the church's power and authority cannot be dismissed as minor differences of theological opinion. They teach an entirely different Jesus to the one found in Scripture. How do you think Jesus views that? How would the apostle Paul respond to such teaching?

For if he who comes preaches another Jesus whom we have not preached, or if you receive a different spirit which you have not received, or a different gospel which you have not accepted—you may well put up with it! (2 Corinthians 11:4).

The apostle John declared:

He [Jesus] must increase, but I must decrease (John 3:30).

Kevin Reeves, former elder of a *Latter Rain* church warns:

These are critical days for the Body of Christ. We are in the epoch [period of time] of church history spoken of by the apostle Paul as *"perilous times"* (2 Timothy 3:1). What makes the danger all the more imminent is that not much of the church believes it. Many of us have owned the glorious but erroneous vision of an end-times remnant walking in unconquerable power, transforming entire societies. The result has been nothing short of catastrophic. How soon we forget. Every cult in the world has sprouted from the fertile soil of deception, always initiated by a drastic move away from the primacy of the Word of God into the nebulous [obscure and vague], self-defining atmosphere of experience.

LOGOS OR RHEMA?

The new "apostles" and "prophets" of the *Prophetic Movement* that hold so much influence over today's charismatic/evangelical church claim their spiritual authority by creating a false distinction between the *logos* of God and the *rhema* of God that does not exist in the Bible. The premise of their authority to speak new "revelation" – even when it contradicts the Bible – is that the *logos* is the written Word of God and the *rhema* (Greek for "utterance" or "to speak") is the spoken word of God, and they have the "anointing" from God to speak the *rhema* of God, which supersedes the *logos*; God provides new revelation through His *rhema* that is not contained in His *logos*. In *Engaging the Enemy*, C. Peter Wagner states:

> Pentecostal theologians have made the helpful suggestion of distinguishing the logos word of God from the rhema word of God... The rhema is regarded as a more immediate word from God which we do not find in the 66 books of the Bible (page 15-16).

This lie is so clever yet so evil that it can only come from the father of all lies (John 8:44), because it enables these lying false "apostles" and "prophets" to declare a belief in the orthodox Christian position of all Scripture being inspired by God, but by implication of their extra-Biblical direct words from God, deny the sufficiency of Scripture; in their warped theology, the *rhema* supersedes the *logos*.

Francis Frangipane does his best to find a Biblical justification for this dangerous nonsense by claiming the Bible describes the "sword of the Spirit" as being double-edged because one edge is Scripture and the other is "the living Word of God [rhema]: what the Spirit is saying now to the church". Frangipane was an "apostle" himself of the Church of the Living Word, which was infamous for its new revelations through false prophets, occult manifestations and immorality. Frangipane never renounced his involvement so it is clear that his attempt at apologetics in support of members of the *Prophetic Movement* is an attempt to justify his own actions and beliefs.

As previously mentioned, the Bible does **not** make this distinction and these two terms are used interchangeably in the New Testament. However, whilst professing a belief in the inspiration and inerrancy of the written Word (*logos*) of God, creating this false distinction enables these new "apostles" and "prophets" to encourage their followers to listen to and accept their supposed *rhema* as the **true** Word of God, rather than actually study the Bible, even when it makes God look like He can arbitrarily change His mind and speak with a forked tongue. This view is well illustrated by a section in Wendy Alec's book, *Journal of the Unknown Prophet,* which she claims was spoken by Jesus Himself:

> For the Word alone is yesterday's manna and even they [prophetic teachers] have seen deep in their hearts that it is no longer enough to feed my people (page 84).

This is terribly dangerous stuff, because Wendy Alec is claiming that Jesus is telling Christians the Word of God is no longer sufficient for them! And if that was not bad enough, the specific description of the Word of God being "yesterday's manna" exposes the depth of disdain Alec has for the Word of God. Manna was of course the food God supernaturally provided for the Israelites in the wilderness to sustain them on a daily basis; they were told to collect just enough for each day, because Exodus 16:20 tells us that manna left until the following morning (i.e. "yesterday's manna") became worm infested and stank. Alec is describing the written Word of God as worm infested and stinking, **and** claiming Jesus is telling her so! Welcome to the apostasy where blatant blasphemy tickles the ears of those who profess to love the Lord Jesus.

But Alec's attitude of the written Word of God being obsolete and insufficient is by no means an isolated one within the *Prophetic Movement*; it is shared by many of the new "prophets" and "apostles". For example, in the introduction to his 1998 bestselling book, *The God Chasers*, Tommy Tenney states:

> God chasers don't just want to study from the moldy [sic] pages of what God has done.

The *logos* is just mouldy pages telling us what God has done, but the *rhema* is telling us what God is doing!

"Prophet" Scott Hicks, whose words are regularly found in the "Elijah List", posted the following in the discussion section of the "signofjonah" blog:

> The Bible we have "NOW" is translated text – while it is generally holy and inspiring, and full of old "love letters" there are still errors due to translational issues during translation – However, how can God's Rhema word be with error if it comes straight from the throne? – It can't! God is without error… did it occur to you that if translated Scripture is with error – then perhaps God does use men to speak through. So that all can have a clear message?...

Hicks regards the Bibles (*logos*) we have today "generally holy and inspiring", but unreliable; certainly far less reliable than God's *rhema* which, through new "prophets" like him, "comes straight from the throne". Contrast Hick's view of the written Word of God with Jesus, who declared:

> *Heaven and earth will pass away, but My words will by no means pass away* (Matthew 24:35; Luke 21:33; Mark 13:31).

So, we have the written Word of God described as "yesterday's manna", "moldy pages" and containing "errors", in stark contrast to how God regards it. For example, David declares:

> *For you have magnified Your Word above all Your name* (Psalm 138:2).

The false and unbiblical distinction between the *logos* and *rhema* of God is responsible for much of the charismatic/evangelical church today continuing to fall away from the fundamentals of the faith and into apostasy, mainly through ignorance of what the Bible actually teaches. I was interested to note the following comment from Bono (a man who claims to be a Christian and is revered by the Emergent Church) in *Rolling Stone Magazine* (3/11/2005) that typifies this problem:

> I don't read it [the Bible] as a historical book. I don't read it as, "Well, that's good advice." I let it speak to me in other ways. They call it the rhema. It's a hard word to translate from Greek, but it sort of means it changes in the moment you're in. It seems to do that for me.

The inerrancy and infallibility of the **true** Word of God is replaced by a faith in the inerrancy and infallibility of the words of men. This is no better than a Catholic following the words of the Pope. The result is the same, in that the true authority of Scripture is undermined.

BEYOND QUESTION

These new "apostles" and "prophets" (and their followers) have become very proficient at defending themselves against those who would question them by testing their "words" and "prophecies" against the Word of God. The following is a selection of defence strategies I have had personal experience of. Followers of these false teachers can be quite aggressive and unpleasant, as I have found time and time again. For example, in response to a series of articles I had published on Bill Johnson's doctrine, a number of his supporters were very aggressive and vitriolic; amongst other things, I was accused of being "autistic", and even "a worker of Satan" for questioning Bill Johnson's teaching. Very tellingly, not one of them even attempted to defend Bill Johnson's doctrine from the Word of God, but instead just attacked me on a personal level. They could not attack the message, so instead attacked the messenger.

TOUCH NOT THE LORD'S ANOINTED

The premise of this defence is of course that the "apostles" and "prophets" of the *Prophetic Movement* are specially anointed by God and therefore should be above Question. Proponents of this particular defence appeal to Psalm 105:15 and 1 Chronicles 16:22:

> Do not touch the Lord's anointed ones (Psalm 105:15).

> Do not touch My anointed ones (1 Chronicles 16:122).

An extract from Rick Joyner's 1996 book, *The Final Quest*, provides a good example of how this claim is used against anyone who questions the new "apostles" and "prophets". Joyner tells the story of the time he met with a man on one of his many visits to the third heaven:

> I began to touch the Lord's anointed, and to do His prophets harm….I did not do it myself, but I incited men under me to investigate others and do my dirty work…. We sowed fear and division throughout the church, all in the name of protecting the truth….And we always comforted ourselves by actually thinking that we were doing God a favor when we attacked His own children…They really do not understand that they are doing the work of the Accuser (page 107-109).

The first thing to point out about this defence of these new "apostles" and "prophets" is that **every** reference used comes from the Old Testament when certain people did receive an anointing from God for a specific purpose such as king, prophet, priest or even builder. The New Testament teaches that **all** Christians are anointed and permanently indwelt by the Holy Spirit, and there is no special anointing taught in the way these new "apostles" and "prophets" claim. This is a vital point when understanding what the Bible says in its proper context, because *'the Lord's anointed'*, is a reference to the kings of national Israel (1 Samuel 12:3,5; 24:6,10; 26:9,11, 16,23; 2 Samuel 1:14,16; 19:21; Psalm 20:6; Lamentations 4:20). Prophets are mentioned in Psalm 105:8-15 and 1 Chronicles 16:15-22, but these are references to the Old Testament patriarchs.

Having established the correct context, the second thing to point out is that the word "touch" actually refers to physical harm; no physical harm is to be inflicted on the Lord's anointed. It does **not** mean that God's anointed were exempt from criticism (public or private).

How do we know this?

Because that is exactly what David did with Saul. It was David who said he would not harm God's anointed, who was King Saul at the time, but He did speak out publicly against him. David was not the only person to speak out against Saul either, because Samuel (a **true** prophet of God) also spoke out against him (1 Samuel 15).

To summarise, in the context of defending the false teaching and practices of these new "apostles" and "prophets", the mantra of "touch not the Lord's anointed" is complete and utter rubbish, because the New Testament teaches they have **no** special anointing over and above **every** Christian, and the context of the Old Testament passages used is doing no physical harm to God's anointed, not speaking out against them. Even in the Old Testament, God's truly anointed were not beyond question.

YOU PHARISEE!

Those who test the words of these new "apostles" and "prophets" against the word of God are often accused of being a Pharisee. What they mean by that is the person exposing their error is "legalistic" and too "orthodox" and as a result, whilst they understand the Word, they have strangled and suffocated the work of the Holy Spirit, thereby rendering it lifeless. A perfect example of this can be found in Rick Joyner's 2003 book, *Overcoming Evil in the Last Days*:

> The Lord had little trouble with demons while He walked on the earth. They quickly recognised His authority and begged for mercy. It was the conservative, zealous, religious community [the Pharisees] that immediately became His greatest enemy. Those who were the most zealous for the Word of God crucified the Word Himself when He became flesh to walk among them. The same is still true (page 133).

Joyner's attack on conservative evangelical Christianity by comparing them to the Pharisees is very clear, and is made even more incendiary when it is combined with rhetoric about the Pharisees being the ones who killed Christ. Joyner is by no means alone in applying this tactic. For example, Mike Bickle does exactly the same thing in an audio message titled *Contending for the Power of God* (CD1):

> It was the ones pressing into biblical orthodoxy that murdered Christ.

Was the Pharisees' problem that they were too Biblically orthodox?

Was their sin really to hold the Scriptures in too high esteem?

Was it the Pharisees who killed Jesus?

Rather than take Rick Joyner's and Mike Bickle's word for it (as they would love everyone to do), perhaps we should test their claims against what Scripture actually tells us about the Pharisees. For example, a careful look at Matthew 15:1-9 and John 5:45-47 clearly tells us that the Pharisees problem was **not** that they held the Scriptures in too high esteem, thereby rendering them lifeless; quite the opposite is true. Their problem was that they knew the Scriptures, but were willing to cancel them out in favour of their own doctrine. So who exactly is being a Pharisee then?! That sounds more like what the "apostles" and "prophets" of the *Prophetic Movement* do!

And by the way, whilst they claim it was the Pharisees who murdered Jesus, did Jesus say it was the Pharisees who murdered Him? The answer is found in John 10:17-18:

> *Therefore My Father loves Me, because **I lay down My life** that I may take it again. **No one takes it from Me, but I lay it down of Myself**. I have power to lay it down, and I have power to take it again. **This command I have received from My Father** (emphasis added).*

Jesus is crystal clear that no one took His life, but He gave it willingly in accordance with His Father's command. Christ's life could not be taken; it had to be given, and God the Father gave it:

> *For God so loved the world that **He gave** His only begotten Son, that whoever believes in Him should not perish but have everlasting life* (John 3:16).

NOT QUALIFIED TO QUESTION

Many of these new "apostles" and "prophets" go as far as to claim that they can only be corrected or questioned by someone else who holds the same office, which basically prevents them from feeling obliged to listen to or be corrected by anyone outside their movement. Furthermore, as the only people claiming to be new "prophets" and "apostles" already share the same premise regarding these offices, they are hardly likely to challenge a fellow "apostle" or "prophet" in any way, because doing so would undermine their own position. This can be seen in practice by reading the bizarre things published within the "Elijah List" newsletter, which are never challenged or corrected.

DEMONS OUT!

Another common strategy employed to deflect the teachings of these new "apostles" and "prophets" from being tested Biblically is to imply a demonic influence on those who would try, and C. Peter Wagner's theology and methodology on Spiritual Warfare very conveniently provides the foundations for this; just consider how Stephanie was treated at IHOP for questioning what she was being subjected to.

Many who openly question are accused of doing so out of having a "religious spirit". This is perfectly illustrated within the pages of *Overcoming the Religious Spirit*, by Rick Joyner:

> A religious spirit will usually give a counterfeit gift of discernment of spirits. This counterfeit gift thrives on seeing what is wrong with others rather than seeing what God is doing so that we can help them along. This is how a religious spirit does some of its greatest damage to the church. Its ministry will almost always leave more damage and division than healing and reconciliation. It is wisdom rooted in the Tree of the knowledge of Good and Evil and though the truth may be accurate, it is ministered in a spirit that kills.

Not surprisingly, Joyner provides absolutely no Biblical evidence to support his claim that a "religious spirit" even exists, let alone that it gives a counterfeit gift of discernment of spirits, but then as far as these new "apostles" and "prophets" are concerned anyone asking for Biblical evidence demonstrates they have a "religious spirit"! Joyner even says that when the discernment of error is accurate, it should still be dismissed because it is ministered "in a spirit that kills".

Worse still, is the accusation of having a "Jezebel spirit", which tends to be applied to those who will not yield to the authority of these new "prophets" and "apostles" and again, I will allow Rick Joyner to provide the definition:

> Basically, the spirit of Jezebel is a combination of a religious spirit and the spirit of witchcraft that is the spirit of manipulation and control… This spirit attacks the prophetic ministry because that has always been the primary way in which the Lord gives timely, strategic direction to His people (*A Prophetic Vision for the 21st Century*, page 148).

Queen Jezebel practised witchcraft, sought to control and manipulate the king (Ahab) for her own ends and attacked the true prophets of God, so what Joyner is saying about people who question these new "apostles" and "prophets" is very clear, very offensive and **very** unbiblical.

GOD WILL JUDGE YOU!

If being accused of having a "religious spirit" or even a "Jezebel spirit" is not intimidating enough, these new "apostles" and "prophets" will go even further in their attempt to quash dissent by claiming God will judge those who oppose them; God is on their side, so we had better be also, or else! For example, the following prophecy by Apostolic Pastor and member of the ICA, Dutch Sheets about what would happen in 2006 can be found on the "Elijah List" website:

> Opposition to the apostolic and prophetic [specifically **their** definition of both] will also be the greatest this year [2006]… he is going to expose wineskins (new or old), and religious spirits, taking off the masks of those who oppose His move. Those who refuse to move in current truth [meaning their teaching and words of prophecy] will begin to openly criticise leaders in the Body of Christ that are moving in the flow of the apostolic and the prophetic. Some have been doing so in a very subtle way but this year it will become obvious. When they do, **God is going to begin to judge them** (emphasis added).

If these new "apostles" and "prophets" were actually continuing the mantle ("anointing") of the Old Testament prophets or New Testament apostles, then I have no doubt God would indeed judge those who criticise and oppose them, because they **did** speak with God's authority, but the reality is that these new "apostles" and "prophets" do not, and God will ultimately judge **them** for claiming they do.

By attacking those Christians who test the words of these new "apostles" and "prophets" by holding them up to the light of the Word of God (as the Bible encourages believers to do), they succeed in creating an environment in which too many Christians passively accept the authority of their words over the authority of the Word of God; through a combination of manipulation, coercion, intimidation and even flattery, they succeed in convincing too many Christians to lay down the very weapon that God has given us to defend ourselves against false teaching and the strategies of Satan: *"the Sword of the Spirit, which is the Word of God"* (Ephesians 6:17).

UNITY VERSUS DIVISION

Another common strategy used by false teachers is to erroneously claim that Christians should forget about their differences in doctrine, because doctrine divides;

they should just love one another instead, as though those two are consistent goals, when in reality the only way we can love right is to live right, and the only way to live right is to believe right. Is doctrine divisive? Is it an obstacle to unity? Consider the words of Rick Joyner in *There Were Two Trees in the Garden*, Rick Joyner writes:

> We must first understand that our unity is not based on doctrines. Such unity is superficial at best. Our unity can only be found in Jesus. To focus our attention on Him and learn to love and cover one another is far more important than agreeing on all doctrines. Having like doctrines is not basis for unity… it is a basis for division (page 31).

Amos 3:3 says, *"Can two walk together, unless they are agreed?"*, so which Jesus does Joyner say our unity can only be found in? The Mormon Jesus? The *New Age* Jesus? One can only answer that question with right **doctrine**.

The only way doctrine divides is by dividing truth from error and according to Paul in Romans 16:17, the division is caused by those who teach *"contrary to the doctrine which you learned"*, **not** by those who point out their heresy. Joyner's unbiblical claim illustrates how false teachers seek unity at the expense of truth by minimising the importance of doctrine, whereas true unity can only be achieved through the recognition and agreement of Biblical truth; not necessarily agreement on every Biblical doctrine, but certainly the fundamental truths as an absolute minimum requirement. And herein lies the problem with much of today's charismatic/ evangelical church, because under the influence of the *Prophetic Movement* (whether implicitly or explicitly) the problem goes much deeper than doctrines that could be considered non-fundamental to the faith; it is fundamental doctrines that are in error in many people's ministries without many Christians even realising it; is not William Branham's denial of the doctrine of the Trinity fundamental? Not according to the multitude of false teachers today who acknowledge him as a true man of God and a gifted prophet. In contrast, Paul would have noted him and avoided him (Romans 16:17)!

HEAD KNOWLEDGE, NOT HEART KNOWLEDGE

This is a common accusation laid at the feet of Christians who are not willing to disengage their brain in order to blindly accept a "prophecy" or experience or "word from God" without first testing it against God's Word; they are accused of allowing their "head knowledge" of God to stifle their "heart knowledge" of God. I have heard time and time again from charismatics/evangelicals who repeat the following like it has been plucked right out of the pages of Proverbs:

God offends the mind to reveal the heart.

This is **not** Biblical and the Bible does **not** treat the intellect as a problem. The heart and mind are frequently used interchangeably in Scripture. Jesus Himself said the greatest commandment was:

> *You shall love the LORD your God with all your heart, with all your soul, with all your strength, and with all your **mind*** (Luke 10:27).

The claim that "God offends the mind to reveal the heart" is a way for false "apostles" and "prophets" to say, "You think too much to accept the extra-Biblical garbage I'm trying to feed you." It is a way of accusing those Christians who **do** engage their brain and judge all things by His Word of being less "spiritual" than those who just blindly accept what they are fed. Again, this is utterly unbiblical, as Paul tells us in 1 Corinthians 2:15 that:

> *He who is spiritual judges all things.*

God says those who judge all things are the spiritual ones! How do we judge all things? By the Word of God. Christians who do not judge all things against the Word of God have no effective weapon with which to overcome Satan. They are like a soldier with a broken sword (Ephesians 6:17; Hebrews 4:12) and vulnerable to Satan's attack; they will not even have the belt of Truth to hang their broken sword on (Ephesians 6:14).

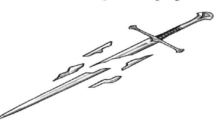

This is how apostasy has infiltrated the church and continues to do so at an alarming rate. Satan has been extremely successful in blunting the swords of many Christians in the charismatic/evangelical church, with its many false teachers contaminating the Christian faith. The effective wielding of *"the sword of the Spirit"* (the Word of God) would easily overcome all these deceptions, which is precisely why Satan has tried so hard to undermine the trust Christians place in it.

In contrast to the general attitude of indifference displayed toward knowledge by too many professing Christians, it would be difficult to overstate the importance the Bible puts on it (as well as wisdom, which is knowing how to apply knowledge); the Bible speaks a lot about knowledge and how having knowledge can save, but having a lack of knowledge can leave people open to destruction. For example:

> *For the LORD is the God of **knowledge*** (1 Samuel 2:3).

> *And Hezekiah gave encouragement to all the Levites who taught the good **knowledge** of the LORD* (2 Chronicles 30:22).

*Teach me good judgment and **knowledge**, for I believe Your commandments* (Psalm 119:66).

*²² "How long, you simple ones, will you love simplicity? For scorners delight in their scorning, and fools hate **knowledge**. ²³ Turn at my rebuke; surely I will pour out my spirit on you; I will make my words known to you* (Proverbs 1:22-23).

*Then you will understand the fear of the LORD, and find the **knowledge** of God* (Proverbs 2:5).

*For the LORD gives wisdom; from His mouth come **knowledge** and understanding* (Proverbs 2:6).

*When wisdom enters your heart, and **knowledge** is pleasant to your soul* (Proverbs 2:10).

*…that you may preserve discretion, and your lips may keep **knowledge*** (Proverbs 5:2).

*They are all plain to him who understands, and right to those who find **knowledge**. Receive my instruction, and not silver, and **knowledge** rather than choice gold* (Proverbs 8:9-10).

*Wise people store up **knowledge**, but the mouth of the foolish is near destruction* (Proverbs 10:14)

*…through **knowledge** the righteous will be delivered* (Proverbs 11:9).

*Whoever loves instruction loves **knowledge**…* (Proverbs 12:1).

*A prudent man conceals **knowledge**, but the heart of fools proclaims foolishness* (Proverbs 12:23).

*Every prudent man acts with **knowledge**…* (Proverbs 13:16).

*The simple inherit folly, but the prudent are crowned with **knowledge*** (Proverbs 14:18).

*The tongue of the wise uses **knowledge** rightly, but the mouth of fools pours forth foolishness* (Proverbs 15:2).

*The lips of the wise disperse **knowledge**, but the heart of the fool does not do so* (Proverbs 15:7).

*The heart of him who has understanding seeks **knowledge**, but the mouth of fools feeds on foolishness* (Proverbs 15:14).

The heart of the prudent acquires knowledge, and the ear of the wise seeks **knowledge** (Proverbs 18:15).

…it is not good for a soul to be without **knowledge** (Proverbs 19:2).

There is gold and a multitude of rubies, but the lips of **knowledge** *are a precious jewel* (Proverbs 20:15).

Apply your heart to instruction, and your ears to words of **knowledge** (Proverbs 23:12).

By **knowledge** *the rooms are filled with all precious and pleasant riches* (Proverbs 24:4).

So shall the **knowledge** *of wisdom be to your soul; if you have found it, there is a prospect, and your hope will not be cut off* (Proverbs 24:14).

…by a man of understanding and **knowledge** *right will be prolonged* (Proverbs 28:2).

The righteous considers the cause of the poor, but the wicked does not understand such **knowledge** (proverbs 29:7).

…the excellence of **knowledge** *is that wisdom gives life to those who have it* (Ecclesiastes 7:12).

Because the preacher was wise, he still taught the people **knowledge** (Ecclesiastes 12:9).

And I will give you shepherds according to My heart, who will feed you with **knowledge** *and understanding* (Jeremiah 3:15).

They are wise to do evil, but to do good they have no **knowledge** (Jeremiah 4:22).

Everyone is dull-hearted, without **knowledge** (Jeremiah 10:14).

Therefore my people have gone into captivity, because they have no **knowledge** (Isaiah 5:13).

Wisdom and **knowledge** *will be the stability of your times, and the strength of salvation* (Isaiah 33:6).

He gives wisdom to the wise and **knowledge** *to those who have understanding* (Daniel 2:21).

My people are destroyed for lack of **knowledge** (Hosea 4:6).

*For I desire mercy and not sacrifice, and the **knowledge** of God more than burnt offerings* (Hosea 6:6).

*For the earth will be filled with the **knowledge** of the glory of the LORD* (Habakkuk 2:14).

*For the lips of a priest should keep **knowledge**, and the people should seek the law from his mouth* (Malachi 2:7).

The New Testament also places an importance on knowledge that too many Christians simply ignore:

*To give **knowledge** of salvation to His people by the remission of their sins* (Luke 1:77).

*Woe to you lawyers! For you have taken away the key of **knowledge*** (Luke 11:52).

*And even as they did not like to retain God in their **knowledge**…* (Romans 1:28).

*Now I myself am confident concerning you, my brethren, that you also are full of goodness, filled with all **knowledge**, able also to admonish one another* (Romans 15:14).

*…that you were enriched in everything by Him in all utterance and all **knowledge*** (1 Corinthians 1:5).

*Now thanks be to God who always leads us in triumph in Christ, and through us diffuses the fragrance of His **knowledge** in every place* (2 Corinthians 2:14).

*For it is the God who commanded light to shine out of darkness, who has shone in our hearts to give the light of the **knowledge** of the glory of God in the face of Jesus Christ* (2 Corinthians 4:6).

*…by purity, by **knowledge**, by longsuffering, by kindness, by the Holy Spirit, by sincere love* (2 Corinthians 6:6).

*But as you abound in everything – in faith, in speech, in **knowledge**, in all diligence, and in your love for us* (2 Corinthians 8:7).

*…that the God of our Lord Jesus Christ, the Father of glory, may give to you the spirit of wisdom and revelation in the **knowledge** of Him* (Ephesians 1:17).

*And this I pray, that your love may abound still more and more in **knowledge** and all discernment* (Philippians 1:9).

*…ask that you may be filled with the **knowledge** of His will in all wisdom and spiritual understanding… being fruitful in every good work and increasing in the **knowledge** of God* (Colossians 1:9-10).

*…and have put on the new man who is renewed in **knowledge** according to the image of Him who created him* (Colossians 3:10).

*² Grace and peace be multiplied to you in the **knowledge** of God and of Jesus our Lord, ³ as His divine power has given to us all things that pertain to life and godliness, through the **knowledge** of Him who called us by glory and virtue, ⁴ by which have been given to us exceedingly great and precious promises, that through these you may be partakers of the divine nature, having escaped the corruption that is in the world through lust. ⁵ But also for this very reason, giving all diligence, add to your faith virtue, to virtue **knowledge**, ⁶ to **knowledge** self-control, to self-control perseverance, to perseverance godliness, ⁷ to godliness brotherly kindness, and to brotherly kindness love. ⁸ For if these things are yours and abound, you will be neither barren nor unfruitful in the **knowledge** of our Lord Jesus Christ* (2 Peter 1:2-8).

*For if, after they have escaped the pollutions of the world through the **knowledge** of the Lord and Saviour Jesus Christ…* (2 Peter 2:20).

*…but grow in the grace and **knowledge** of our Lord and Saviour Jesus Christ* (2 Peter 3:18).

*..who desires all men to be saved and to come to the **knowledge** of the truth* (1 Timothy 2:4).

Paul even makes a point about people who have a zeal for God, but one not based on knowledge:

*For I bear them witness that they have a zeal for God, but not according to **knowledge*** (Romans 10:2).

How true that is of so many professing Christians in today's charismatic/evangelical church.

Further, Paul tells us how **learning** the Scriptures gives us hope and peace:

For whatever things were written before were written for our learning, that we through the patience and comfort of the Scriptures might have hope (Romans 15:4).

The things which you learned and received and heard and saw in me, these do, and the God of peace will be with you (Philippians 4:9).

I appreciate that quoting so many Bible verses about the value of knowledge may seem like I am labouring a point, but the reality is in spite of the importance that God places on knowledge in His Word, there is a definite weaning of professing Christians away from knowledge of, an understanding of and a dependence upon the Word of God. I was recently struck by just how relevant for today something Charles Spurgeon said in one of his many sermons (no. 1017):

> What if I were to say that most of you church members do not read your Bibles; would I be slandering you? You hear on the Lord's Day a chapter read, and you perhaps read a passage at family prayer, but a very large number never read the Bible privately for themselves; they take their religion out of the monthly magazine, or accept it from the minister's lips. Oh for the Berean spirit [of Acts 17:11] back again, to search the Scriptures whether these things be so. I would like to see a huge pile of all the books, good and bad that were ever written, prayer-books, sermons and hymn books, all smoking like Sodom of old, if the reading of those books keeps you away from the reading of the Bible; for a ton weight of human literature is not worth an ounce of Scripture; one single drop of the essential tincture of the word of God is better than a sea full of our commentings and sermonisings, and the like. We must live upon the word, the simple, pure, infallible word of God, if we are to become strong against error and tenacious of truth. Brethren, may you be established in the faith, rooted, grounded and built up; but I know you cannot be unless you search the Scriptures continually.

Spurgeon saw in his day how there was a progressive dumbing down of the flock through down grading (as Spurgeon's magazine described it) the importance of doctrine that was producing Biblically illiterate Christians who had little or no defence against *"ravenous wolves"* (Matthew 7:15) coming forth teaching all kinds of error and performing extra-Biblical "signs and wonders". That situation has only progressed further down the slippery slope since Spurgeon's day and has left much of the modern-day evangelical/charismatic church defenceless against error to the point where many are not even concerned whether or not something is Biblical. Consider for example, the following words of Mike Bickle from a 1989 teaching tape titled *Divine Appointment*:

> … and they [apostles and prophets] do things that you have no frame of reference for understanding because, believe me, what's going to be coming down in the next twenty years you and I have no frame of reference for understanding. It is so unusual you are not going to be able to look at the word for every manifestation and find one there because the Spirit of the Lord has so many manifestations that you and I know nothing about.

As Bickle has already said that the supernatural manifestations he is predicting will not be found in the Word of God, how are believers supposed to be obedient in testing **all** things in accordance with 1 Thessalonians 5:21, and testing the spirits to see whether they are of God in accordance with 1 John 4:1? If not the Word of God, what **are** we supposed to test **all** things against? Bickle's words mirror those of Paul Keith Davies in *Early Supernatural Models* (referred to earlier), when speaking of William Branham:

> Branham had several supernatural experiences for which he had no frame of reference or ability to understand.

Testing Branham's supernatural experiences against the Word of God would have provided clear understanding on their origins. That can also be said for events at Azusa Street, the *Sharon Bible School* and every so-called "revival" that has been founded on *Latter Rain* teaching.

An example of **how** the Word of God is down graded is provided by Francis Frangipane, a man I would describe as **the** apologist for false teachers and false prophets. In his book, *The House of the Lord*, he writes:

> We have instructed the church in nearly everything but becoming disciples of Christ. We have filled the people with doctrines instead of Deity; we have given them manuals instead of Emmanuel (page 36).

Frangipane's clever but empty sound-bite creates a false tension between doctrine and God (Deity), like they are mutually exclusive with one preventing the believer from having the other. Based on his statement, one must conclude that Frangipane is oblivious to the fact that teaching people to become disciples of Jesus Christ **requires** doctrinal instruction. In fact, giving people doctrinal instruction fulfils the second part of the Great Commission commanded by Jesus:

> *…teaching them to observe all things that I have commanded you…* (Matthew 28:20).

Frangipane's attitude towards doctrine is a far cry from the early church in Acts 2 which *"continued steadfastly in the apostle's doctrine"* (Acts 2:42).

Frangipane then goes on to say:

> Let us not look for the apostasy anywhere else but in the areas of our own hearts (page 84).

This is utterly false teaching camouflaged in false humility, because whilst we should indeed examine our own doctrine and faith first in accordance with Paul's instruction in 2 Corinthians 13:5, suggesting that examination should go no further than ourselves completely contradicts the many warnings we find in the Word of God about false teachers and false prophets, and the instruction from Paul to judge other believers (1 Corinthians 5:12-13).

LIMITING GOD

The following is another common claim I hear from the lips of charismatic/ evangelical Christians immersed in extra-Biblical spiritual activities, as if it is a Proverb:

> God is greater than His Word and we limit Him by testing our experiences of Him against Scripture.

This is in fact **precisely** what John Wimber claimed almost four decades ago, and is still used as a mantra to this day by those following in his footsteps. In his 1981 Church Planting Seminar Audio Tape (volume 5), he declared:

> God is greater than His word.

This claim requires careful inspection, because the root of it is the previously mentioned artificial tension created between the *logos* and *rhema* of God created by these false "apostles" and "prophets" of the *Prophetic Movement*.

Do we really limit God by testing our experiences of Him against Scripture?

On the contrary! Through Paul's writings God commands us to, *"test all things; hold fast what is good"* (1 Thessalonians 5:21). This command is to *"test **all** things"*; not just the things we **think** may be a bit *"dodgy"*, but *"**all** things"* including the things that are of God. In this passage there is a direct implication that God is confident that the things that are genuinely of Him will stand the test.

So do we limit God by testing Him? Absolutely not; testing is what He commands.

Further to this, John instructs us:

> *...do not believe every spirit, but test the spirits, whether they are of God; because many false prophets have gone out into the world* (1 John 4:1).

God's Word is clear that we should not just assume, or blindly take someone's word that what we are being told or experiencing is from God. But sadly, the litmus test used by so many professing Christians is how it **feels**. Rather than subjective feelings and emotions being present as a **result** of the adherence to sound Biblical doctrine, feelings have become the **judge** of whether or not something is of God. There is a widespread assumption that if it is happening to people who claim to be Christians, it must be from God.

We are **not** limiting God by testing our experience of Him against Scripture; we are taking God at His Word, and taking God at His Word is the very essence of faith.

Again, much of today's charismatic/evangelical attitude about limiting God by testing our experience against Scripture can be traced back to John Wimber. For example, in his Healing Seminar Series he claimed:

> ...it's evil when you don't recognise God. It's evil when you don't see Jesus in the things that are going on. It's evil when you hide behind doctrinal beliefs that curtail and control the work of the Spirit... The church today is committing evil in the name of sound doctrine. And, they are quenching the work of the Holy Spirit. And they are turning against the work of the Holy Spirit.

The modern-day charismatic/evangelical church has turned the Biblical model on its head, with too many Christians going from place to place like little "spiritual butterflies" seeking their next "experience of God", like a drug addict desperate for their next fix. In contrast, the Biblical model shows us people who were first seeking God, who then had an experience. For example, Peter and John were not seeking an experience as they *"went up together to the temple at the hour of prayer"* (Acts 3:1). They first sought God in prayer, who then drew their attention to *"a certain man lame from his mother's womb"* (Acts 3:2). The experience of the lame man being healed came as a result of seeking God first.

So then, we move on to the next issue: Is God greater than His Word?

You may be forgiven for initially thinking that this claim is one that honours and magnifies God, but no matter how good it may sound, is it true? If we do as Paul instructs us to do and test this claim against God's Word, we find the answer very easily. For example:

> *In the beginning was the Word, and the Word was with God, and the Word was God* (John 1:1).

How does the claim that "God is greater than His Word" stand up to what John states above? If the Word was with God, and the Word **was** God, how can God be above Himself? He cannot! The Bible exposes the claim that "God is greater than His Word" to be a deceptive lie. In fact, Psalm 138:2 tells us the exact opposite of this claim:

> *For You have magnified Your word above all Your name.*

God has chosen to reveal Himself to humanity through words that He divinely and supernaturally inspired men to write down. In like manner, our worship of Him should be according to His Word. As John declares:

> *Sanctify them by Your truth. Your word is truth* (John 17:17).

We must accept that God has chosen to reveal His rhema (*"utterance"*) through His *logos* (written word) with good reason, and that reason is simply because He knows best. Perhaps it is because words are best suited to convey precisely what He wants mankind to know. Words have definite meanings and can be interpreted objectively. The Bible is not about our feelings, but is about God's truth and our knowledge, understanding **and** experience of our Lord and Saviour Jesus Christ is increased by studying the Bible, not stifled by it. Studying His written Word ensures our knowledge of Him is first of all **personal**. We must know Him personally and directly, not through someone else's experience of Him. That would be like trying to get to know one's spouse by just relying on what someone else tells you about them! We must have a personal knowledge of God.

Secondly, the deepening of our personal knowledge of God will in turn deepen our **intelligent** knowledge of Him. We do not rely on visions or dreams, but instead as He chose to reveal Himself through his Word. We should have an intelligent knowledge and understanding of all of Christ's offices as Prophet, Priest and King. We should have an intelligent knowledge and understanding of His nature, His attributes, His works and His glory.

Thirdly, the deepening of our intelligent knowledge of God will in turn deepen our **affectionate** knowledge of Him; the inevitable consequence of having a true and Biblical knowledge of Jesus is that it will deepen our love for Him.

Fourthly, the deepening of our affectionate knowledge of God will in turn deepen our **exciting** knowledge of Him; the more we know Jesus, the more we should want to know. Professing to have an excitement about God without having a true Biblical knowledge of Him is precisely what Paul warned about in Romans 10:2:

> *…they have a zeal for God, but not according to knowledge.*

Personal knowledge; intelligent knowledge; affectionate knowledge; exciting knowledge. All these aspects of the knowledge of God are the result of studying His written Word and faithfully keeping within the boundary of it; a boundary graciously given to us by God for our protection and so we can objectively determine what is and is not from Him. Those who remain within this boundary are identified as being obedient followers of Jesus. There are however, people who claim to be followers of Jesus, but want to break the boundary down. They want knowledge, and particularly experience of God that goes beyond His written Word; they claim (either explicitly or implicitly) that His written Word is not quite enough. Bill Johnson provides a perfect example of this in his globally successful book, *When Heaven Invades Earth*, he writes:

> A powerless word is the letter not the Spirit. And we all know, 'The letter kills, but the Spirit gives life' (page 116)

Whilst Johnson does not say so in his book, this is a direct reference to 2 Corinthians 3:6, where Paul writes:

> ...*who also made us sufficient as ministers of the new covenant, not of the letter but of the Spirit; for the letter kills, but the Spirit gives life.*

The false implication made by Johnson is that studying the Bible will kill you spiritually. This misrepresentation of what Paul means has been used time and time again to promote extra-Biblical practices and experiences within the Church that cannot be justified when tested against the Word of God. The true context of the passage shows Paul was speaking of the letters written on stone, meaning the Ten Commandments, and this is clearly shown in verse 3:

> ...*clearly you are an epistle of Christ, ministered by us, written not with ink but by the Spirit of the living God, not on tablets of stone but on tablets of flesh, that is, of the heart.*

In Romans 7:5-6 Paul explains how the law (letter) "kills" because of our sinful passions it exposes, **not** because it is studied to understand what it means, as Johnson implies.

On page 76 of *When Heaven Invades Earth*, Johnson writes:

> Those who feel safe because of their intellectual grasp of Scripture enjoy a false sense of security. None of us has a full grasp of Scripture, but we all have the Holy Spirit. He is our common denominator who will always lead us into truth. But to follow Him, we must be willing to follow off the map – to go beyond what we know.

Johnson is basically claiming that we cannot know Scripture, but we can know what the Holy Spirit is saying by other means. In contrast, the Bible claims that Scripture is the Holy Spirit speaking to the church; Scripture is inspired by the Holy Spirit:

> *All Scripture is given by inspiration of God, and is profitable for doctrine, for reproof, for correction, for instruction in righteousness* (2 Timothy 3:16).

In 1 Corinthians 4:6, Paul tells us **not** to go beyond what is written, but on page 93 of *When Heaven Invades Earth*, Johnson writes:

> But in reality, the Bible is a closed book. Anything I get from the Word without God will not change my life. It is closed to insure that I remain dependent on the Holy Spirit.

This is just a thinly veiled attempt to use the Holy Spirit as an excuse for rejecting Biblical doctrine and objective study of the Bible in favour of subjective mystical experience. The Bible is the Holy Spirit talking to us and provides believers with the best possible defence against extra-Biblical teaching and experiences. Jettison this God-given defence and you end up being where God does not want you, but exactly where Satan wants you: defenceless and open to deception.

BE NOT DECEIVED – WHO, ME?

So many professing Christians seem to take the attitude that because they are indwelt by the Holy Spirit, they are immune from the threat of being deceived, and therefore any spiritual experience they have must be from God. But if that is true why would there be so much warning in Scripture to believers about the threat of being deceived? Why warn of something that cannot happen? John warned:

> *Beloved, do not believe every spirit, but test the spirits, whether they are of God; because many false prophets have gone out into the world* (1 John 4:1).

If it were not possible to be deceived by demonic spirits, why would we need to test the spirits to see whether they are from God?

Jesus warned His **disciples** not to be deceived; warning in fact that shortly before His return the deception will be so great that even the elect will succumb to it:

> *4 And Jesus answered and said to them: "Take heed that no one deceives you. 5 For many will come in My name, saying, 'I am the Christ,' and will deceive many* (Matthew 24:4-5).

> *For false christs and false prophets will rise and show great signs and wonders to deceive, if possible, even the elect* (Matthew 24:24).

Of all the future events Jesus gave His disciples to look out for as signs of His return, He warned them about deception the most; believers being deceived is a key sign of Jesus' impending return. He warned of wars and rumours of wars, famines, earthquakes and even signs in the sun, moon and stars, but what He warned most about was coming deception as a key sign of His return.

Peter warned the **church**:

> *8 Be sober, be vigilant; because your adversary the devil walks about like a roaring lion, seeking whom he may devour. 9 Resist him, steadfast in the faith, knowing that the same sufferings are experienced by your brotherhood in the world* (1 Peter 5:8-9).

Paul warned the church of the dangers of being deceived:

> *3 But I fear, lest somehow, as the serpent deceived Eve by his craftiness, so your minds may be corrupted from the simplicity that is in Christ. 4 For if he who comes preaches another Jesus whom we have not preached, or if you receive a different spirit which you have not received, or a different gospel which you have not accepted—you may well put up with it!* (2 Corinthians 11:3-4).

13 For such are false apostles, deceitful workers, transforming themselves into apostles of Christ. 14 And no wonder! For Satan himself transforms himself into an angel of light.15 Therefore it is no great thing if his ministers also transform themselves into ministers of righteousness, whose end will be according to their works (2 Corinthians 11:13-15).

Do not be deceived, God is not mocked; for whatever a man sows, that he will also reap (Galatians 6:7).

Paul exhorted believers to:

Test all things; hold fast what is good (1 Thessalonians 5:21).

Why would we need to test all things if all things experienced by believers are always only good? The answer is obvious, yet many believers have the attitude that deception is "for other people". But the question is: which other people?

Paul warned:

Now the Spirit expressly says that in latter times some will depart from the faith, giving heed to deceiving spirits and doctrines of demons (1 Timothy 4:1).

It is absolutely clear that Christians **can** be deceived, and that a sign of Jesus' Second Coming getting closer will be that believers **will** be deceived. There is no better example of this than the deceptions infiltrating today's charismatic/evangelical church at the hands of the "apostles" and "prophets" of the *Prophetic Movement*.

The fact that Scripture warns **believers** about being deceived is very important, because there are many well-respected Christians who take a stand against the kind of ministries I have mentioned by concluding none of the people involved are really saved. For example, at the *Strange Fire Conference* held at John MacArthur's *Grace Community Church*, Sun Valley, California, Todd Friel of Wretched Radio (acting as host) asked the assembled panel how should Christians express their concern to people they know who are involved in the (charismatic) ministries being examined at the conference. Steve Lawson answered by saying they should simply preach the gospel to them because they cannot possibly be saved if following such ministries. MacArthur wholeheartedly agreed and added, "We are trying to identify the Body of Christ and show that these people are not part of it". His comment was met with rapturous applause by the audience, and another panellist expressed agreement with MacArthur's assertion by declaring, "They are not our brothers and sisters in Christ". Todd Friel also concluded that, "These people are just lost". Likewise, whilst discussing the *Strange Fire Conference* on his *Dividing Line* radio programme, Reformed theologian and fellow cessationist, James White, said he "found it difficult to conceive of any true believer in Jesus Christ being influenced by Todd Bentley" (just one of the many people discussed during the conference).

Explaining away the excesses and extremes taking place within so many charismatic/ evangelical churches by simply claiming those involved are not saved and therefore not part of the Body of Christ, is arrogant, simplistic, shallow, naïve **and** unbiblical. But sadly that is the only answer a card-carrying cessationist has to these difficult questions. It is an answer that allows the cessationist to avoid engaging properly with the issue, because doing so would expose the short-comings in their cessationist position.

Whilst I have no doubt there are many unsaved people involved in the churches and ministries I have mentioned (because a diluted or distorted gospel will always produce false converts), to dismiss everyone involved as being unsaved is completely wrong and ignores the warnings given in Scripture to **believers** about being deceived; warnings given to the Body of Christ. For example, the church at Corinth had such dreadful problems (such as division, sexual immorality, doctrinal deviations and even abuse of the Lord's Supper) that Paul warns them about receiving a *"different spirit"*, but Paul still regards them as believers; he opens his letter to the church at Corinth:

> *To the church of God which is at Corinth, to those who are sanctified in Christ Jesus, called to be saints, with all who in every place call on the name of Jesus Christ our Lord, both theirs and ours* (1 Corinthians 1:2)

Paul calls them, *"the church of God... sanctified in Christ Jesus, called to be saints"*. He warns the church at Corinth about receiving a *"different spirit"*, not unbelievers; Paul warns, *"If **you** receive a different spirit"* (2 Corinthians 11:4). This is precisely what millions of Christians (as well as unbelievers) have done through the false doctrines and false practices so common within charismatic/evangelical churches today. I believe every person involved in the kind of doctrines and practices I have referenced in this book should certainly do as Paul told the church at Corinth and, *"Examine yourselves as to whether you are in the faith"* (2 Corinthians 13:5), but that could also be said for many who sit in the pews of many churches that hold to a cessationist position on the gifts of the Spirit.

Whilst some of the manifestations occurring within charismatic/evangelical churches can legitimately be put down to man-made causes (i.e. the over-exuberance of the **human** spirit), even the most hardened cessationist acknowledges this cannot explain everything that is manifested; they have no choice but to acknowledge a demonic (supernatural) element to at least some of what is occurring. However, that puts the cessationist in a very awkward position, because it means they are acknowledging that Satan continues to perform the supernatural at the same time as denying God does. Try squaring that circle.

However, for those who defend these supernatural manifestations there is a no less awkward question to answer. Mother Etter, Charles Parham, William Seymour, William Branham, Franklin Hall, Lonnie Frisbee, John Wimber, Bill Haman, Bob Jones, Rick Joyner, Todd Bentley, Mike Bickle, Bill Johnson etc etc. If the supernatural phenomena manifested by these people (and many others) is really from God and is not a demonic deception perpetrated through *"a different spirit"*, then the conclusion has to be that God "anoints" with the most power those who are least faithful, both in their moral practices and Biblical doctrine. But if that was true, it would contradict God's Word and make Him a liar. People who follow the ministry of these men and women need to consider this carefully and stop judging the authenticity of their power by the experience that power manifests; experience can be deceptive.

NOTE AND AVOID

There is absolutely no doubt that most charismatic/evangelical Christians today show far more tolerance toward false doctrine and those who teach it than God does. If that were not true the false teachers of today would not be so successful, because if there were not people prepared to buy into their false doctrine, the ministries of false teachers would very quickly die off. The Bible **never** says we are to tolerate false doctrine or false teachers under grace or love. We are told *"Love will cover a multitude of sins"* (1 Peter 4:8), but nowhere does Scripture suggest this includes false doctrine. Paul tells us our love should abound in more and more knowledge and all discernment (Philippians 1:9), clearly indicating real love cannot abound unless it does so in doctrinal truth and discernment of what is true and false. In Romans 16:17 Paul instructs true believers to:

> …**note** those who cause divisions and offenses, contrary to the doctrine which you learned, and **avoid** them (emphasis added).

Paul says we should note and avoid false teachers, not overlook their false teaching with the excuse that you are sure they "have a pure heart to serve the Lord" or "they love Jesus". Jesus said His true followers demonstrate their love for Him by being obedient to His Word.

Just how serious does the false doctrine have to be for a Christian nowadays to be obedient to Paul's instruction to note and avoid false teachers? Followers of William Branham during his lifetime were happy to overlook his claim that the doctrine of the Trinity is "of the Devil". Is that not serious enough? Would Paul have been so lenient? I do not think so. But what about Branham's modern-day followers in charismatic/evangelical churches? Do they just overlook his claim that the doctrine of the Trinity is "of the Devil", or do they themselves fail on the fundamental doctrine of the identity of God? This is after all **the** most fundamental doctrine in the Christian faith, so anyone deviating from *"the doctrine which you learned"* on the deity of Jesus Christ must be noted and avoided. With that in mind, let us lay aside for a moment all their other well-documented false doctrines, promotion of demonic manifestations and signs that make you wonder, and focus on the view of Jesus' deity held by just two of the men I have referred to: Rick Joyner and Bill Johnson.

RICK JOYNER

On page 59 of *There were Two Trees in the Garden*, Rick Joyner denies the two natures of Jesus Christ:

> There is a tendency to continue relating to Him as **'the MAN from Galilee.'** Jesus is not a man. He was and is Spirit. He took the form of a servant and became a man for a brief time (emphasis in the original).

This is a direct denial of a fundamental Christian doctrine called the Hypostatic Union. The word "hypostatic" derives from the Greek word *hupostasis*, meaning "giving substance or reality to". Hypostatic Union describes the personal union of Jesus' two natures: divine and human. Jesus is God in the flesh (John 1:1, 14; 10:30-33; 20:28; Philippians 2:5-8; 1 Timothy 3:16; Hebrews 1:8). He was born into this world in a physical body, had a (perfected) physical body after His resurrection and continues to be in perfect physical form now at the right hand of the Father in heaven. Joyner's claim that Jesus was a man for only a brief time is seriously wrong.

Jesus is fully God and fully man:

> *For in Him [Christ] dwells all the fullness of the Godhead bodily* (Colossians 2:9)

Jesus has two natures: God and man. He is not half God and half man. He is 100% God and 100% man. Jesus never lost His divinity.

Jesus continued to exist as God when He became a physical man and added human nature to Himself (Philippians 2:5-11). There is a union therefore of a full human nature and a full divine nature in the person of Jesus Christ.

To be incarnate means to become flesh. The incarnation of Jesus is when the human nature (Jesus the man) was added to the nature of God, the second person of the Trinity. It is where God became a man (John 1:1, 14; Philippians 2:5-8). It was the voluntary act of Jesus to humble Himself so that He might die for our sins (1 Peter 3:18). Thus, Jesus has two natures: divine and human, known theologically as the Hypostatic Union.

This error by Joyner is **critical** because the New Testament links Jesus' on-going work as intercessor and mediator to His humanity:

> For there is one God and one Mediator between God and men, the Man Christ Jesus (1 Timothy 2:5).

Would the apostle Paul have embraced Rick Joyner or would he have noted and avoided him?

BILL JOHNSON

Bill Johnson is a man I have mentioned frequently throughout this book, because he is arguably the most prominent and influential figurehead in the modern-day *Prophetic Movement* and NAR. His doctrine on the identity and nature of Jesus should therefore be examined carefully. For example, in *When Heaven Invades Earth*, Johnson states:

> He [Jesus] laid his divinity aside as He sought to fulfil the assignment given to Him by the Father (page 79).

Whilst Jesus operated His earthly ministry as a man, rather than as God, Scripture **never** suggests He laid aside His divinity; Jesus was always both fully God and fully man. Jesus laid aside His "Majesty", the glory that His position of being God demanded, but He did **not** lay aside His divinity. He laid aside His divine privileges, not His divine attributes. Look at Philippians 2:6-10:

> who, being in the form of God, did not consider it robbery to be equal with God, but made Himself of no reputation, taking the form of a bondservant, and coming in the likeness of men. And being found in appearance as a man, He humbled Himself and became obedient to the point of death, even the death of the cross. Therefore God also has highly exalted Him and given Him the name

which is above every name, that at the name of Jesus every knee should bow, of those in heaven, and of those on earth, and of those under the earth.

He goes on to state:

The anointing is what linked Jesus, the man, to the divine...

This is the same "anointing" that men like William Branham and Todd Bentley are claimed to have, and relegates Jesus' uniqueness completely. Johnson further undermines the uniqueness of Jesus by claiming He had to be **born again**, not resurrected. Johnson makes this claim often within his teaching, and the foundation of this is the heretical belief that Jesus laid aside His divinity whilst on earth; not in just the way He carried out His mission on earth, but that Jesus actually **became** a man, suffered in hell as a man and had to be born again because He was a man, not God. Johnson claims Jesus laid aside His divine nature.

When Bill Johnson says, "Jesus was born again" people need to understand the **huge** false doctrine behind that very small sentence. It is a heresy that denies the very nature of Christ and therefore attacks the central tenet of the Christian faith; there is no doctrine more important than having a correct Christology. Jesus was **not** born again, but was **resurrected** because death had no hold on Him, and death had no hold on Him because He was without sin of His own. He paid for **our** sins, but had **no** sin of His own to pay for so He did **not** have to be born again, but was resurrected. Look at what the three Gospels say:

He is not here; for He is risen, as He said. Come, see the place where the Lord lay (Matthew 28:6)

But he said to them, "Do not be alarmed. You seek Jesus of Nazareth, who was crucified. He is risen! He is not here. See the place where they laid Him (Mark 16:6)

He is not here, but is risen! Remember how He spoke to you when He was still in Galilee (Luke 24:6)

All three accounts tell us that the angel declared Christ to be *"risen"*. The Greek word used is *anastasis*, meaning "rising up", and is from where the word "resurrection" is derived. The term "born again" is derived from a completely different Greek word - *gennao*. For example, in John 3:3 Jesus tells Nicodemus:

Unless one is born again [gennao], he cannot see the kingdom of God.

The root of Johnson's error that "Jesus was born again" is the Word of Faith heresy that Jesus died spiritually as well as physically, and the divinity of Christ was destroyed, thereby meaning He had to be born again. Divinity is not something that is subject to change. In John 3:6 Jesus says:

That which is born of the flesh is flesh, and that which is born of the spirit is spirit.

Jesus was conceived not by flesh, but of the Holy Spirit. Furthermore, Hebrews 13:8 tells us that:

Jesus Christ is the same yesterday, today, and forever.

Johnson shares this heretical doctrine with some very unsavoury bed-fellows such as Kenneth Copeland, Kenneth Hagen, Benny Hinn, Oral Roberts and of course E. W. Kenyon.

Johnson also teaches that Jesus "became sin", which seems at first glance much closer to orthodox Christian doctrine than his statement that "Jesus was born again". But as these two statements are inextricably linked in his theology, it is important we look at what Johnson is **really** saying. The teaching that Jesus became sin is mainly based on 2 Corinthians 5:21:

For He made Him who had no sin to be sin for us, that we might become the righteousness of God in Him.

The original Greek word used for sin in 2 Corinthians 5:21 is *hamartia*, which can be translated as either *"sin"* or *"sin offering"*; it is the very same word used in the Greek translation of the Old Testament (Septuagint) in Isaiah 53:10, which renders *hamartia* as *"sin offering"* or *"offering for sin"*:

Yet it pleased the LORD to bruise Him; He has put Him to grief. When You make His soul an offering for sin, He shall see His seed, He shall prolong His days, and the pleasure of the LORD shall prosper in His hand.

So which rendering of the Greek word hamartia is correct when used by Paul in 2 Corinthians 5:21; did Jesus become sin or a sin offering? To start to answer that question it is worth noting that the word *"sin"* (*hamartia*) is used twice by Paul in 2 Corinthians 5:21. It would therefore perhaps be unreasonable to presume that Paul would use two different renderings of the same word in one short sentence like 2 Corinthians 5:21. For example, if the meaning of *"sin offering"* is used for both occasions when *hamartia* is found in 2 Corinthians 5:21 the passage would read as follows:

For He made Him who knew no sin offering [hamartia] to be a sin offering [hamartia] for us.

Does that really make sense of the passage? I do not think so. However, just because "sin" makes more sense than *"sin offering"* when translating *hamartia* in 2 Corinthians

5:21, that is not evidence enough to conclude that the word *hamartia* should **always** be translated as *"sin"*, rather than *"sin offering"*. I do not believe it is a case of either/or, but is a case of and/as well; Christ became both sin for us and a sin offering, and we should not shy away from accepting that Jesus "became sin" just because it seemingly (on the surface at least) lends weight to Bill Johnson's heretical claim that "Jesus was born again" **because** He "became sin" for us.

The **huge** problem lies with what Johnson really means when he says "Jesus became sin"; as with so many false teachers, he uses the same vocabulary as orthodox Christian doctrine, but uses a **very** different dictionary. When Johnson says "Jesus became sin" he actually means Jesus **became sinful**, which goes well beyond what Scripture says about Christ's atoning sacrifice and means Johnson is guilty of doing exactly what Paul warned us **not** to do in 1 Corinthians 4:6 when he declared, *"do not exceed that which is written."* Jesus could only **become sinful** if He took sin into His own nature by committing sin Himself, which would of course cancel out Christ's perfection and nullify His atoning sacrifice. How then you might ask, does Johnson believe Jesus **became sinful**, but still believe in the validity of His atoning sacrifice? The answer lies squarely in the other part of Johnson's declaration that **"Jesus was born again"**. Johnson believes that Jesus **had** to be born again just like me and you **because** He not only became sin, but actually **became sinful** in nature like us. This is standard Word of Faith heresy. How many poor souls reading Johnson's books or attending *Bethel School* will understand the heresy Johnson is preaching (and the origin of it) when he says that seemingly simple statement: "Jesus was born again"? This is **serious, serious error**, but you will not find this within the *Bethel* website statement of faith, you have to listen to his sermons and read his books to fully understand the depth of his heresy, and from where it originates.

These misrepresentations of Christ's identity and nature taught by Rick Joyner and Bill Johnson are an attack on **the** fundamentals of the Christian faith, and would certainly have prompted Paul to note them (i.e. point them out!) and avoid them in accordance with Romans 16:17. Sadly however, these doctrines are commonplace within large sections of the charismatic/evangelical church, but the swords of these false teachers and of those who follow them, are so badly broken that they don't know how serious their error is.

A MIXTURE

Not **everything** the modern-day "apostles" and "prophets" teach is false; if everything they said was false they would be much easier to note and avoid, but they sugar-coat much of their error with a thin veneer of truth which, at least on the surface, makes their error and deception look like truth. That is what makes it so deceptive and attractive! Just as the best forgery looks very much like the genuine article, so too the most convincing (and therefore dangerous) deception looks like truth. A forger will never bother forging a £3 note or a $7 bill because the original does not exist, meaning the forged £3 note or $7 bill would be very easily recognised as a fake. The forger will only counterfeit that which already exists, and so too with Satan.

The most convincing and seductive (and therefore dangerous and toxic) deception is always mixed with an element of truth. It is a mixture, and because of its strength to deceive, the Bible makes very clear God's attitude toward the mixture. From the forbidden garments of wool and flax in the Old Testament to the warning of Peter in 2 Peter 2:1-3 of how false prophets and false teachers will *"secretly bring in destructive heresies"*. The Greek word translated in English as *"secretly bring in"* is pareisaxousin, which more accurately means "to bring into alongside of" or "to smuggle in". It has the meaning of mixing true doctrine with false.

Paul warns in Galatians 5:9 that:

A little leaven leavens the whole lump.

The Canadian-American Bible teacher, preacher and pastor H.A. Ironside (1876-1951) describes error as follows:

Error is like leaven, of which we read, "A little leaven leaveneth the whole lump." Truth mixed with error is equivalent to all error, except that it is more innocent looking and, therefore more dangerous. God hates such a mixture! Any error, or any truth-and-error mixture, calls for definite exposure and repudiation. To condone such is to be unfaithful to God and His word and treacherous to imperilled souls for whom Christ died.

What false teachers say will be a mixture of truth and error and the problem is that even if those Christians who follow their teaching can actually recognise the error mixed in with the truth (which I very much doubt), they naively think they can digest the truth, but spit out the error. They cannot, because it is all mixed together – even if they manage to recognise within the mixture which bits are true and which bits are in fact error. As a way of illustrating this point, imagine someone has a cup of tea with milk in. If that person does not like milk, they cannot drink the tea and not the milk; it is all mixed in together and cannot be separated. A teaching or ministry containing a mixture will do nothing more than produce a mixture in others, and that is my deep and grave concern for the millions of Christians who follow the teaching and ministries of so many within the charismatic/evangelical church today.

Jesus spoke of false doctrine as *"the leaven of the Pharisees"* in Matthew 16:6 and Luke 12:1. In Biblical typology, leaven represents spiritual pride and the sin resulting from it. Let us be clear that false doctrine is no small matter; it is sin and always involves spiritual pride. Most of what the Pharisees believed was Biblically true, but it only took the little bit that was false to lead the people astray. In the same way, some of what the "apostles" and "prophets" of the *Prophetic Movement* teach is true, but the parts that are not true *"leavens the whole lump"* as far as God is concerned.

The Biblical basis for purity is the truth of right doctrine. This is why the New Testament contains more exhortation to right doctrine than it does to right conduct; God does not judge our faithfulness by our sincerity, He judges our faithfulness by our obedience. God takes right doctrine very seriously, but many Christians nowadays believe doctrine is not important because it brings division. On the contrary, as I have already mentioned earlier, it is those not adhering to right doctrine that bring division:

> *Now I urge you, brethren, note those who cause divisions and offenses, contrary to the doctrine which you learned, and avoid them* (Romans 16:17).

THE PROBLEM

Whilst the false "apostles" and "prophets" of the *Prophetic Movement* are certainly a huge problem for the charismatic/evangelical church of today, not all the blame is to be laid at their feet, because they are not the root of the problem. We have established that the root of the *Prophetic Movement* is toxic, but not even that is the real root of the problem; the real root goes much deeper. The real root of the problem is those who profess to love and follow Jesus, but refuse to obey Him. Jesus declared, *"If you love Me, keep My commandments"* (John 14:15) and *"If anyone loves Me, he will keep My Word"* (John 14:23). John declared, *"This is love, that we walk according to His commandments"* (2 John 1:6). Those who love and follow Jesus demonstrate they love and follow Him by keeping His commandments, and conversely, *"He who says, 'I know Him' and does not keep His commandments, is a liar, and the truth is not in Him"* (1 John 2:4). No matter how much someone professes a love for Jesus, it is a profession void of any substance or meaning if they will not be obedient and submit their will and desires to God. The real root of the problem is professing Christians who pursue their own desires; they refuse to endure sound doctrine because of personal desires. Paul warned such a time would come:

> *For the time will come when they will not endure sound doctrine, but according to their own desires, because they have itching ears, they will heap up for themselves teachers* (2 Timothy 4:3).

If certain Christians did not **want** to have their itching ears tickled, false teachers would not have an audience and would not survive; those who **want** to have their itching ears tickled are the oxygen false teachers need to breathe and survive and it would be very easy to cut off their oxygen supply if there were not Christians who **want** to *"heap up for themselves teachers"* who will tickle their itching ears. If only their priority was God's Word, rather than their own desires. Proverbs 14:7 declares:

> *Go from the presence of a foolish man, when you do not perceive in him lips of knowledge.*

Too many Christians do the exact opposite to this wise instruction and intentionally pursue and follow foolish men who they are aware have no knowledge of the truth, but do so nevertheless because they say what their itching ears want to hear.

The cold hard truth is that many Christians following the ministries of false teachers are being deceived **willingly**, and have merely found teachers who enable them to articulate and express that which has always been in their heart. They **want** to believe what these "apostles" and "prophets" say; they **want** to believe they have a special "anointing" of supernatural power; they **want** to believe they are part of the great End-Time breed of "elite" Christians who are greater than those who have gone before; they want to believe they are the generation that will invite Jesus to return. Supernatural power; dominion and authority over both the earth and the spiritual realm; victory over sin; health and wealth. All this certainly sounds wonderful, but has nothing to do with how Jesus said it would be immediately prior to His return:

> *When the Son of Man comes, will He really find faith on the earth?"* (Luke 18:8).

They **wilfully** replace Biblical absolutes with an experience based faith of their own design; making the *rhema* (spoken Word of God) supersede the *logos* (the written Word of God); this gets Christians into serious trouble.

Rather than being the best and greatest there has ever been, the final church immediately prior to the return of Jesus Christ is characterised by apostasy; it will be the worst ever! The apostle Paul describes this End-Time church:

> *Now, brethren, concerning the coming of our Lord Jesus Christ and our gathering together to Him, we ask you, ² not to be soon shaken in mind or troubled, either by spirit or by word or by letter, as if from us, as though the day of Christ had come. ³ Let no one deceive you by any means; for that Day will not come unless the falling away comes first...* (2 Thessalonians 2:1-3).

The Greek word translated *"falling away"* is apostasia, from where we derive the English term apostasy. It describes a general defection from the true God of the Bible and His commands and teachings. Every age has had its defectors, but the falling away of the End-Time church will be complete and worldwide.

Jeremiah was a prophet at a time when the nation of Israel was descending into apostasy through the empty words of false prophets, and much of what he had to say to Israel remains disturbingly relevant for the church today. For example:

> *The prophets prophesy falsely, and the priests rule by their own power; and My people love to have it so. But what will you do in the end?* (Jeremiah 5:31).

> *Your dwelling place is in the midst of deceit; through deceit they refuse to know Me, says the Lord* (Jeremiah 9:6).

> *And the Lord said to me, "The prophets prophesy lies in My name. I have not sent them, commanded them, nor spoken to them; they prophesy to you a false vision, divination, a worthless thing, and the deceit of their heart* (Jeremiah 14:14).

> *Thus says the Lord of hosts: "Do not listen to the words of the prophets who prophesy to you. They make you worthless; they speak a vision of their own heart, not from the mouth of the Lord"* (Jeremiah 23:16).

In Revelation 3:14-22 we read about the church at Laodicea; Jesus has nothing good to say about Laodicea and threatens to spit it out because it is neither hot nor cold. This is yet again a description of how much God hates the mixture. The historical city of Laodicea was located near some hot mineral springs at Hierapolis (approximately five miles south) and cold water springs at Colossae. Archaeology of the ancient city shows Laodicea had an aqueduct system that carried water from the hot mineral spring that would have mixed with the cold water and resulted in being lukewarm by the time it reached the city, thus rendering it unpalatable. Jesus uses this to illustrate how the church was neither hot nor cold, so He would vomit them out of His mouth; He hates the mixture and for that reason Jesus says He is outside the church; He is not inside where the members of the church at Laodicea presume He is. What a terrifying indictment!

The first step towards solving a problem is recognising there is one, and Laodicea did not **know** it was Laodicea; it did not **know** Jesus was outside the church; it did not **know** it was an apostate church. Because of its position of material wealth it presumed it was also spiritually wealthy, but Jesus declared:

> *Because you say, 'I am rich, have become wealthy, and have need of nothing'—and do not know that you are wretched, miserable, poor, blind, and naked* (Revelation 3:17).

Who says the prosperity teachers are not in the Bible!

The problem with much of today's charismatic/evangelical church is that it is so self-deceived it does not know it is apostate. This is a desperately dangerous position to be in and is why I write this book with such a heavy heart.

A. W. Tozer made the following observation about self-deception:

> Of all forms of deception, self-deception is the most deadly, and of all deceived persons the self-deceived are the least likely to discover the fraud [because] he is his own enemy and is working a fraud upon himself. He wants to believe the lie and is psychologically conditioned to do so. He does not resist the deceit but collaborates with it against himself. There is no struggle, because the victim surrenders before the fight begins. He enjoys being deceived.

This describes perfectly my friend I referred to in the forward to this book, as well as literally millions of professing Christians today who are self-deceived to their apostasy.

Charles Haddon Spurgeon warned:

> A time will come when instead of shepherds feeding the sheep, the church will have clowns entertaining the goats.

The clowns have been entertaining the goats for quite some time now, because that is exactly how the goats want it. The *"falling away"* which Paul prophesied would come has been progressively growing in strength and gathering momentum for quite some time as a result of charismatic/evangelical Christians first tolerating and then embracing false teachers. As John Wesley (1703-1791) warned:

> What one generation tolerates, the next generation will embrace.

How much false teaching will you embrace, or even just tolerate?

END NOTES

[1] It is bad enough to be accused of quenching the work of the Holy Spirit, but being accused of blaspheming the Holy Spirit is even worse, because Scripture describes it as the unpardonable sin. This is therefore an incredibly serious and threatening accusation for one believer to make against another. It is also an incredibly stupid accusation to make, because blaspheming the Holy Spirit is **not** a sin the New Testament believer in Jesus Christ can commit. The concept of blasphemy against the Holy Spirit is mentioned in Mark 3:22-30 and Matthew 12:22-32. The context is that Jesus had just performed a miracle. A demon-possessed man had been brought to Him and He had cast out the evil spirit and healed him of his blindness and muteness. The Old Testament prophecies about the coming Jewish Messiah state He would perform such miracles as evidence of His identity as Messiah, so the witnesses to the miracles began to wonder if Jesus was the Messiah prophesied about by the Old Testament prophets. However, the Pharisees quickly tried to quash such speculation by attributing Jesus' actions to "Beelzebub, the ruler of the demons". Jesus deals with this claim and speaks of blaspheming the Holy Spirit, i.e. accusing Jesus of being demon-possessed instead of spirit-filled. This kind of blasphemy **cannot** be duplicated today. The Pharisees were in a particular and unique moment in history: they had the Law and the Prophets, they had the Holy Spirit stirring their hearts and they had the Messiah physically standing in front of them performing the very miracles that their own Scriptures prophesied would identify the Messiah; no one has ever been blessed with such divine revelation than the religious leaders of Jesus' time, yet they attributed the work of the Holy Spirit to the Devil. In response, Jesus declared their wilful blindness unpardonable; their blasphemy against the Holy Spirit was their final rejection of God's grace and it was from that point onwards Jesus began to teach in parables, so only a select few would be blessed with understanding what He was teaching.

[2] Cessationism – The doctrine within Christianity that the charismatic gifts (healing, speaking in tongues, interpretation of tongues, words of knowledge, words of wisdom etc.) ceased with the closing of the canon of Scripture and/or the death of the last apostle (the closing of the "apostolic age"). This is not true. Paul declares:

> *But whether there are prophecies, they will fail; whether there are tongues, they will cease; whether there is knowledge, it will vanish away.* [9] *For we know in part and we prophesy in part.* [10] *But when that which is perfect has come, then that which is in part will be done away* (1 Corinthians 13:8-10).

Paul makes very clear that prophesies, tongues and (words of) knowledge will continue until *"that which is perfect has come"*, which of course refers to the Second Coming of Jesus Christ. I have heard well-respected cessationists such as John

MacArthur actually use the above passage in defence of their position by arguing that when Paul says *"that which is perfect has come"* he is referring to the first advent of Jesus. But this cannot be the case because Paul is very obviously referring to a **future** event; Paul says, *"**When** that which is perfect **has** come".*

The fact is that there is so little in Scripture for a cessationist to appeal to in defence of their position that it always falls back to, "Well, that is not my experience". They do not see that they are basing their theology on their experience (or lack thereof), which is absolutely no better (or different) to the hyper-charismatic who justifies a spiritual manifestation not from Scripture, but by their experience of it.

The excesses of the charismatic/evangelical church cannot be used as an argument for the cessation of real and Biblical charismatic gifts. I have personally experienced (but not participated in) such charismatic excesses many times as a young Christian, but nevertheless still affirm the gifts of the Spirit **are** for today. Why? Because the Word of God tells me they are. I have lost count of the number of times as a young Christian people have insisted on laying hands on me to release me into the gift of speaking in tongues. In combination with the (no doubt sincere and) passionate prayers declared over me, I was told to repeat out loud, "Abba, Abba, Abba, Abba, Abba......." until the tongues came forth from my mouth. They never did, and even as young as I was at the time I just thought that a real gift of the Spirit would not need to be "manufactured" like that; particularly in a way that violated a direct command from Jesus not to use *"vain repetitions"* (Matthew 6:7).

2nd century historical records and beyond clearly showing that the gifts of the Spirit continued beyond the time of the apostles. For example, not only did Quadratus write a defence of the Christian faith to Emperor Hadrian in 125AD, in which he emphasised the existence of miracles of healing, consider also the following quotes, some of which are from people that cessationist Christians would honour as part of their Reformed heritage:

Justin Martyr (100AD-165AD):

> For the prophetical gifts remain with us even to the present time. Now it is possible to see among us women and men who possess gifts of the Spirit of God.

Irenaeus (125AD-200AD):

> In like manner we do also hear many brethren in the church who possess prophetic gifts and through the Spirit speak all kinds of languages. ... Yes, moreover, as I have said, the dead even have been raised up, and remained among us for many years.

Tertullian (150AD-240AD):

> For seeing that we too acknowledge the spiritual charismata, or gifts, we too have merited the attainment of the prophetic gift… and heaven knows how many distinguished men, to say nothing of the common people, have been cured either of devils or of their sicknesses.

Novation (210AD-280AD):

> This is he [the Holy Spirit] who places prophets in the church, instructs teachers, directs tongues, gives powers and healings, does wonderful works… and arranges whatever gifts there are of the charismata; and thus making the Lord's church everywhere, and in all, perfected and completed.

Origen (185AD-284AD):

> Some give evidence of their having received through this faith a marvellous power by the cures which they perform, invoking no other name over those who need their help than that of the God of all things, along with Jesus and a mention of his history.

Augustine (354AD-430AD):

> In his work *City of God*, Augustine tells of healings and miracles that he has observed first-hand and then says, "I am so pressed by the work that I cannot record all the miracles I know".

Consider more recently the biographies of D. L. Moody (the man who led Queen Victoria to Christ) and R. A. Torrey, who both testified to being baptised in the Holy Spirit and speaking in tongues.

John Wesley (1703-1791), revivalist and founder of the Methodist movement, wrote:

> I do not recollect any Scripture wherein we are taught that miracles were to be confined within the limits of the apostolic age or the Cyprian age, or any period of time, longer or shorter, even till the restitution of all things.

Wesley was absolutely correct.

[3] *Star Wars* – I mention the following because for the last 30 years *Star Wars* Bible Studies have been used in many charismatic/evangelic churches as a way of explaining the Christian message. *Star Wars* church services are also not uncommon, where people are invited to attend dressed as their favourite *Star Wars* character.

Not only did *Star Wars* have an impact on the entertainment industry, it also opened the eyes of the Western world to pantheism. It is the belief that the impersonal God is one essence with the universe; God inhabits all things; the universe is God and God is the universe. In other words, God is not separate from the universe but is contained within it and **is** it. This worldview lies at the foundation of most Hindu, Buddhist, and *New Age* religions. This worldview gained popularity in the sixties, at a time when Eastern ideas began to enter the West. It drew public attention through celebrities such as *The Beatles* and Shirley McClain who embraced the teachings of the Eastern religions. *Star Wars*, with its success, continues to stir interest in the ideas of pantheism.

In a *Discovery Channel* documentary entitled "The Science of *Star Wars*," George Lucas admitted that his influence for creating the Jedi was studying the Shaolin monks of China. The Shaolin monks are priests known for originating and becoming the masters of the Martial Arts. Their fighting skills were legendary throughout the land of China, which came from their mastery of the use of the *Chi* force.

The "religion" of the Jedi created by George Lucas for his *Star Wars* films is pantheistic and directly reflects his own view of "God". In a *Time Magazine* interview Lucas admitted that the Force was "God". He claimed that the simple message of the movie was that:

> There is a God and there is both a good side and a bad side [to God]. You have a choice between them, but the world works better if you're on the good side.

Lucas openly acknowledged that:

> I put the Force into the movie in order to try to awaken a certain kind of spirituality in young people – more a belief in God than a belief in any particular religious system.

In making the movies Lucas surrounded himself with people who shared his worldview. For example, Irvin Kershner, the director of *The Empire Strikes Back*, is a Zen Buddhist. Kershner admitted of the film:

> I wanna introduce some Zen here because I don't want the kids to walk away just feeling that everything is shoot-cm-up, but there's also a little something to think about here in terms of yourself and your surroundings.

Lucas' biographer, Dale Pollock, acknowledges that Yoda's philosophy was deliberately Buddhist.

Some Christians have equated the Force with the Holy Spirit and therefore suggested that Star Wars contains Christian themes that can be drawn on and used to evangelise. However, there are several major differences. First, the Force is an impersonal energy field whereas the Holy Spirit is a personal being, the third member of the Trinity. He has a personality, intelligence, and will. Second, the Force is made up of all living things in the universe while the Holy Spirit is not contained in the universe. The Holy Spirit is an eternal being who was involved in creating the universe out of nothing (Genesis 1). Being God, the Holy Spirit is involved in the universe but He is not contained in the universe and exists independent of living things. Third, the Force can be manipulated by the Jedi who use it to accomplish their will, but the Holy Spirit cannot be manipulated by those He indwells. Instead He guides, teaches, and empowers them to do the will of God the Father. Christians do not master the Holy Spirit to accomplish their will, but rather the Holy Spirit guides them to do His will. Finally, the Force has a good side and a dark side which exist in a state of balance while the Holy Spirit has no dark or evil side but only the attributes consistent with a holy and good God.

[4] The Down Grade – Authorship of the original article published in *The Sword and the Trowel* is often wrongly attributed to Charles Spurgeon. It was published anonymously, but was written by Spurgeon's close friend, Robert Shindler.

[5] Are those who have not spoken in tongues without the Holy Spirit? There are three occasions in the book of Acts where speaking in tongues accompanied the receiving of the Holy Spirit—Acts 2:4, 10:44-46, and 19:6. However, these three occasions are the only places in the Bible where speaking in tongues is an evidence of receiving the Holy Spirit. Throughout the book of Acts, thousands of people believe in Jesus and nothing is said about them speaking in tongues (Acts 2:41, 8:5-25, 16:31-34, 21:20). Nowhere in the New Testament is it taught that speaking in tongues is the only evidence a person has received the Holy Spirit. In fact, the New Testament teaches the opposite. We are told that **every** believer in Christ has the Holy Spirit (Romans 8:9; 1 Corinthians 12:13; Ephesians 1:13-14), but not every believer speaks in tongues (1 Corinthians 12:29-31).

So, why was speaking in tongues the evidence of the Holy Spirit in those three passages in Acts? Acts 2 records the apostles being baptized in the Holy Spirit and empowered by Him to proclaim the gospel. The apostles were enabled to speak in other languages (tongues) so they could share the truth with people in their own languages. Acts 10 records the apostle Peter being sent to share the gospel with non-Jewish people. Peter and the other early Christians, being Jews, would have a hard time accepting Gentiles (non-Jewish people) into the church. God enabled the Gentiles to speak in tongues to demonstrate that they had received the same Holy Spirit the apostles had received (Acts 10:47, 11:17). Acts 10:44-47 describes this:

> *⁴⁴ While Peter was still speaking these words, the Holy Spirit fell upon all those who heard the word. ⁴⁵ And those of the circumcision who believed were astonished, as many as came with Peter, because the gift of the Holy Spirit had*

been poured out on the Gentiles also. [46] For they heard them speak with tongues and magnify God. Then Peter answered, [47] "Can anyone forbid water, that these should not be baptized who have received the Holy Spirit just as we have?"

Peter later refers back to this occasion as proof that God was indeed saving the Gentiles (Acts 15:7-11).

Nowhere is speaking in tongues presented as something all Christians should expect when they receive Jesus Christ as their Saviour and are therefore baptised in the Holy Spirit. In fact, out of all the conversion accounts in the New Testament, only two record speaking in tongues in that context.

It must be said that the vast majority of believers who claim to practice the gift of speaking in tongues today do not do so in agreement with what the New Testament teaches about it. For example, Paul states in 1 Corinthians 14:27-28:

If anyone speaks in a tongue, let there be two or at the most three, each in turn, and let one interpret. [28] But if there is no interpreter, let him keep silent in church, and let him speak to himself and to God (1 Corinthians 14:27-28).

Paul then declares in only a few verses further on in the same passage:

[33] For God is not the author of confusion but of peace, as in all the churches of the saints (1 Corinthians 14:33).

The vast majority of so-called speaking in tongues I have witnessed in my forty or so years as a Christian attending charismatic/evangelical churches has been nothing more than confusing and meaningless babble that has received no interpretation. Whilst I do **not** believe the gift of tongues has ceased for the present day, the reality is that genuine manifestations of this gift are a rarity.

[6] Is hell eternal? - There are still those today who deny the eternal nature of hell, and do so by claiming the words translated *"eternal"* in relation to hell's duration, such as the noun *aion* and the adjective *aionios*, only mean *"age"*. Aion and aionios can mean an *"age"* or *"all eternity"*, just in the same way "bat" can mean something you hit a ball with or the winged rodent variety. Context is therefore **everything** in understanding the intended meaning of these terms. For example, in the Olivet Discourse, after revealing that He will separate the righteous from the wicked like a shepherd separates sheep from the goats (Matthew 25:31:45), Jesus states that the wicked:

Will go away into everlasting [aionios] *punishment, but the righteous into eternal* [aionios] *life* (Matthew 25:46)

Jesus used the same adjective to describe the duration of hell as he did for heaven. If hell is merely temporary, then so is heaven. And if heaven is not a real place, it makes a nonsense of Christ's promise in John 14:3:

And if I go and prepare a place for you, I will come again and receive you to Myself; that where I am, there you may be also.

The Greek word *aionion* is used no less than 50 times to describe the eternal life of the believer (e.g. John 3:15-16, 10:28; Romans 5:21, 6:23) and it is used repeatedly to describe God's eternal nature (e.g. Romans 16:26; 1 Timothy 6:16; Hebrews 9:14). It is also used to emphasise the unending eternity we will experience as believers, in contrast to the temporary age of the present material world. If hell is not eternal (or real), then neither is heaven.

[7] The *Manifest Sons of God* movement takes its name from a misinterpretation of Romans 8:19, where Paul declares:

For the earnest expectation of the creation eagerly waits for the revealing of the sons of God.

Taken in the proper context of the surrounding verses instead of taking it in isolation and therefore out of context, Paul is referring to the bodily return of Jesus Christ, which will reverse the curse of futility imposed on God's creation (by God) since the fall (see verse 20). However, the *Manifest Sons of God* have reinterpreted Romans 8:19 to mean an elite group of Christians, meaning fallen creation is no longer waiting for the return of Jesus Christ, but instead this elite group of believers, who are glorified through progressive revelation of their "sonship". In this teaching the identity of Jesus Christ and the identity of the Body of Christ (the church) are utterly confused; the *Manifest Sons of God* see themselves **as** Christ. Some within the movement even teach an on-going incarnation of Christ and imply that Christ has to come within us before He can come to us. But then this is only the logical conclusion of a doctrine that transfers to an elite part of the church the rights and responsibilities that in Scripture are the sole remit of the resurrected Jesus Christ.

[8] Throughout the first two decades of the 20th century, apostasy began to take hold of more and more seminaries and ministry schools, so much so that in 1910, in an effort to stem the tide of growing apostasy, the General Assembly of the Presbyterian Church issued the *Five Fundamentals of the Faith*, which included:

1. The inspiration of Scripture

2. The virgin birth

3. The substitutionary atonement

4.   The resurrection of Christ

5.   The miracles of Christ

(They should have really issued a sixth fundamental of the faith: the Second Coming of Christ!).

Those who subscribed to the *Five Fundamentals of the Faith* were labelled "Fundamentalists", and so a new term was coined: the **Christian Fundamentalist**. Those who denied these fundamentals were regarded as Modernists or Liberals. The General Assembly reaffirmed these fundamentals in 1916 and 1923 in the face of continued and growing apostasy.

[9] Bob Jones - in 1991, Bob Jones was found to be having women undress in his office in order to "receive prophecy" (Olathe Daily News, USA 13/11/1991). He was exposed to be working out of a **demonic** spirit later in the 1990s by Clifford Hill (Clifford Hill audio tape, *Occult Links with Toronto Blessing*); something his associates acknowledged, but rather than deal with him in the appropriate Biblical way, he was allowed to continue in ministry after a short period of "reflection" by people who chose to be blinded to the demonic origins of the "signs and wonders" he was performing, instead of testing them against Scripture.

Jones claimed to have his own "portal" to the third heaven that he could use whenever he liked ("Beam me up Scottie!"). Anyone with a knowledge of the Eastern mystery religions and the *New Age Movement* will immediately recognise Jones' accounts of his visits to the third heaven as being experiences of astral projection, and nothing to do with the Word of God. During these many "translations" to the third heaven, Jones claimed to have been given revelations that are not only contrary to the clear teaching of Scripture, but can in fact very easily be identified as being *New Age* and occult in origin (www.youtube.com/watch?v=kGCTMEoifqQ). He even used a form of palm reading to discern matters! (www.youtube.com/watch?v=rOtI2H59vto).

Up until his death in 2014, Bob Jones continued to become more and more influential in charismatic circles to the point where he was treated as a wise old "elder-statesman" figure, instead of the demonised false prophet and false teacher he really was.

[10] Promise Keepers arose from within John Wimber's Vineyard movement in 1990 and was led by University of Colorado football coach Bill McCartney under the direction of his pastor James Ryle, who teaches the Beatles were "anointed by God" but lost their anointing when they broke up in 1970. According to researcher Russ Bellant, Ryle "believes Promise Keepers, of which he is a board member, is the fulfilment of the biblically prophesied End-Time army described in the Book of Joel, 'a terrifying army from which there is no escape.'"

At a Promise Keepers male-only rally in Colorado in 1993, 50,000 copies of the book, *The Masculine Journey: Understanding the Six Stages of Manhood* by Robert Hicks were distributed to attendees with the intention of this book being used as a handbook for living (an official study guide was also made available to guide small groups through the book). The content of this book is full of New Age phallic symbolism that has nothing to do with Biblical Christianity. Hicks states men should "worship God as phallic kinds of guys" and described Jesus as having "all the inherent phallic passions", and blames feminists for neutering Christ and downplaying the penis that made Christ "very much masculine" (page 181). Hicks says that the church needs to establish masculine initiation rites, because men experience more gender role conflict than women do. He urges church elders to congratulate young men on passing milestones of masculinity, and to wink at behaviour (such as premarital sex) that the Bible condemns as sin (page 176). Exactly what happens to the young women confessing similar indiscretions is not spelled out.

Promise Keepers promotes a form of male bonding that is **not** Biblical; male bonding is a homosexual concept and a *New Age* concept, but not a Biblical concept; the Bible teaches male fellowship. Male / female bonding is clearly outlined in Scripture where the Hebrew term *devek* (meaning "cling to") is used in Genesis 2:24.

The *Seven Principles of Promise Keepers* are not even Biblical, meaning anyone can adopt them. Membership of Promise Keepers is therefore full of men who are not born-again and are not even told they need to be.

[11] The word *apocrypha* means "hidden," while the word *deuterocanonical* means "second canon." The Apocrypha/Deuterocanonicals were written primarily in the time between the Old and New Testaments; the period known as the "400 silent years" or "intertestamental period" (meaning "between the testaments"), which began with the last words of Malachi written in 397BC. It is called the "400 silent years" specifically because during this period there was no new prophetic word from God, no divine visitations and no more Holy Scripture written, until God sent the angel Gabriel to announce the birth of John the Baptist and began to divinely inspire people to write the New Testament. The books of the Apocrypha are 1 Esdras, 2 Esdras, Tobit, Judith, Wisdom of Solomon, Ecclesiasticus, Baruch, the Letter of Jeremiah, Prayer of Manasseh, 1 Maccabees, and 2 Maccabees, as well as additions to the books of Esther and Daniel. Most, but not all of these books are included in Catholic Bibles.

Jews treated the Apocryphal books with respect, but never accepted them as true books of the Hebrew Bible; some of the Apocryphal books were (and still are) used by Jews for the historical information contained (only that which can be corroborated by other historical documents), but never for doctrine; there are many proven errors and contradictions in the doctrine contained in the Apocrypha.

The early Christian Church debated the status of the Apocrypha, but because it contradicted Old Testament Scriptures time and time again, few early Christians believed they belonged in the canon of Scripture. Whilst Roman Catholics treated the Apocrypha as a legitimate part of Scripture for centuries before, the Roman Catholic Church **officially** embraced it at the Council of Trent in the mid 1500sAD, mainly in response to the Protestant Reformation. The Apocrypha supports some of the Roman Catholic practices which cannot be supported from Scripture itself. For example, praying for the dead, petitioning "saints" in heaven for their prayers, worshiping angels, and "alms giving" atoning for sins.

[12] Pantheism is the view that God is everything and everyone and that everyone and everything is God. Pantheism is similar to polytheism (the belief in many gods), but goes beyond polytheism to teach that everything is God; God is all and in all. A tree is God, a rock is God, an animal is God, the sky is God, the sun is God, you are God, etc. Pantheism is the supposition behind many cults and false religions such as Hinduism, Buddhism (to an extent), the various unity and unification cults, and "mother nature" worshipers.

Does the Bible teach pantheism? No, it does not. What many people confuse as pantheism is the doctrine of God's omnipresence. Psalm 139:7-8 declares:

> *Where can I go from your Spirit? Or where can I flee from your presence? If I ascend into heaven, you are there; if I make my bed in hell, behold, You are there.*

God's omnipresence means He is present everywhere. There is no place in the universe where God is not present. This is not the same as pantheism. God is everywhere, but He is not all and in all; He is separate from His creation. Pantheism is not Biblical. Pantheism is addressed further within the section covering the teaching and philosophies of Agnes Sanford.

[13] Theosophical Society - In 1875, Helena Blavatsky (1831-1891) founded the *Theosophical Society* to specifically advance the spiritual principles of *theosophy*, literally meaning "god-wisdom" or "divine wisdom" from the Greek word *theosophia*. The purpose of the *Theosophical Society* was to strip away what was seen as the bigoted dogmas of Christianity and replace them with occult practices to achieve a state of "inner enlightenment" or of "divine wisdom." *Theosophy* teaches that all religions contain elements of "Ancient Wisdom" and that wise men throughout history have held the secret of spiritual power. Those who have been enlightened by the divine wisdom can access a transcendent spiritual reality through mystical experience. This is of course nothing new, it is the ancient heresy of Gnosticism. Like Hinduism, *theosophy* teaches reincarnation and a belief in karma.

Theosophists place their trust in Mahatma's, also referred to as Great Masters or the Adepts – those who have reached an exalted state of existence and who possess the sum of the world's accumulated knowledge. According to the *theosophists*, the Mahatmas are directing the spiritual evolution of mankind.

Theosophists contend that their philosophy is compatible with Christianity (and with Buddhism, Hinduism and all other religions), yet in reality it denies basic Christian doctrines such as the existence of a personal, infinite God and the need for repentance and forgiveness. It teaches that Christ was a "Great Soul" who inhabited the body of a man named Jesus for a few years (this also is an ancient Gnostic heresy).

The above is the seal of the *Theosophical Society*, which incorporates (amongst other things) the following symbols:

Ouroboros, the symbol of the serpent eating its own tail to signify continuation (or "the eternal return")

Star of David

Ankh, the Egyptian key of life

The Hindu sacred symbol of OHM, representing the greatest of all the Hindu mantras

Swastika, an ancient Hindu occult symbol that Blavatksy embraced long before the Nazis did

In 1887 Blavatsky founded **Lucifer**, a monthly magazine designed, as stated on its title page, "to bring to light the hidden things of darkness."

The fact that the *Theosophical Society* endorses Agnes Sanford's books should tell you all you need to know about the source of her theology and practice, yet John Wimber was happy to promote her books.

In her book, *The Secret Doctrine*, Blavatsky writes:

> Lucifer represents life... thought... progress... civilisation... liberty... independence... Lucifer is the logos, the Serpent, the Saviour.

> It is Satan who is the real God of our planet and only God.

> The celestial virgin which thus becomes the Mother of God and devils at one and the same time; for she is the ever loving beneficent deity. But in antiquity and in reality Lucifer or Luciferius is the name. Lucifer is the divine and terrestrial light, the 'Holy Ghost' and Satan at one and the same time.

Today, there are branches of the *Theosophical Society* all over the world and Blavatsky's influence on the advancement of the occult in the West cannot be underestimated. The following is a quote from the editors of the 1991 *New Age Almanac*:

> Madame Blavatsky ... stands out as the fountainhead of modern occult thought, and was either the originator and/or populariser of many of the ideas and terms which have a century later been assembled within the New Age Movement. The Theosophical Society, which she cofounded, has been the major advocate of occult philosophy in the West and the single most important avenue of Eastern teaching to the West (page 16).

Whilst most "ordinary" people have never heard of Helena Blavatsky, her influence on modern-day society is too significant and widespread to cover within the pages of this book, but just a couple of fascinating examples will suffice:

1. Elvis Presley was so taken with Blavatsky's book *The Voice of Silence* - which contains the supposed translation of ancient occultic Tibetan incantations - that he was known to sometimes read from it onstage in the middle of performances; and was even directly inspired by it to name his own gospel group, *Voice*.

2. Blavatsky's deeply occult ideas pervade the ideological fabric of J. K. Rowling's *Harry Potter* books and films, where she is even mentioned by name under the very thinly veiled anagram of Cassandra **Vablatsky**. Vablatsky's book titled *Unfogging the Future* is a required textbook for students taking Divination Classes at Hogwarts School of Witchcraft and Wizardry. Even J. K. Rowling's choice of Cassandra for her first name is a carefully chosen substitute for Helena, because in Greek mythology Cassandra was a Trojan princess who was given the power of prophecy by Apollo, but after she spurned his advances, he cursed her so nobody would believe the truth she spoke. As J. K. Rowling studied Greek mythology as part of her Classics degree at Exeter University, she would be very well aware of this, and has cunningly used the Harry Potter stories as a "Trojan horse" to influence millions of children with the occult teachings of Helena Blavatsky. Should anyone be sceptical of that fact, they can find articles on the *Theosophical Society of America* website enthusiastically acknowledging the Blavatsky teaching contained within the *Harry Potter* stories, and that Cassandra Vablatsky is a thinly veiled reference to its founder, Helena Blavatsky. In one particular telling scene from one of the *Harry Potter* movies, Harry shouts out, "Isis unveiled!" as he casts a spell, which just happens to be the title of one of Blavatsky's books (authored in 1877) in which she outlines her theosophical world-view.

No Christian parent should allow their children within a thousand miles of Harry Potter.

[14] Shekinah Glory - The word shekinah does not appear in the Bible, but the concept clearly does. The Jewish rabbis coined this extra-Biblical expression, a form of a Hebrew word that literally means "he caused to dwell," signifying that it was a divine visitation of the presence or dwelling of the Lord God on this earth. Exactly when the Shekinah was first evident in Scripture is the subject of a certain amount of debate, with some suggesting it is in Genesis 1:3 when God declared, *"Let there be light"*, while others suggesting it was in the burning bush of Exodus 3. Others still suggest the Shekinah was first evident when the Israelites set out from Succoth in their escape from Egypt. Exodus 13:20-22 outlines how the Lord appeared in a cloudy pillar in the day and a fiery pillar by night.

God spoke to Moses out of the pillar of cloud in Exodus 33, assuring him that His Presence would be with the Israelites (v9). Verse 11 says God spoke to Moses "face to face" out of the cloud, but when Moses asked to see God's glory, God told Him, *"You cannot see My face; for no man shall see Me, and live"* (v20). So, apparently, the visible manifestation of God's glory was somewhat muted. When Moses asked to see God's glory, God hid Moses in the cleft of a rock, covered him with His hand, and passed by. Then He removed His hand, and Moses saw only His back. This would seem to indicate that God's glory is too awesome and powerful to be seen completely by man, i.e. significantly more awesome and powerful than a bit of sparkly glitter coming from the air vents at Bill Johnson's *Bethel Church*.

The visible manifestation of God's presence was seen not only by the Israelites but also by the Egyptians:

> *During the last watch of the night the LORD looked down from the pillar of fire and cloud at the Egyptian army and threw it into confusion. He made the wheels of their chariots come off so that they had difficulty driving. And the Egyptians said, 'Let's get away from the Israelites! The LORD is fighting for them against Egypt'* (Exodus 14:24-25).

Just the presence of God's Shekinah glory was enough to convince His enemies that He was not someone to be resisted.

In the New Testament, Jesus Christ is the dwelling place of God's glory. Colossians 2:9 tells us that *"For in Him dwells all the fullness of the Godhead bodily"*, causing Jesus to exclaim to Philip, *"He who has seen Me has seen the Father"* (John 14:9). In Christ, we see the visible manifestation of God Himself in the second person of the Trinity. Although His glory was also veiled, Jesus is nonetheless the presence of God on earth. Just as the divine Presence dwelled in a relatively plain tent called the "tabernacle" before the Temple in Jerusalem was built, so did the Presence dwell in the relatively plain man who was Jesus. *"He has no form or comeliness [the quality of being good looking]; and when we see Him, there is no beauty that we should desire Him"* (Isaiah 53:2).

In conclusion, not only is God's Shekinah Glory infinitely more awesome and powerful than a bit of sparkly glitter coming from the air vents at *Bethel*, there is actually no need for God to show New Testament believers His Shekinah Glory. Whatever is manifesting at *Bethel*, it is demonstrably **not** God's presence.

[15] Oral Roberts (24/1/1918-15/12/2009) was a self-proclaimed healing evangelist who made an art-form out of scamming people out of money through mailshots in the post. He claimed a 900-feet tall Jesus personally appeared to him and told him God had chosen him to find a cure for cancer. This "revelation" came during a "seven-hour long conversation" he had with Jesus, who **instructed** him to ask each of his thousands of so-called "prayer partners" to send him $240.00 to complete the medical centre that would be set up for the purpose of curing cancer. Robert's "prayer partners" funded the project which cost over $200million. History proves this was a completely false vision and prophecy. There were no miracles, no cure for cancer, and the medical centre that **Jesus told** him to build soon went into bankruptcy. Yet did any of this adversely affect his reputation and influence within charismatic circles? Of course not.

Robert's claimed he discovered the sick would be healed if he touched them with his right hand; not with his left, just his right. Justification for this "gift" cannot be found anywhere in the Word of God, but is not uncommon in occult practices, and is very similar to the healing "gift" William Branham had (whom Roberts knew and revered).

In his book, *Miracle of Seed Faith* published in 1970, Robert's claimed God revealed to him that the principle of sowing and reaping observed in the physical world was also true in the spiritual world. One could "plant" a monetary gift in a ministry and "reap" miracles in return. This was the birth of the utterly false doctrine of "seed faith" that has made countless "faith teachers" grotesquely wealthy at the expense of gullible and deceived Christians.

Oral Roberts was a money-hungry false prophet and if he did have a "gift" for healing in his right hand, it was demonstrably **not** from God, but that did not prevent Bill Johnson from asking Roberts for his healing "anointing". And just so you know, four hours after Oral Roberts claimed a complete healing at the hand of Paul Crouch on television, he was admitted to hospital with a major coronary. And as for Bill Johnson, in spite of him refusing to create a theology that allows for sickness, his father died of cancer, his son is 90% clinically deaf and he himself wears spectacles!

[16] The Desert Fathers were a group of semi-mystics trying to escape the growing worldliness of the pre-Nicean church by adopting a hermit lifestyle in the deserts of the Middle East (mainly in the Scetes desert in Egypt). These so-called "Desert Fathers" based their spiritual practices not on the teachings and practices of the first century apostles, but on the priests and monks of the pagan mystery religions they came into contact with (such as Buddhism and Hinduism). The mystical monastic traditions derived from the practices of the Desert Fathers is from where the Roman Catholic Church gets almost all its spiritual practices, such as the use of prayer ropes (rosary beads), prayer labyrinths, lectio divina and contemplative/centering prayer; all of which have been embraced by the Emergent Church in more recent years and packaged as "Vintage Christianity". It is nothing of the sort; it is nothing more than vintage paganism.

Cardinal John Henry Newman (1801-1890), regarded as the greatest Catholic thinker Britain has ever produced, who Rome want to canonise as a saint (he converted from Anglicanism), stated:

> At least seventy percent of the rights, rituals, customs and traditions of Roman Catholicism are of pagan origin.

[17] John G. Lake (18/3/1870-16/9/1935) is regarded as a significant contributor to the development of Pentecostalism and is very much revered by many of today's

charismatic Christians. He spent time in ministry at John Alexander Dowie's city of Zion, and actively promoted Dowie's theology on healing. It was John G. Lake who first opened "healing rooms", which remain so popular today with many charismatic/evangelical Christians (which were directly influenced by Dowie's "faith cure homes"). Did Jesus or any of his apostles need to open a healing room? Mike Bickle has stated that Lake influenced him "more than any man other than Jesus", and the complete works of John G. Lake are available for purchase at IHOP. However, Lake's doctrine was far from orthodox. For example, the following statements come from his own sermons recorded in a book titled *John G. Lake: His Life, His Sermons, His Boldness of Faith*, published in 1994 by Kenneth Copeland Publications:

> The power of God, the Holy Ghost, is the Spirit of Dominion, it makes one a god (page 13).

> God was in Christ, wasn't he? An incarnation. God is in you, an incarnation, if you were born again. You are incarnate (page 196).

> God's purpose through Jesus Christ is to deify the nature of man (page 304).

You can see why Kenneth Copeland would publish Lake's sermons!

One of the most bizarre teachings of John G. Lake was something that is very plainly forbidden in Scripture: communication with the dead. He taught that communication with the dead was perfectly acceptable as long as it involved calling them down from heaven and not calling them up from hell! The Bible makes no such distinction and forbids any kind of communication with the dead. For example, Isaiah 8:19-20 could not be any clearer on this matter. Lake was very open about how he communicated with his dead wife, never once considering the possibility it was a deceiving spirit impersonating his dead wife.

Equally bizarre and unbiblical was Lake's belief that you could receive sin impulses from other people if they laid hands on you.

In addition to his numerous very false doctrines, he was also exposed as a fraud. According to the *Oregonian* (24/7/1921 and subsequent issues), Lake was arrested, charged and forced to settle out of court for a fraud in which he promised members of his congregation stock in a mining company in return for paying their tithe to the church in a lump sum. He never delivered on this promise.

The same newspaper reported on 25th August 1921 that Lake had been arrested and had to post a $100 bond for impersonating a police officer.

On 21st November 1933, Lake placed an advert in the *Oregonian* for an Arab healer called Abdul Ben Shinandar visiting his church. Only four days after the advert was placed by Lake, the Oregonian exposed Lake as the Arab healer in costume.

Even more disturbingly, on 24th May 1920 the *Oregonian* recorded the arrest of Lake after the death of Hanna Anderson, who died of neglect after his attempt to heal her of flu failed and no medical treatment was administered because her illness was not reported. Not only did Lake fail to heal Hanna, but he committed a criminal offense by failing to report the illness to authorities.

[18] "Dominion" theology teaches that the church will take dominion of the earth by subduing and conquering the "seven cultural mountains" of this world:

1. Religion
2. Family
3. Education
4. Government
5. Media
6. Arts and Entertainment
7. Business

[19] Who are the 144,000 described in Revelation 7? Paul Cain attributes to the church just about everything and anything described in the book of Revelation. I dealt within the main body of the book the blasphemy of believing the "man child" of Revelation 12 is the church, but I want to address here Cain's claim that the 144,000 described in Revelation 7 is also the church, because this is not a belief exclusive to the *Prophetic Movement*; it is a teaching broadly accepted by most of the church and is merely a symptom of the wider problem of the church being taught that it has replaced Israel in the plans and purposes of God.

Revelation 7:4 states:

> *And I heard the number of those who were sealed. One hundred and forty-four thousand of all the tribes of the children of Israel were sealed:*

As if that is not clear enough, Revelation 7:5-8 then goes on to specifically list 12,000 from each of the 12 tribes of Israel. Revelation 7:3 says these 144,000 are sealed on their foreheads, which gives them divine protection from all of the judgments of God, and from the Antichrist, to perform their mission during the tribulation period (see Revelation 6:17, in which people will wonder who can stand from the wrath to come). The tribulation period is a future seven-year period of time in which God will enact divine judgment against those who reject Him and will complete His plan of salvation for the nation of Israel. All of this is according to God's revelation to the prophet Daniel (Daniel 9:24–27). The 144,000 Jews are a sort of "first fruits" (Revelation 14:4) of a redeemed Israel which has been previously prophesied (Zechariah 12:10; Romans 11:25–27), and their mission will be to evangelize the world after the church is raptured and proclaim the gospel during the tribulation period. The 144,000 is **not** the church, but will be God's witness to the world once the church has been raptured; the church is **never** identified as the tribes of Israel **anywhere** in the Bible.

As a result of the witness of the 144,000 sealed Jews, millions will come to faith in Christ, and this is referenced in Revelation 7:9-10:

> *After these things I looked, and behold, a great multitude which no one could number, of all nations, tribes, peoples, and tongues, standing before the throne and before the Lamb, clothed with white robes, with palm branches in their hands, [10] and crying out with a loud voice, saying, "Salvation belongs to our God who sits on the throne, and to the Lamb!"*

For the sake of thoroughness it is worth noting that when looking at the tribal names listed, some have concluded the tribe of Ephraim is missing, but this is not accurate. In place of the name of Ephraim there is the name of his father Joseph (verse 8), but it is the same tribe.

One tribe however is missing, namely the tribe of Dan, and the reason why has been the cause of much speculation. A popular theory is that it is because either the Antichrist or False Prophet will arise out of the tribe of Dan, but there is absolutely nothing to indicate this in Scripture anywhere.

[20] Hillsong may be financially rich with income of $100 million a year from its tax exempt Australian operations, but it is spiritually bankrupt (Revelation 3:17). Many examples could be given to demonstrate this, but just one will suffice. In a sermon transmitted on Hillsong.com/TV in March 2015 (and widely available on YouTube), Brian Houston, leader of the global Hillsong megachurch empire, preached the following:

> Do you know – take it all the way back to the Old Testament and the Muslims and you, we actually serve the same God. Allah to Muslims, to us Abba Father God.

This blasphemous declaration should have had the entire congregation stampeding for the exit (closely followed by the cancellation of their heavy tithing commitment), but instead it was met by rapturous applause and approving nods from the thousands of people sat there happy to have their itching ears scratched with false doctrine. In an interview with Brian Houston recorded in the *Sydney Morning Herald* on 3oth January 2003, a reporter asked Houston why his church was so successful in Australia, which is a long way away from the American Bible belt. Houston replied, "We are scratching people where they are itching". Indeed they are doing just that, which is literally fulfilling prophecy:

For the time will come when they will not endure sound doctrine, but according to their own desires, because they have itching ears, they will heap up for themselves teachers (2 Timothy 4:3).

Let us be clear, Allah is **not** YAHWEH. Islam claims God has no son; it claims Jesus was just a prophet who did not die on the cross or rise from the dead, but Paul declares:

And if Christ is not risen, your faith is futile; you are still in your sins! (1 Corinthians 15:17).

According to 1 John 2:22 Islam is an antichrist religion:

Who is a liar but he who denies that Jesus is the Christ? He is antichrist who denies the Father and the Son.

[21] People often ask why Nebuchadnezzar's dream referenced only four specific kingdoms when (secular) history records many more kingdoms and empires. For example, why did his dream not include the great Indian Empire, or the Chinese Empire? The answer is simple: out of all the kingdoms that have come and gone throughout history, these specific kingdoms are referenced in Nebuchadnezzar's dream because they are relevant to **Israel**; all the kingdoms referenced in Nebuchadnezzar's dream at one time or another held control of **Israel**.

APPENDIX 1
DOWIE'S LEGACY ON HEALING

John Alexander Dowie's theology on healing remains the absolute bedrock of both modern-day Pentecostalism and the Charismatic Movement it subsequently spawned (which is now the dominant force driving evangelical Christianity). Its continuing prominence can be evidenced by examining the theology of a man who is at the very forefront of the charismatic/evangelical world: *Bethel's* Bill Johnson.

Amongst the many sermons of Johnson I have read and watched on video, I came across a video of a question and answer session in which Johnson was asked if God ever causes sickness. He started to answer the question by making reference to the time when Jesus was sleeping in the boat and a great storm began. He made no reference to where this story occurs in Scripture, and I can only surmise this is because he did not want anyone realising that he then goes on to directly misquote it for the purpose of answering the question. The story he referred to is in Matthew 8:23-27; Mark 4:35-40 and Luke 8:22-25, so for the purpose of fairness let us look at the relevant passages in all three gospels:

> *Now when He got into a boat, His disciples followed Him. And suddenly a great tempest arose on the sea, so that the boat was covered with the waves. But He was asleep. Then His disciples came to Him and awoke Him, saying, "Lord, save us! We are perishing!" But He said to them, "Why are you fearful, O you of little faith?" Then He arose and rebuked the winds and the sea, and there was a great calm. So the men marvelled, saying, "Who can this be, that even the winds and the sea obey Him?"* (Matthew 8:23-27).

> *Then He arose and rebuked the wind, and said to the sea, "Peace, be still!" And the wind ceased and there was a great calm. But He said to them, "Why are you so fearful? How is it that you have no faith?"* (Mark 4:39-40).

> *And they came to Him and awoke Him, saying, "Master, Master, we are perishing!" Then He arose rebuked the wind and the raging of the water. And they ceased, and there was a calm* (Luke 8:24).

In the video Johnson said that:

> Jesus slept through the storm because the world He was sleeping in had no storm; He was living in a realm of kingdom reality and actually living in a realm called peace.

This pseudo-spiritual clap-trap sounds lovely, but is not based in the reality of Scripture. Jesus lived in and through the very same world and experiences (and temptations) that his disciples did (Hebrews 4:15), but still overcame them (Hebrews 2:18). If that were not so it would render His sacrifice as utterly pointless and without power.

Johnson then goes on to explain that, "The disciples woke Jesus up and He **released peace** onto the storm to still it." This is utter rubbish and a total and deliberate misquoting of Scripture. Matthew 8, Mark 4 and Luke 8 all say that Jesus *"rebuked the winds and the sea"*; He did not quell the storm by releasing peace onto it, He **rebuked** it. Mark 4 certainly tells us that Jesus said, *"Peace, be still!"*, but after He had **rebuked** it to be still; He **commanded** the storm to **be** still. He did not **release** peace onto, or into, the storm.

This deliberate misquoting of Scripture by a world famous teacher and pastor who is at the forefront of the charismatic/evangelical world is bad enough in itself, as it completely misrepresents the Biblical truth of what happened and what Jesus actually did, but the reason why Johnson misrepresented Matthew 8, Mark 4 and Luke 8 is even worse. He did it in an attempt to find Biblical justification for his wider false doctrine that God cannot and does not cause sickness—one bad premise is used to justify another bad premise; the only way he can find Biblical justification for his Dowie's theology on healing is to misquote and misrepresent Scripture.

Returning to the question of whether or not God can ever cause sickness, Johnson went on to explain that, "You can only give away what you have, and this is why Jesus was able to give away peace in order to calm the storm" (ignoring of course the misquoting and misrepresentation of the story about Jesus and the storm and that Jesus in fact **rebuked** the storm and did not calm it by releasing peace onto it). He then asked the question, "Can God give away sickness?", and then answered his own question by smugly saying, "No, God cannot get sick, therefore God cannot give away sickness, because you can only give away what you have."

We all agree with the first part of Johnson's statement: "God cannot get sick". However, as with so much of his teaching, this little truth is then mixed in with a huge untruth by claiming God therefore cannot give sickness, which then creates a false principle about God that Scripture itself totally contradicts. Here are just a few examples from the Bible of God **giving** (causing) sickness, which Dowie and Johnson blissfully ignore:

> *But the hand of the Lord was heavy on the people of Ashdod, and He ravaged them and struck them with tumours* (1 Samuel 5:6).

> *So the anger of the Lord was aroused against them, and He departed. And when the cloud departed from above the tabernacle, suddenly Miriam became leprous, as white as snow. Then Aaron turned toward Miriam, and there she was, a leper* (Numbers 12:9-10).

So the Lord said to Moses and Aaron, "Take for yourselves handfuls of ashes from a furnace, and let Moses scatter it toward the heavens in the sight of Pharaoh. And it will become fine dust in all the land of Egypt, and it will cause boils that break out in sores on man and beast throughout all the land of Egypt." Then they took ashes from the furnace and stood before Pharaoh, and Moses scattered them toward heaven. And they caused boils that break out in sores on man and beast (Exodus 9:8-10).

Then Uzziah became furious; and he had a censer in his hand to burn incense. And while he was angry with the priests, leprosy broke out on his forehead, before the priests in the house of the Lord, beside the incense altar. And Azariah the chief priest and all the priests looked at him, and there, on his forehead, he was leprous; so they thrust him out of that place. Indeed he also hurried to get out, because the Lord had struck him (2 Chronicles 26:19-20).

So on a set day Herod, arrayed in royal apparel, sat on his throne and gave an oration to them. And the people kept shouting, "The voice of a god and not of a man!" Then immediately an angel of the Lord struck him, because he did not give glory to God. And he was eaten by worms and died (Acts 12:21-23).

Daniel 4 tells us that Nebuchadnezzar was driven to madness by God, and John 9:1-3 even gives us an example of God allowing disease – blindness – not as a punishment, but to reveal Himself and His mighty works through that blindness and the subsequent healing by Christ:

Now as Jesus passed by, He saw a man who was blind from birth. And His disciples asked Him, saying, "Rabbi, who sinned, this man or his parents, that he was born blind?" Jesus answered, "Neither this man nor his parents sinned, but that the works of God should be revealed in him".

A further New Testament example is provided in Acts 13:4-12 where Paul inflicts blindness on the sorcerer Bar-Jesus.

So, does God have tumours, or leprosy, or boils, or madness, or blindness? Of course not! God gave all these things (and more) to people, but does not have them Himself, thus proving without question that Johnson's doctrine is not Biblical. This error is the very basis for his theology that causes him to claim: "I refuse to create a theology that allows for sickness." But then Johnson does not follow a Biblical doctrine on sickness, he follows the false doctrine of John Alexander Dowie.

To further disprove Johnson's false claim that God cannot give away what He does not have (being of course used to try to persuade us that God does not cause sickness), let us briefly look at the subject of evil spirits. The Bible is clear that God is not evil. He does not have any evil in Him, so by Johnson's logic and doctrine that means God cannot send evil spirits to people. However, Scripture is clear that God **did** send evil spirits to people to be used for His divine purposes:

> *Now the distressing spirit from the Lord came upon Saul as he sat in his house with his spear in his hand* (1 Samuel 19:9).

> *God sent a spirit of ill will between Abimelech and the men of Shechem; and the men of Shechem dealt treacherously with Abimelech* (Judges 9:23).

> *Therefore look! The Lord has put a lying spirit in the mouth of all these prophets of yours, and the Lord has declared disaster against you* (1 Kings 22:23).

I could use other examples from Scripture, but will allow the above to suffice for the sake of brevity.

Johnson's claim that God cannot cause sickness because He cannot get sick is utter rubbish and relies on his audience knowing less about Scripture than he does; and judging by the whooping and clapping by the watching audience in response to his ridiculous statement, that was clearly the case in the video I watched.

Men like Bill Johnson can "refuse to create a theology that allows for sickness" if they want, but it is entirely something else when they teach other people this unbiblical error. James 3:1 warns that teachers will be judged more severely. It is undeniable that God **does** sometimes intentionally allow, or even **cause** sickness to accomplish His sovereign purposes. While sickness is not directly addressed in the passage, Hebrews 12:5-11 describes God disciplining those He **loves** (verse 6) to *"produce a harvest of righteousness"* (verse 11). Psalm 23:4 speaks of the Shepherd (God) using both the rod and the staff with the flock. The rod is used to discipline and the staff is used to guide.

Being in a relationship with God is not all about us demanding blessing from Him; we work out our salvation *"with fear and trembling"* (Philippians 2:12). Sickness **can** be a means of God's **loving** discipline. It is difficult for us to comprehend why God would work in this manner, but it is nevertheless clear from Scripture that He can and does. One of the clearest examples of this in Scripture is found is Psalm 119. Notice the progression through verses 67, 71, and 75:

> *Before I was afflicted I went astray, but now I obey your word...It was good for me to be afflicted so that I might learn your decrees...I know, O LORD, that your laws are righteous, and in faithfulness you have afflicted me.*

The author of Psalm 119 is doing what Johnson fails to do: he looks at suffering from **God's** perspective. It was good for the Psalmist to be afflicted. It was faithfulness that caused God to afflict him. The result of the affliction was that he could learn God's decrees and obey His Word.

Clearly sickness is not part of God's **eternal** plan for His creation, but neither is sin and death and Christians still sin and die! We were not originally made to die and leave our bodies and be unclothed spirits (2 Corinthians 5:1-4), so let me state categorically that sickness and death are tragic and I long for the day when that last enemy is put under the feet of King Jesus (1 Corinthians 15:26). However, just like Dowie before him, Johnson's theology on healing demands **now** that which God has planned to be totally fulfilled only later in eternity, i.e. the total eradication of all sickness. Just like Dowie, Johnson puts the proverbial "cart before the horse" by trying to apply to earth now what God has planned for His eternal Kingdom. This false theology makes demands of God now, and if those demands are not met, the problem must reside with the person who remains in sickness. Does God heal? Of course He does. Do I pray for healing? Of course I do; but it is **not** necessarily God's will to heal every time we ask. Furthermore, healing is **not** automatically a part of salvation, as Johnson (and many others) claim; I have already demonstrated how God can and does use sickness to fulfil His purposes. Johnson's refusal "to create a theology that allows for sickness" is of course rooted in Dowie's doctrine of "healing in the atonement" i.e. his understanding and interpretation of the meaning of that phrase – "healing in the atonement".

HEALING IN THE ATONEMENT

Dowie claimed that healing is a **right** and something God is obligated to do for every Christian through "healing in the atonement". This false doctrine claims Christ died for our sins and suffered for our healing. It divides the atonement up between what Christ did on the cross and the suffering He experienced prior to going to the cross. This is based on a misrepresentation of Isaiah 53:5:

> *But He was wounded for our transgressions, He was bruised for our iniquities; the chastisement for our peace was upon Him, and by His stripes we are healed.*

"By His stripes we are healed" - The context here is of healing from **iniquity (sin)**. Christians who believe in the doctrine of "healing in the atonement" in the way taught by Dowie and those who followed him completely ignore the obvious context; they take the text out of its context, isolate it from its cotext and create a pretext. Isaiah 53 v 5 is quoted twice in the New Testament:

1. Romans 4 v 25, where the context is again Jesus' suffering for our **sins**.

2. 1 Peter 2 v 24-25, where the context is again that of healing from **sin**.

It is clear Johnson is aware of the New Testament use of the Greek word *sozo* for salvation, because he runs a specific ministry by that name. On the *Bethel* website sozo is claimed to mean "saved, healed and delivered" – *Sozo* contains the whole package of being made whole or well." *Sozo* actually more accurately means "to save, keep safe and sound, to rescue from danger or destruction". It is derived from an obsolete Greek word *saos* that simply meant "safe". It is a verb that is translated as "to save" and the noun form, *soteria*, is translated "salvation". The big question is: is there physical healing in the atonement? I would have to say yes, there is a physical aspect to salvation, and whilst the use of the Greek word *sozo* in the New Testament is mainly in the context of spiritual healing from sin, it can and does have a physical application. Matthew 8:16-17 testifies to this:

> *When evening had come, they brought to Him many who were demon-possessed. And He cast out the spirits with a word, and healed all who were sick, that it might be fulfilled which was spoken by Isaiah the prophet, saying: "He Himself took our infirmities and bore our sicknesses.*

What Jesus did in Matthew 8:16-17 was in fulfilment of Isaiah 53. This proves that the atonement cannot be divided up as people like Johnson teaches. The events described in Matthew 8:16-17 occurred **before** Calvary; they were **before** the atonement. Christ did take upon Himself our infirmities and bore our sicknesses as He looked forward to what He would achieve **on the cross**. Christ atoned for our sins **and** our physical infirmities **on the cross**. Scripture makes absolutely no distinction or separation between how Christ paid the price for our sins and how He physically suffered for our physical infirmities; a distinction between the two has to be read **into** Scripture in order for people like Johnson to cling to Dowie's false doctrine and to say he "refuses to create a theology that allows for sickness" because he believes God is obligated to heal all Christian's physical ailments through Christ's physical suffering - *"by His stripes we are healed"*.

Everything Christ atoned for was done on the cross and everything Christ did on the cross was for sin. All the physical ailments that come to mankind are as a result of sin, and Christ dealt with sin on the cross. Is there, therefore, healing in the atonement? Yes, but not in the way men like Johnson (and many like him) claim. It is not because of Christ's suffering i.e. *"His stripes"* healing us, and it is not something God is obligated to provide for every Christian here and now.

Salvation means that we will all be truly and fully saved from all our enemies: the Devil, death, sickness, sin etc., but not all now. Part of this has an eternal aspect that Johnson refuses to accept. We can say we are saved (*sozo'd*) now, because it has already been accomplished in Christ's death and His being risen. We still look in faith to the **future** manifestation of it when we too are raised in our glorified bodies and are fully and eternally set free from sickness and death. This is what Romans 8:22-25 teaches:

> For we know that the whole creation groans and labours with birth pangs together until now. Not only that, but we also who have the first fruits of the Spirit, even we ourselves groan within ourselves, eagerly waiting for the adoption, the redemption of our body. For we were saved in this hope, but hope that is seen is not hope; for why does one still hope for what he sees? But if we hope for what we do not see, we eagerly wait for it with perseverance.

I cannot imagine that any Bible-believing Christian would disagree when I say that Paul was as complete a Christian as there will ever be on this earth, yet he said his condition was that of groaning within himself, "**waiting** *for the redemption of the body*". He said the redemption of the body was a hope, not a present possession. In Romans 8:10 Paul says the body is dead because of sin. The Christian has eternal life; his sins are forgiven; his name is written in heaven; he is a child of God. However, the Christian lives in a body that is under the curse of death, and the Christian lives in a world which is still under the curse of God because of sin—a world which "*groans and labours*". Therefore, whilst the Christian can live a life of victory and fruitfulness through the power of the indwelling Holy Spirit, he is still under the influence of the troubles and pains of this wicked and corrupt world. Whilst God can and does heal the sick, the full release from the troubles of the flesh will come at the "*redemption of the body*" (Romans 8:23). Making a doctrine that says anything more than that is just plain wrong. Even Jesus Himself only performed healings when "*the power was present*" (Luke 6:17). For us to command from God healing on people at our will is something even Christ did not do. We should not blame people who remain sick, as if it is somehow their fault.

In his 2009 autobiography, Chuck Smith writes:

> Grace does not shield the cruel realities of a world damaged by the fall. We are not in heaven yet and God does not spare us from the crushing blows that come to everyone. We lose people we love, we suffer, we grieve, we journey on, but we are not abandoned.

This is the reality for every believer in Jesus Christ whilst on earth, including those who professed otherwise; Dowies' daughter died from severe burns; Mother Etter's life was characterised by personal tragedy, with all her children predeceasing her; William Seymour suffered from small pox, which left him blind in one eye; Charles Parham spent much of his life sick and both his sons died prematurely from illness;

Smith Wigglesworth's wife and two sons died of illness, his daughter was deaf and he himself suffered from gallstones; Aimee Semple McPherson died from an overdose of the medications she was taking for the various conditions she suffered from; Kathryn Kuhlman suffered from a heart condition that eventually killed her; Bill Johnson's son Eric is clinically deaf and has a speech impediment (and both Bill and Beni Johnson of course wear spectacles). If Dowie's theology of healing in the atonement is correct, none of these things would happen in this lifetime.

But sadly, Dowie's legacy lives on.

APPENDIX 2
WOMEN CHURCH LEADERS

In addition to Mother Etter, Aimee Semple Mcpherson and Kathryn Kuhlman all being divorcees (and God's view of divorce is clear from Scripture), and their ministries being founded on John Alexander Dowie's erroneous understanding of healing in the atonement (which also underpins the modern-day Word of Faith Movement), they also each pastored a church and exercised spiritual authority over men, which the Bible forbids. In spite of the Bible being very clear on this issue, there is barely a denomination within Christianity that has not been disobedient on this matter.

This is not an issue of women's rights, or a question of gender equality; it is a matter of being obedient to the will of God. There is no issue with women holding positions of authority over men in the business world, but the church is not to be run in the way one would run a secular business. Sadly however, that is exactly what is being done in all too many churches today; the clear Biblical teaching on women pastors is all too often judged in the way the world sees it, rather than by how God sees it.

Paul declares:

> *I do not permit a woman to teach or to have authority over a man, but to be in silence* (1 Timothy 2:12)

The context of what Paul is declaring is the **church**; women should not have authority over men in the church. Why? He provides the answer in the following verse:

> *For Adam was formed first, then Eve. And Adam was not deceived, but the woman being deceived, fell into transgression* (1 Timothy 2:13-14).

Consider also 1 Timothy 3:1-7:

> *This is a faithful saying: If a **man** desires the position of a bishop, **he** desires a good work. ² A bishop then must be blameless, the **husband of one wife**, temperate, sober-minded, of good behaviour, hospitable, able to teach; ³ not given to wine, not violent, not greedy for money, but gentle, not quarrelsome, not covetous; ⁴ one who rules **his** own house well, having his children in submission with all reverence ⁵ (for if a **man** does not know how to rule **his** own house, how will **he** take care of the church of God?); ⁶ not a novice, lest being puffed up with pride **he** fall into the same condemnation as the devil. ⁷ Moreover he must have a good testimony among those who are outside, lest **he** fall into reproach and the snare of the devil (emphasis added).*

The number of masculine pronouns (*"he"* and *"his"*) speaks for itself. The role of an elder/overseer must be filled by a man. The phrase *"husband of one wife"* further makes clear that the office of elder is intended to be fulfilled by men. The same points are also made in the parallel passage of Titus 1:5-9.

God assigns different roles for men and women in the church and women should not have spiritual authority over men within church because of the way sin entered the world. This includes preaching to them, teaching them publicly, and exercising spiritual authority over them. Mother Etter, Aimee Semple McPherson and Kathryn Kuhlman all did exactly the opposite, as do many women in ministry today.

A common argument against Paul's instruction in 1 Timothy is that it is not directed at women today and was only intended for the women of the first century, who were (it is claimed) typically poorly educated. This is however an argument out of total silence, because nowhere does Paul mention the issue of education. In fact, if education was the qualification for ministry, most of the men Jesus chose as His apostles would have also been excluded from ministry.

As 1 Timothy was written to Timothy, who was the pastor of the church at Ephesus, a further common objection to Paul's instruction is that it was specifically intended for the women at Ephesus only, which was a place where women did have spiritual authority over men at the pagan temple dedicated to Artemis (known as Diana in the Roman pantheon of gods). It is therefore argued that Paul is merely reacting to the female-dominated pagan practices that were so prevalent in Ephesus at the time, and is trying to draw a clear distinction between Christian and pagan practices. Again however, this is an argument out of silence, because Paul does not mention Artemis anywhere in his epistle to Timothy, nor does he make reference to the practices of Artemis worshipers as a reason for his restrictions on women.

A third common objection is that the context of what Paul is saying is husbands and wives, and therefore not women in general, and indeed the Greek words used in 1 Timothy 2 **could** refer to husbands and wives. However, the basic meaning of the words is in fact broader than that, and the same Greek words are used in 1 Timothy 2:8-10:

> *I desire therefore that the men pray everywhere, lifting up holy hands, without wrath and doubting; in like manner also, that the women adorn themselves in modest apparel, with propriety and moderation, not with braided hair or gold or pearls or costly clothing, but, which is proper for women professing godliness, with good works.*

Is Paul saying only **husbands** are to lift up holy hands in prayer without wrath and doubting? Is Paul saying only **wives** should dress modestly, do good works and worship God? Of course not. Paul's instruction is clearly directed at all men and women, not just husbands and wives.

But what about women who did hold positions of authority and leadership in the Bible? For example, what about Miriam, Deborah and Huldah from the Old Testament, whom God chose to fulfil special service to Him? Whilst these women from the Old Testament are to be held up as models of faith and leadership, they are of absolutely no relevance to the issue of pastoral authority in a New Testament church; the church was a new concept and structure that was only revealed through the epistles of the New Testament. The authority structure of the New Testament church is unique to the New Testament church and what God did in the Old Testament for the nation of Israel has no relevance; you cannot build a doctrine for the church from the Old Testament, particularly when it contradicts the New Testament!

But what about women mentioned in the New Testament, such as Priscilla and Phoebe? Supporters of women pastors make much of the fact that in Acts 18 where Priscilla and Aquila are mentioned as being faithful ministers in Christ, Priscilla's name is mentioned first, perhaps indicating she was the more prominent of the two in ministry. This is yet again merely an argument out of silence, because the Bible does not say Priscilla pastored a church, taught publicly or had any spiritual authority over a congregation of believers. In fact, even if one's argument is based on which name is mentioned first, it is worthy of note that in Acts 18:26 when Priscilla and Aquila took Apollos to one side and explained the gospel to him, it is Aquila who is mentioned first, not Priscilla.

Proponents of women pastors appeal to Romans 16:1 where Phoebe is called a servant in the church, because some Bible versions use the term "deacon". However, as with Priscilla, there is no mention at all of Phoebe being a pastor, or teacher of men in the church. 1 Timothy 3:1-13 and Titus 1:6-9 gives being able to teach as a qualification for elders within a church, not deacons (servants).

The structure of 1 Timothy 2:11–14 makes the reason why women cannot be pastors perfectly clear. Verse 13 begins with *"for,"* giving the cause of Paul's statement in verses 11–12. Why should women not teach or have authority over men? Because *"Adam was formed first, then Eve. And Adam was not deceived; but the woman…"* (verse 13–14). God created Adam first and then created Eve to be a "helper" for Adam. The order of creation has universal application in the family (Ephesians 5:22–33) and in the church, and ignoring this creates significant challenges for both the structure and success of families and churches.

The fact that Eve was deceived is also given in 1 Timothy 2:14 as a reason for women not serving as pastors, or having spiritual authority over men. This does not mean that women are gullible, or they are all more easily deceived than men. If all women are more easily deceived, why would they be allowed to teach children (who are themselves easily deceived) and other women (who are supposedly more easily deceived)? The text simply says that women are not to teach men, or have spiritual authority over men because Eve was deceived. God has chosen to give men the primary teaching authority in the church, with women having other gifts such as hospitality, mercy, teaching, evangelism, and helps. The effectiveness of the church depends on both men and women exercising their gifts and callings as God determines. Women in church are not restricted from public praying or prophesying (1 Corinthians 11:5), only from having spiritual teaching authority over men. The Bible nowhere restricts women from exercising the gifts of the Holy Spirit (1 Corinthians 12). Women, just as much as men, are called to minister to others, to demonstrate the fruit of the Spirit (Galatians 5:22–23), and to proclaim the gospel to the lost (Matthew 28:18–20; Acts 1:8; 1 Peter 3:15).

But God has ordained that only **men** are to serve in positions of spiritual teaching authority in the church, and this very simple instruction was ignored by Mother Etter, Aimee Semple McPherson, Kathryn Kuhlman, and countless women since. This is not because men are necessarily better teachers, or because God thinks women are inferior or less intelligent, but because it is simply the way God designed the church to function. In their lives, words and spiritual leadership, men are to set the example, with women taking a less authoritative role, and when that is violated the Devil has every right to gain a foothold. Women are encouraged to teach other women (Titus 2:3–5), and God does not restrict women from teaching children. The only activity women are restricted from is teaching, or having spiritual authority over men. This precludes women from serving as pastors to men. This does not make women less important in any way, but rather gives them a ministry focus more in agreement with God's plan and His gifting of them.

APPENDIX 3
TODD BENTLEY

I have given Todd Bentley his very own appendix because I am firmly convinced he is the most demonised individual claiming to be a Christian since William Branham; they do indeed have the same anointing, but **not** an anointing from God.

Todd Bentley was born in 1976 in the small town of Sechelt, located on the lower Sunshine Coast of British Columbia, Canada. His parents divorced while Bentley was very young and from an early age he was involved in drugs and alcohol. At the age of 15, he was convicted of sexually abusing a 13 year old boy and spent time in several different prisons. At the age of 17, Bentley was hospitalised after an overdose of amphetamines and hallucinogenic pills. He was a very troubled young man.

Just like his spiritual mentor, William Branham, so too Bentley had deep experience of the occult and contact with demonic spirits during his formative years. For example, on pages 47-48 of his book, *Journey into the Miraculous*, Bentley writes:

> I wasn't a satanist, but dabbled in many areas of the occult… Because of my drugs and growing communication with evil spirits, there was a high level of demonic activity in my home. Once, while getting a glass of water, something violently, physically shook my mother – even though she was alone. [A friend of Todd's father] George held garage sales every Sunday in a big old house. When he died, a spirit posing as his ghost grabbed me and awoke me at night. Even after I left home, my mother continued to have weird demonic encounters, because I'd opened the door to that realm.

> I would communicate with spirits from the grave and ask different ones to visit and empower me. Whole high, a familiar spirit that I believed to be the

presence of Jim Morrison [who was a self-confessed Satanist], would visit me. Though I never actually saw the spirit, I'd feel its presence. It would fill me with mystic feelings, and I actually believed that when I died, I'd spend eternity in bliss with Jim.

I'd also, for a time, get high on speed or acid, and listen to his group, *The Doors* for six-hour stretches, and also watch his movie repeatedly. I loved and worshiped the guy! That's not just a figure of speech – I literally felt that way toward him.

One day, I met a girl who also liked *The Doors*. Together, we'd get high on acid, and on one of our "trips", we acted out one of the [satanic ritual] scenes from the movie… We weren't even talking with our own voices and freaked everyone out so badly, they didn't want us around anymore!

My quest for the ultimate high and sexual ecstasy propelled my involvement with the occult, and I'd make deals in my heart with the devil for those reasons. I thought about giving myself to him if he could increase my pleasure. Although I did never make an actual covenant, I did make that deal in my heart by calling on different sexual demons.

I was so hungry for the spirit world and so fascinated by ghosts, demons, and horror movies, that I'd go and get high and drunk in cemeteries… **Today, people ask me if my involvement with the occult and my hunger for the dark side had anything to do with how quickly I eventually grew in the anointing. I believe that those demonic experiences did help me become more sensitive to the spirit realm** (emphasis added).

I mention the above account by Bentley not to judge the actions of the young Todd Bentley, because in reality his need for God's forgiveness and saving grace in his life is no less than my own need (or anyone else's for that matter), and I praise God when anyone is **genuinely** saved from their sins. I mention the above because it demonstrates that his self-confessed hunger for the supernatural before his (alleged) conversion was no different to his hunger after his conversion; demons were simply replaced by angels in Bentley's mind. He even acknowledges that his involvement in the occult pre-conversion helped his spirituality post-conversion! What is clear from reading his testimony is that demonic activity remained in his life **after** his conversion, and he could not (and still cannot) discern whether what he was experiencing was divine or demonic. For example, on pages 77-78 of Journey into the Miraculous, he describes an experience he had after his conversion:

I often heard demons growl and scrape on the walls of my home. For several days in a row, in the early morning hours of 1 or 2AM, I'd hear a commotion from my mother's bedroom; voices, banging, crashing, and clanging, as well as "people" fighting and hitting each other. However, when I'd run into her room, it would all stop, and Mom would be soundly sleeping. Strangely, her body would be turned 90 degrees so that she lay horizontally along the headboard, her legs on the bedside table. She'd startle when I awoke her, but have no idea what had transpired.

Bentley's own writings provide evidence of his inability to discern between what is divine and what is demonic in origin. For example, on pages 84-85 of his aforementioned book he writes:

> I had a visitation of the person of the Holy Spirit. My body shook and I felt electricity [a sensation common in the occult, but never found in Scripture]. Once while I was under a heavy anointing my friend stopped by and yelled to me, "Come on, let's go". It was all I could do to shout back, "I'm in my room". When he opened the door to my room and saw me, he said, "Why are you shaking?"

> [Bentley replied] "I don't know. I think it's the Holy Spirit".

> "Why would the Holy Spirit make you shake?" [his friend replied].

> "I don't know but he's been doing it for about three hours".

> "Get up off your bed".

> "I can't. I can't move. My whole body is numb, and I'm sinking into my mattress".

> "This is a demon possessing you. You can't even do what you want to do. That's not the Lord".

> "**I don't know, but it feels good**", I said as my friend tried to pull me from the bed" (emphasis added).

Is this not the same disturbing attitude displayed by too many professing Christians toward so many spiritual experiences? What happened to John's instruction to test the spirits? (1 John 4:1). Bentley's inability to discern between the divine and the demonic is at the very root of his ministry, and has resulted in him leading multitudes of professing Christians into having direct contact with demonic powers masquerading as angels of light (2 Corinthians 11:13-15). Bentley is literally doing the Devil's work, whether he knows it or not. This is the fruit by which all Christians should judge the authenticity of his conversion and ministry, instead of the signs that should make every true believer wonder.

At the age of 19, Bentley claims he had a conversion experience and almost immediately began a ministry of evangelising and giving his testimony in churches at special revival meeting. In 1998, Bentley gave his testimony at a group called *Fresh Fire Ministry*, and very shortly after was asked to lead it; he was just 22 years old. Bentley's reputation for "revival meetings" grew quickly and came to the attention of Stephen Strader, pastor of *Ignited Church* in Lakeland, Florida. Strader invited Bentley to lead a series of these revival meetings at his church. Through the meetings in Lakeland being both streamed live online and televised by GOD TV, news of what was happening there spread across the world, prompting millions of people to travel thousands of miles just to experience the "Toronto" style supernatural manifestations as a result of Bentley's "imparting" and "anointing", and to witness his unorthodox "healing methods" that really should have rang alarm bells with anyone claiming to be a follower of Jesus Christ. For example, Bentley claimed in a service that when he asked the Lord why revival had not come yet to the church, his visionary Jesus replied it was because he had not "punched an older man in the stomach yet". *Irish Central News* reports in an article explaining why Bentley was banned from entering Britain (and praise God he was), that he said the Holy Spirit told him to kick a sweet old lady worshiping the Lord in the face. Bentley can be heard in video footage of the incident telling the audience:

> And the Holy Spirit spoke to me, the gift of faith came on me. He said, 'kick her in the face with your biker boot'. I inched closer and I went like this – BAM! And just as my boot made contact with her nose, she fell under the power of God.

In a separate incident, Bentley was caught on video punching a man in the stomach who had come up on stage to receive Bentley's "anointing" of healing; the man had stage four stomach cancer and Bentley punched him in the stomach so hard he can be seen doubling up in pain. Bentley told the man, "Sometimes when you are being healed it gets worse before it gets better". His behaviour was so outrageous that it was as if he (and/or the demon influencing him) was taunting people with just how far they would let him go in the "name of the Lord".

For the very few people who actually went to hear what Bentley had to say, rather than just experience the bizarre manifestations, in between the many outrageous stories and self-affirming testimonies of healings, angelic encounters, revelations, prophecies, supernatural manifestations and even people raising from the dead, they would have clearly heard Bentley expound his Manifest Sons of God and Dominion theology. But let us face it, just as it was with William Branham, who really cared what Bentley actually taught when he could do such apparent supernatural things? Bentley had become the "golden boy" of the *Prophetic Movement;* the new William Branham the movement had always been looking for.

In June 2008, ten of the "apostles" and "prophets" of the New Apostolic Reformation (NAR) held an internationally televised commissioning service for Bentley, laying hands on him and prophesying over him in the name of the Lord. The men conducting this ceremony included John Arnott of Toronto Airport Christian Fellowship, Bill Johnson of *Bethel Church* in Redding, Che Ahn, pastor of Harvest Rock Church in Pasadena, Rick Joyner and C. Peter Wagner. These self-aggrandising men, all puffed up with their own self-importance as "apostles" and "prophets", all took turns to prophesy over Bentley, confirming God's "anointing" and blessing on Bentley and his ministry. This was at a time when a small number within the charismatic/ evangelical church were expressing concern over Bentley's actions and theology, but instead of these concerns being taken seriously, these self-appointed "apostles" and "prophets" publically declared God's blessing on Bentley and his ministry. As an example, consider the following declared by head "apostle" C. Peter Wagner (and was recorded in *Charisma* Magazine):

> This commissioning represents a powerful spiritual transaction taking place in the invisible world. With this in mind, I take the apostolic authority that God has given me and I decree to Todd Bentley, your power will increase, your authority will increase, your favour will increase, your influence will increase, your revelation will increase.

> I also decree that a new supernatural strength will flow through this ministry. A new life force will penetrate this move of God. Government will be established to set things in their proper order. God will pour out a higher level of discernment to distinguish truth from error. New relationships will surface to open the gates to the future.

Bentley himself responded to all the powerful words spoken over him by such impressive men of God by declaring:

> I am no church historian, but I do not know of any other time in history, since the book of Acts, have so many different apostles and so many different prophets and movements and leaders [been represented].... The Devil is shaking in his boots because the apostles are gathering and the prophets are gathering... I believe last night was truly historic and a true sign of unity. Many streams converged and I know last night's commissioning will truly help bring God's outpouring to a much larger part of the body (*Charisma* magazine)

Did any of the prophecies about Bentley given by these self-appointed "apostles" and "prophets" in the name of God come true? Did Bentley's commissioning by these men bring God's outpouring to a much larger part of the body? Was the Devil shaking in his boots? The answer is an emphatic **NO** to all those questions. In fact I think the Devil was probably laughing his proverbial socks off at what happened next, because within a week of the commissioning service it came to light that Bentley had been visiting bars and getting drunk and had been in a long term extra-marital affair with his children's nanny. If these self-appointed "apostles" and "prophets" were genuinely in touch with God and given authority to speak on behalf of God as they claim, why did God not reveal to them the serious and habitual sin that was in Bentley's life? The whole pompous commissioning service just exposed the spiritual bankruptcy of these men:

> And the LORD said to me, "The prophets prophesy lies in My name. I have not sent them, commanded them, nor spoken to them; they prophesy to you a false vision, divination, a worthless thing, and the deceit of their heart (Jeremiah 14:14).

Rather than being restored to relationship with his wife, Bentley left his wife and children and married his mistress, who is now regarded as a "prophetess" who has "visions" direct from God. One of her most notable "visions" from God was of a dancing elephant whose long trunk was called "discernment". This would be hilarious if it was not for the fact that she claims her "visions" are from God and so many within the charismatic/evangelical church **believe** her! Her testimony about this divine "vision" can be found on YouTube in which you will witness her shaking her head violently for prolonged periods of time as a manifestation of her being "in the Spirit". However, anyone with even an ounce of Bible knowledge and discernment will see this is not a manifestation of the Holy Spirit, but in fact is identical to how the kundalini awaking is manifested.

ANGELIC ANOINTING

Todd Bentley's ministry is powered by the "anointing" given to him by a **female** angel named Emma; by Bentley's own admission, the same angel who was with William Branham (and John G. Lake before him). Furthermore, this is the same angel who Bob Jones claimed started the whole *Prophetic Movement* in Kansas in the 1980s. Jones described the angel Emma as "a mothering-type angel that helped nurture the prophetic"[1]. Bentley is quoted as saying about this angel:

> She glided into the room, emitting brilliant light and colours. Emma carried these bags and began pulling gold out of them. Then, as she walked up and down the aisles of the church, she began putting gold dust on people. "God, what is happening?" I asked. The Lord answered: "She is releasing the gold, which is both the revelation and the financial breakthrough that I am bringing into this church. I want you to prophesy that Emma showed up in this service-the same angel that appeared in Kansas city- as a sign that I am endorsing and releasing a prophetic spirit in the church."

See, when angels come, they always come for a reason; we need to actually ask God what the purpose is. Within three weeks of that visitation, the church had given me the biggest offering I had ever received to that point in my ministry. Thousands of dollars! Thousands! Even though the entire community consisted of only three thousand people, weeks after I left the church the pastor testified that the church offerings had either doubled or tripled.

During this visitation the pastor's wife (it was an AOG church) got totally whacked by the Holy Ghost- she began running around barking like a dog or squawking like a chicken as a powerful prophetic spirit came on her. Also, as this prophetic anointing came on her, she started getting phone numbers of complete strangers and calling them up on the telephone and prophesying over them. She would tell them that God gave her their telephone number and then would give them words of knowledge. Complete strangers. Then angels started showing up in the church[2].

Bentley proudly acknowledges the influence of William Branham on his life and ministry on the Elijah List website:

[Branham] was a forerunner of this type of signs and wonders ministry. In 1946 an angel visited him and ignited what we call The Voice of Healing revival. This revival really took off in the 50s and 60s with Oral Roberts, Jack Coe, A. A. Allan, R. T. Ritchie, Gordon Lindsay and The Voice of Healing newsletter… It all started with this poor, uneducated, stuttering man who had an angelic visitation and received a healing anointing… He moved in more accurate realms of revelations than almost anybody else that I know of, other than Jesus.

When you read Bentley's numerous books (which I would not recommend!) it becomes clear that he sees his ministry and anointing a continuation of both William Branham's and John G. Lake (see end note 17).

MARKED MAN

Bentley has covered his body in a fascinating array of tattoos **after** he claims he gave his life to Christ; he claims God told him to do it, in spite of God's Word specifically forbidding the permanent marking of the body in Leviticus 19:28:

You shall not make any cuttings in your flesh for the dead, nor tattoo any marks on you: I am the LORD.

For those Christians who would argue that this Old Testament commandment does not need to be adhered to in our New Testament faith, I would respectfully ask them to prayerfully consider two important points. Firstly, just because a commandment in the Old Testament is not repeated in the New Testament, it does not automatically mean that we should ignore and dismiss it. For example, in the verse directly after the instruction not to tattoo our bodies, Leviticus 19:29 commands us not to prostitute our daughters. This is the only place in the Bible where it commands us not to prostitute our daughters. Does this therefore mean we New Testament Christians have the freedom and liberty to prostitute our daughters? Of course not. A further example is that "bestiality" is only forbidden in the Old Testament. Does that therefore mean New Testament Christians have freedom and liberty to engage in sexual contact with animals? Of course not. Just because the commandment not to tattoo our bodies is not repeated in the New Testament, it does not mean we have the freedom and liberty to ignore the commandment.

The second point to prayerfully consider is the origin of tattooing the body, which is precisely **why** God forbids the practice. Throughout history the tattoo bears the mark of paganism, demonism, Baal worship, shamanism, mysticism, heathenism, cannibalism and just about every other pagan belief known to man. The tattoo has **never** been associated with God's people, whether that be the Jews and national Israel, or Bible believing Christians that make up the Body of Christ. The only exception to that is within the 20th and 21st Centuries as professing Christians have moved **away** from Biblical Christianity towards **pagan** practices.

Like it or not, the permanent marking of the body very clearly has spiritual implications and spiritual consequences, and God gave us these commandments to keep us from bondage and idolatry. But Todd Bentley wilfully disobeyed this command **after** he was supposedly saved.

The photo clearly shows a number of Bentley's tattoos, including a demon god on his shin and a hexagram and the all-seeing eye of Horus on his right forearm. The hexagram is used in religious and cultural contexts within Jewish identity, Hinduism, Islam and the occult. The context of its use is  therefore generally established by the symbols used with it, and in this case Bentley has the hexagram situated above the all-seeing eye of Horus. Horus is the Egyptian sun-god and, according to former Satanist, William Schnoebelen in his book,

Masonry: Beyond The Light, in Egyptian mythology Horus **is** Lucifer (page 197). This is further confirmed by Satanist Aleister Crowley, who preached of the coming of Satan's kingdom in the context of "the age of Horus."

The context of the hexagram on Bentley's arm is pretty clear then! But these are not the most disturbing of Bentley's tattoos. Let us consider the tattoos on his left arm (see below):

These are three large Japanese Kanji symbols. Kanji are Chinese-style characters that the Japanese adopted around the fifth century AD. Each Kanji character represents an entire object, idea or meaning in a visual character. Many Kanji symbols are similar to each other and some can have different meanings, depending on context.

The first letter on Bentley's is **DAI**, meaning "big" or "great". The middle letter is **EI**, meaning "protect" or "defend". The third letter is **OU**, meaning "king" or "monarch". In Japanese, **DAIOU** is often added to provide honour to the subject. In proper order Bentley's tattoo would appear to read "Protect Great King". However, not only is the order wrong, but the middle character is wrongly rendered, so it does not make sense in Japanese. It is not unusual for Western tattoo translations to be in error. However, there is an expression used commonly in the Japanese culture: "Emma Daioh" meaning "Emma, the Great King" This Japanese "god" is sometimes simply called "Emma-sama" (sama added to emphasise respect) or just "Emma". Buddhists recognise Emma-sama as *Yama*, ruler of the spirits of the dead in *Naraku* (hell). Those more familiar with the Japanese language suggest that Bentley's tattoo can be translated as giving honour to Emma the god of *Naraku* (hell), and the tongues of flames surrounding the tattoo symbols would lend weight to that translation. It simply cannot be a coincidence that Bentley claims to have an angel called Emma.

In spite of the fact that Bentley's tattoos advertise just how heavily demonised he is, he still remains broadly accepted by the charismatic/evangelical church.

End notes

[1] *Angelic Hosts* (2003) by Todd Bentley (exerts printed in *The Berean Call* 29/5/2008 and in *True and False Revival* by Andrew Strom.

[2] Ibid

APPENDIX 4
PSYCHOLOGY

The etymology of the word "psychology" derives from two Greek words:

Psycho   - referring to the human mind or soul.

Logos   - from where we derive the ology part, meaning "the study of".

Thus we have psychology – the study of the soul or mind.

N.B. I use the term psychology to include psychological counselling and (non-biological) psychiatry.

The basis of Psychology completely contradicts what the Bible teaches about the nature of man and God's solution for his mental, emotional and behavioural problems, because it regards humanity as intrinsically good, whereas God says, *"all have sinned and fallen short of the glory of God"* (Romans 3:23) and *"the heart [of man] is deceitful above all things, and desperately wicked"* (Jeremiah 17:7).

Psychology (through what is known as psychotherapy) attempts to improve the self through concepts such as self-love, self-esteem, self-worth, self-image, self-actualisation etc. In contrast, the Bible teaches that self is humanity's main problem, not the solution. Jesus declared that if anyone desired to follow Him they would have to deny themselves, not love or esteem themselves (Matthew 16:24; Luke 9:23). Paul exhorted believers to esteem others better than themselves, not esteem themselves, and in Romans 12 he warns believers not to think of ourselves more highly than we should. Rather than esteem himself, Paul described himself as being *"less than least of all the saints"* (Ephesians 3:8), *"the least of the apostles"* (1 Corinthians 15:9) and the chief of sinners (1 Timothy 1:15), so by the standards of modern psychology Paul was desperately in need of help in building up his self-esteem and self-image!

Paul speaks prophetically of how self-love will be a problem in the Last Days:

> *But know this, that in the last days perilous times will come: 2 For men will be lovers of themselves…* (2 Timothy 3:1-2).

How right he was!

In his book, *Absolute Surrender*, South African writer, teacher and pastor, Andrew Murray (1828-1917) wrote:

> Self is our greatest curse; but praise God! Christ came to redeem us from self, and there you have the reason why many people pray for the power of the Holy Ghost, and they get something, but, Oh, so little! Because they prayed

for power for work and power for blessing, but they have not prayed for the power for full deliverance from self.

The solution to the curse of self is not turning to psychology, but turning to Christ. Talking about the Christian who has turned from self to God, A. W. Tozer (1897-1963) said:

> His interests have shifted from self to Christ. What he is, or is not, no longer concerns him. Christ is now where the man's ego was formerly. The man is now Christ-centred, and he forgets himself in his delighted preoccupation with Christ.

Psychology acknowledges only **two** aspects of mans' existence – body and soul, whereas the Bible views man as *imagio Dei*, being made in the image and likeness of the triune God. Man is therefore made of three interconnected elements: body, soul (mind), and spirit. In a Biblical understanding of the inner make-up of man, the spirit is distinct from the soul. However, in psychology (which is based on Eastern philosophy) the spiritual or metaphysical aspect of man is a function of the mind or soul. Hebrews 4:12 makes a distinction between the two:

> *For the word of God is quick, and powerful, and sharper than any two-edged sword, piercing even to the dividing asunder of soul and spirit, and of the joints and marrow, and is a discerner of the thoughts and intents of the heart.*

This makes Christianity distinct and different to psychology (and shamanism, Sufi Islam, Buddhism and Hinduism), which treats soul and spirit essentially as one entity.

Because Psychology regards the spiritual aspect of man as nothing more than a function of the mind or soul, it is incapable of providing a proper diagnosis, let alone a genuine cure. It merely hangs humanistic labels on symptoms that do nothing to address the real root of most (non-biological) mental illness. Because the principles of psychology are diametrically at odds with the Biblical description of body, soul and spirit, and how these elements relate and work together, it rejects the concepts of sin and guilt and regards them as nothing more than an unhealthy preoccupation with relics from a superstitious medieval Christianity. For evidence of this you need look no further than the famous Rorschach ink-blot test, named after its creator, Swiss psychologist, Hermann Rorschach. The test consists of a number of "ink-blots" that were hand drawn by Rorschach himself and meticulously designed to be as ambiguous and "conflicted" as possible. The patient's "real (inner) self" is supposed to be revealed by whatever shapes they see in the ink-blots.

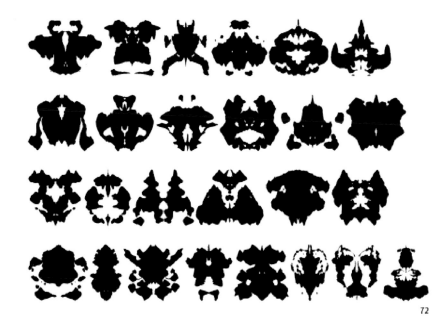

72

In interpreting the results of Rorschach's ink-blot test it is claimed that religious content is virtually never present in the record of "normal" patients. Patients who see religious content in the ink-blots are regarded as having an unhealthy concern with good and evil; concern which, almost always, is interpreted as a screen for and displacement of guilt induced by a suppressed preoccupation with sex. These kinds of responses are regarded as being common among schizophrenics, particularly patients with delusions concerning religion.

I wonder how many Christians have undergone the ink-blot test and had no idea how the examiner was interpreting them seeing religious content in the ink-blots.

OCCULT ORIGINS

Carl Jung (1875-1961) is credited with the creation and development of modern day psychology and psychological profiling.

Carl Jung was heavily influenced by the occult; he was a spiritist, engaging in frequent séances with his mother and two female cousins. Jung was so heavily demonised that at one particular meeting with Sigmund Freud he initiated such terrifying poltergeist activity that Freud fainted in fear.

In was Jung's spirit guide called "Philemon" who gave him his so-called "insights" into the psychology of man; "insights" that contradict the Word of God and therefore lead to the conclusion that the Bible cannot be sufficient for counselling or addressing a believer's mental, emotional and behavioural needs. I wonder who would want to contradict and undermine the Word of God. Genesis 3:1 should provide a clue for anyone not sure. Jung even confessed:

> In cases of difficult diagnosis I usually get a horoscope.

This astonishingly telling admission from Jung was quoted in *Wholemind Newsletter: A User's Manual to the Brain, Mind and Spirit* (Vol. 1, No. 1, page 5), which went on to state that:

> A surprising number of today's psychotherapists are following Jung's advice [about consulting a horoscope].

Jung wrote introductions to some of the first Western editions of books on yoga and Eastern Mysticism. Reflecting the Hindu view that life is merely a dream rather than reality, Jung was obsessed with dreams and their interpretation. In one dream he saw himself in yogic meditation representing his "unconscious prenatal wholeness…" In commenting on the dream, Jung declared:

> In the opinion of the "other side" [referring to communications with his spirit guide] our unconscious existence is the real one and our conscious world a kind of illusion… which seems a reality as long as we are in it. It is clear that this state of affairs resembles very closely the Oriental conception of Maya (C. G. Jung, *Memories, Dreams, Reflections,* pages 323-324).

Maya is the belief in Hinduism that the material world is illusion and the spiritual world is reality; the practice of yoga was specifically developed to achieve escape from this (unreal) world and reach *moksha*, the Hindu heaven through yoking with Brahman, the universal pantheistic "All" of Hinduism. This is what **all** forms of yoga are designed to achieve, without exception, and this is why Jung practised and endorsed yoga; even *hatha* yoga (known in the West as *physical* yoga), which is alleged to be devoid of mysticism. Yoga is yoga and it is **all** designed for yoking with Brahman; yoga means "to yoke". Your average yoga instructor at the local gym will not be aware of the many warnings contained in ancient Hindu texts that *hatha* yoga is a dangerous spiritual tool.

Bearing in mind Jung's personal enthusiasm for Eastern Mysticism, it is no surprise that the practice of meditation has for many years been endorsed and prescribed by many psychologists and psychiatrists for the treatment of any number of conditions. In more recent years, this has spawned an off-shoot of meditation called "mindfulness", which is an attempt to "Westernise" the Eastern practice of meditation by trying to divorce it from its religious/spiritual heritage. With a recent Oxford University study suggesting that "mindfulness" may be as effective as pills for treating depression and anxiety, it is rapidly growing in popularity within the health profession, with many GPs and occupational health professionals happy to refer patients to "mindfulness" sessions as a legitimate form of treatment. Consider for example of *MindUP*, which claims "mindfulness" can, without any religious attachment, be used to train the brain to develop the "social and emotional skills to reduce stress and anxiety for healthier, happier lives". Who would not find that attractive? *Time Magazine* recently featured a cover story on the "mindful revolution", an account of how mindfulness meditation has permeated all walks of American Society. The article explained how the technique is used by "Silicon Valley entrepreneurs, fortune 500 titans, Pentagon chiefs, and more". It is also being used increasingly with children in schools (for example, check out www.mindfulnessinschools.org or www.mindfulteachers.org) and is most often used in conjunction with the practice of yoga.

However, the more popular meditation and "mindfulness" becomes as a form of legitimate secular therapy, the more people are becoming aware of both its origins and dangers. For example, in 2015 *The Washington Post* printed an article titled, *Meditation and Mindfulness* aren't as good as you think, in which it exposed some of the negative side effects that very few want to acknowledge exist. The article quoted Coventry University Psychologist, Dr Miguel Farias, who said:

> Mindfulness is a technique extracted from Buddhism in which one tries to notice present thoughts, feelings and sensations without judgment... What was once a tool for spiritual exploration has been turned into a panacea [universal cure] for the modern age – a cure-all for common problems, from stress to anxiety to depression. By taking this 'natural pill' every day, we open ourselves up to the potential for myriad benefits and no ill effects, unlike synthetic pills, such as antidepressants, with their potential for negative side effects... Mindfulness has been sold to us, and we are buying it... After examining the literature from the last 45 years on the science of mediation, we realised with astonishment that we are no closer to finding out how mediation works or who benefits the most or least from it.

The article went on to state:

> Mindfulness has been separated from its roots [in Buddhism], stripped of its ethical and spiritual connotations and sold to us as a therapeutic tool... Don't consume mindfulness blindly.

Dr Miguel Farias co-authored a book titled T*he Buddha Pill: Can Meditation Change You?* Writing in *New Scientist*, Dr Farias stated:

> Meditating can produce powerful effects on the mind but not all of these are beneficial or peace-generating. The truth is that most of us, including scientists, have beliefs about meditation that are often naïve, and have turned a blind eye to its potential dark side.

The potential dark side of meditation and mindfulness was laid bare in an article published in *The Atlantic* titled, *The Dark Knight of the Soul*: For some, meditation has become more curse than cure. The article interviewed Dr Willoughby Britton who oversees a retreat centre for people recovering from the effects of meditation. Dr Britton is Assistant Professor in Psychiatry and Human Behaviour at Brown University Medical School and is one of the few proponents of meditation who will honestly acknowledge that "meditation is not all peace and calm"; it is "not the 'warm bath' it's been marketed as". *The Atlantic* article stated that Dr Britton "receives regular phone calls, emails and letters from people around the world in various states of impairment. Most of them worry that no one will believe – let alone understand – their stories of meditation-induced affliction. Her investigation of this phenomenon called *The Dark Knight Project*, is an effort to document, analyse, and publicise accounts of the adverse effects of contemplative practices". Dr Britton stated:

> There are parts of me that just want meditation to be all good. I find myself in denial sometimes, where I just want to forget all that I've learned and go back to being happy about mindfulness and promoting it, but then I… meet someone who's in distress, and I see the devastation in their eyes, and I can't deny that this is happening.

Dr Britton acknowledges that the title of her *Dark Knight Project* is taken from the phrase "dark knight of the soul", which can be traced back to a 16th century Spanish poem by the Roman Catholic mystic San Juan de la Cruz, more commonly known as Saint John of the Cross; a man eagerly embraced by both the Roman Catholic Church and the *Emergent Church*. The phrase "dark knight of the soul" is commonly used within Catholic tradition to describe an individual's spiritual crisis in the course of their union with God.

Dr Britton is not the only one to study the negative impact of meditation. One study from the University of California found that an incredible 63% of people who had been on meditation retreats suffered at least one side-effect, ranging from confusion to panic and depression. Other research has flagged up different problems ranging from involuntary twitches, fits and flapping arms, to imitating animals and states of uncontrolled euphoria. Whilst acknowledging the aforementioned negative side-effects of meditation (and "mindfulness"), the scientific community still does not understand or acknowledge the **spiritual** cause of them, because meditation (and "mindfulness") opens the participant up to the spirit world, just as it is intended to do within the Eastern mystery religion of Buddhism it originates from (with yoga originating from Hinduism). The side-effects recorded above have been suffered by practitioners of yoga and meditation for many **centuries** (a fact acknowledged by Dr Britton); they are called "Kriyas", which is the term used to describe the outward physical manifestations of awakened Kundalini, the primal Hindu energy force that is said to be located at the base of the spine that I referred to earlier in the book.

CHRISTIAN PSYCHOLOGY

It is terrifying to see how so much of "Christian" psychology and counselling is based not on the Word of God, but on the teaching of Carl Jung (a man given his "insights" into the psychology of man by a **demon**) and the people Jung influenced like Sigmund Freud, who was very much anti-Christian. For example, in *The Myth of Psychotherapy*, Professor of Psychiatry, Thomas Szasz admitted:

> One of Freud's most powerful motives in life was… to inflict vengeance on Christianity (pages 139 and 146).

Professor Szasz also acknowledges that psychotherapy is:

> Not merely a religion that pretends to be a science… [but] a fake religion that seeks to destroy true religion (page 28).

The evangelical church is in fact a primary referral service for counselling psychologists and psychiatrists. Many large churches have licenced psychotherapists on staff and mission agencies are requiring their missionary candidates to be evaluated and approved by licenced psychological professionals before being considered for service. The church is doing this because it has essentially been sold two **lies**:

1. Psychology and psychotherapy is scientific (much in the way evolution has been sold to the church as being scientific).

2. Christian psychology reconciles science and faith.

In response to the first lie, psychology is **not** scientific; its origin is demonic, as can be seen by how Jung received his "insights" into the psychology of man.

After a thorough study of psychotherapy, Dr Karl Popper (28/7/1902-17/9/1994), regarded as one of the greatest philosophers of science, declared:

> Though posing as science [psychotherapy] had in fact more in common with primitive myths than with science.

In response to the second lie, that Christian psychology reconciles science and faith, it simply does **not**; psychology is **not** a science, nor can it be Christianised. How then do Christian Psychologists function and practice? They selectively draw from the concepts learned during their secular training and try to integrate them into their Christian belief system. This is like trying to mix oil with water. They may appear to be mixing together while they are being vigorously stirred, but they quickly separate as soon as the stirring stops; the concepts of psychology are completely antithetical to the Biblical way of ministering to a believer's problems related to overcoming sin and living a life that is fruitful, productive and pleasing to God. Psychology is part of the *"wisdom of men"* taught by the *"spirit of the world"* which Paul utterly rejects in 1 Corinthians 2:5-14.

In a paper presented at the *Western Association for Psychological Studies* in Santa Barbara in June 1976, the authors J. Sutherland and P. Poelstra (both of whom were Christian Psychologists) stated:

> … there is no acceptable Christian psychology that is markedly different from non-Christian psychology. It is difficult to imply that we function in a manner that is fundamentally distinct from our non-Christian colleagues… As yet there is not an acceptable theory, mode of research or treatment methodology [in psychology] that is distinctly Christian.

In 1,900 years of faithfully studying the Bible on their knees, no true Christian leader until the 20th century saw in Scripture the need for an individual to attain self-esteem.